# DECLARATIONS

## PATRICK MURPHY

Photography by
GRAHAM MORRIS

RINGPRESS

# ACKNOWLEDGEMENTS

The author offers his deepest thanks to all the players who found time in a hectic summer to speak so frankly and at such length.

Thanks also to Peter Smith, John Mountford, Sally Shore and David Hunt.

*Published by Ringpress Books 1989*

*An imprint of Ringpress Limited, Spirella House, Bridge Road, Letchworth, Herts SG6 4ET, United Kingdom.*

Typeset by Area Graphics Ltd
Printed and bound in Great Britain by
Redwood Burn Ltd, Trowbridge, Wiltshire

ISBN 0-948955-85-6

# CONTENTS

# FOREWORD

## By IAN CHAPPELL

A JOURNALIST mate of mine once said: "Sport is about people, not about cars or boats or engines." That fact is borne out in Pat Murphy's extremely readable book, *Declarations*. As a BBC radio man, Pat has used his interviewing skills to capture the character of the game by "drawing out" the different personalities within it. To make it even more interesting, he has chosen a wide range of characters who have experienced different levels of success. From Jack Simmons, the artisan off-spinner, to Dennis Lillee the aristocrat of modern fast bowlers, Pat has chosen well.

As an avid reader, I choose titles by authors whose writing style I admire. Other than that, I read books about people who interest me or have had an interesting life. Pat Murphy scores twice. There is something for all tastes. For a youngster keen to play cricket there is a lot to be learned from the book, especially on the attitude necessary to succeed. One of the great stories of success against all odds is that of Dennis Lillee, who says: "I was like a bull terrier—I wouldn't let go if I had a batsman by the throat." I would prefer to take my chance with a bull terrier any day.

Then there is the example of knowing your limitations. Jack Simmons describes it perfectly when he talks about missing out on the captaincy at Lancashire. "I suppose it is my biggest disappointment in cricket, much more so than not playing for England, because the Lancashire captaincy was more realistic."

There is humour, beautifully encapsulated by the most gentle of fast bowlers, Michael Holding. "We have a saying in the West Indies—if you want a drive, go and rent a car." That is why the fast bowlers drive Mercedes and the batsmen drive Datsuns.

Then there is the philosophy of one of the world's great umpires, Dickie Bird, talking about the reasons for his success. "You see, I'm married to the game. I nearly got wed on two occasions, but it didn't happen and although I would have loved a family, I have no regrets." I will bet a few fast bowlers have queried whether Dickie ever had a father.

I was reading recently a writer who was lamenting the demise of Jimmy Connors at what could well be his last Wimbledon championship. He was also bemoaning the fact that we might not have John McEnroe around much longer to love or hate. This seemed to worry him, because he thought it could well be the end of the characters in tennis. "After all," he wrote, "tennis is a boring game. It is just two guys hitting a ball back and forth over the net, unless they stamp their character on the match."

Well, I have some more bad news for a guy who has somehow managed to miss the character of Wilander, Lendl and Becker: all games can be boring if the players don't stamp their character on the match. To me, there is nothing more mindless than a social match where the cricketers are just going through the motions. It is the heat of battle and the competitiveness that brings out the best and worst in sportsmen and that, along with the contest, is what makes any sport worth watching. Finding out what the characters think and what a far-sighted writer sees in a player or a contest is what makes the game worth reading about. If you want a bunch of statistics hurled at you, go and buy a scorecard. I want the story of the match. The toils and troubles of the players.

They are not always easy to interview. The time has got to be right and the questions need to show a working knowledge of the game and suggest reasonable intelligence. Then the interviewer has a chance of capturing some of the wisdom and the wit of the character who has been chosen. This Pat has achieved. Having been on both sides of such "confrontations" and having had to sit on both sides of a number of Press conferences, it is refreshing to read such informative interviews.

When asked why he never went to Press conferences, the brilliant English sports columnist Ian Wooldridge said: "Because you don't give bad journalists the benefit of answers to good questions." The line of questioning in Pat's book is good. It makes a pleasant change from some of the tedium experienced after play as England capitulated to Australia last summer.

David Gower has been on the receiving end of some strange questioning during the English summer of 1989. On one occasion he walked out of a Press conference and on another he was reduced to banging his head on the table in frustration. I would suggest he read a copy of Pat's interviews to renew his faith in cricket reporting.

This is not a book that simply looks back. It tells us there is much to look forward to as well. I can't wait to see 15-year-old, five-foot four-inch Sachin Tendulkar bat. Ravi Shastri says: "He is sent from upstairs to play the game." I hope I am not called upstairs before Sachin arrives on the International scene! But one should not look on the dark side. As the likeable Graeme Fowler says: "If you want to enjoy yourself have a look around. You will always find something to enthuse about." True about life. True about cricket.

# INTRODUCTION

THE idea for this book has germinated over the years. As a cricket reporter for BBC Radio, I inevitably clock up a fair number of interviews with players over the seasons. Equally inevitably, as any other subscriber to cock-up theories will confirm, the most interesting parts of the interviews rarely get on air. So the listener is told how batsman Smith is pleased to have scored a hundred, while a hat-trick by bowler Jones has him somewhere in the stratosphere, sizing up the moon for a leap over it. It would be rum indeed if either were glum. Very little is heard about alterations in technique and attitude that led to such success; or the amount of mental strength required to surmount psychological and physical setbacks; or even the state of cricket at that time. In other words, the flesh and blood of playing cricket for a living. Perhaps such pearls lurk too far into the tape, with the studio-based editors of the broadcasted extracts displaying the attention span of a stunned stoat. As someone who admires the way professionals can prosper at a sport which regularly reduces me to burning the contents of my cricket coffin, I always start out on their side. Of course, they should be criticised constructively; but at all times we should attempt to understand them. This collection of interviews is an attempt to find out something of the frustrations, tensions and satisfactions of modern professional cricket.

I chose several yeoman players among the *glitterati*, because they provide a balance and perspective that many great players lack; inevitably, selfishness underpins outstanding talent. In the year of Australian carnage, I felt it was worth hearing from several Antipodean notables, while overseas players such as Richard Hadlee, Imran Khan and Ravi Shastri provide a more detached view. From the media, Tony Greig was chosen because he has been influential as both player and broadcaster in the evolution of Test cricket. My desire to hear the views of umpires took me naturally to Dickie Bird, whom Father Time preserve.

I have tried to seal them all into a 1989 time-warp, so that future cricket historians might be able to assess what exercised the minds of those influential figures as we entered the century's last decade. Undeniably, there was widespread admiration for both the manner of Australia's victory in the 1989 series and for the quality and depth of her domestic cricket. In contrast, England's cricket infrastructure was widely damned: too much cricket, far too much travelling, too many competitions, an inordinate interest among county committees in coining a fast buck, deep concern over the quality of pitches and a conviction that many counties prefer parochial success to international prestige. Almost every interview contained a plea for the introduction of four-day cricket on good pitches, so that the best players might prosper and receive a realistic grounding for the Test arena.

There was also tangible disquiet over the way English cricket is being run. It has always been open season on England selectors and administrators at Lord's, but the general opinion is that the current quality of leadership from the Test and County Cricket Board leaves much to be desired. Scapegoats are usually sought when the national side fails as lamentably as in 1989, but the loaded gun seems irresistibly pointed at the foot. Too many committees, too much coagulation of the lifeblood of executive decisions, not enough accountability. There was a great deal of sympathy for Mike Gatting in his various bruising encounters with the game's authorities, and for the cricketers who want to keep open the lines of communication with South Africa.

My view is that English cricket faces a fallow period, in which the public will vote with its feet unless the national side comes up with exciting successors to the likes of Botham, Gatting and Gower. Since 1975, spectators in England have been spoiled. Lillee and Thomson and the first World Cup merged into the glory of Viv Richards and some great West Indian fast bowlers and batsmen. Botham and Willis turned the 1981 summer into one for the scriptwriters. Four great all-rounders kept on sparking each other off in various summers. Gatting, Gower and Gooch batted the 1985 Australians into oblivion with high-class performances. Hardly a series ended in the batting stalemate of yesteryear, when illustrious batsmen were content to "play through the V" for hours, enjoying the technical exercise. Some time in the next century, historians of the game might just acknowledge as another Golden Age the period from the 1975 World Cup to Mike Gatting's 1987 Grand Slam in Australia; not for the overall quality of the play, more for the gallery of charismatic players that kept sponsors, TV producers and public thirsting for more. Since Faisalabad in 1987, the English product has been tarnished and the current relationship between players and authorities does not suggest a revival in the near future.

Predictably, many of the men interviewed distrust the media. Yet it is conveniently forgotten that the media helps build up public interest in cricket, and that in turn attracts the men in suits with cellular phones, whose sponsorship allows baby-faced tyros to drive around with their names plastered all over a two-litre car. Without the media, England players would not earn around £1,750 for six days' work while seeking to establish a public image that leads to several other nice little earners. *Plus ça change*: performers on the stage and the critics should never sup from the same cup. Their tastes must inevitably differ.

In this book, my awareness of the censor's pen means that some remarks from players are perforce elliptical and carefully phrased. The Mike Gatting chapter proved a challenge while it was amusing (and wiser) to emasculate some of Ian Botham's more trenchant observations. Connoisseurs of verbal compromises may enjoy trawling for such examples. I certainly enjoyed talking cricket with these men.

**PATRICK MURPHY**
**OCTOBER 1989**

# IAN
# BOTHAM

**'There is no more dangerous animal than a wounded bear, and that is precisely how I feel. No-one has a clue who will be picking the England team next summer. But I shall make them pick me.'**

IT is a dangerous business to attempt to place a current cricketer in an historical context, but it is safe to name Ian Botham as one of England's most illustrious players of all time. Only Gary Sobers has stronger claims as the greatest all-rounder of all. No Englishman has rivalled Botham's ability to alter consistently the course of a match, and no-one has approached the sheer gusto of his performances. His anarchic, self-indulgent personality at once made him a great cricketer and a character who transcended the mere confines of a sport. Botham is a famous Englishman as much as a famous English cricketer in the way that few others (Grace, Hobbs, Compton, Trueman perhaps) have been. Ian Botham's career has been a parable of our times—a period in which the media has obsessively monitored the private lives of entertainers; a time in which the anti-hero could cultivate a lucrative image; a time in which the attitude to success and failure has become alarmingly one-dimensional. Botham is a social chameleon. Impulsively generous and loyal, yet an implacable enemy; an avowed right-winger, yet libertarian enough to pick up a drugs conviction and enjoy the friendship of rock stars; the champion of Mrs Thatcher's brand of self-help, yet an inspirational supporter of charitable causes. Above all, he is never dull. He will be missed when he stops playing, even by those who blame him for everything from the lbw rule to the destruction of the ozone layer.

For such an individualist, Botham's devotion to the team ethic has been admirable and explains his great popularity in dressing-rooms. He has always wanted to bowl, even on days when the fires have been doused and the batsmen merely have to contend with an old pro's cunning and a range of histrionic gestures that would barely extend a first-year student at drama college. His batting, although founded on orthodox principles, has been spectacular. Few players have hit the ball harder in the game's history, and few have surpassed Botham's ability to halt conversations as the ball is

9

*propelled in his direction. If Botham had been more concerned with personal records, his towering statistical performances would have been even more impressive. The élan he has brought to cricket should never wholly obscure his all-round excellence as a player, which includes his prehensile catching.*

*Botham is no scholar of Robert Browning, and yet Browning's line about "never glad confident morning again" has a poignant significance for Botham. Many felt wistful on his behalf as England's horror show of 1989 rumbled on towards the autumnal knacker's yard. After a year's absence through a back injury that would have finished off a less dedicated sportsman, Botham had battled his way back into the England team at the start of the summer. His pulse quickened at the prospect of yet another turn of the Australian screw at his hands, while television producers once again whipped out the 1981 highlights from the videotape library. It ended in tears. A fractured cheekbone, then a dislocated finger, restricted Botham to just three Tests—and the old embers failed to ignite. He bowled tidily, yet failed to score a hundred in the summer. Then England decided he was not wanted on the Caribbean voyage. It was the first time since his Test debut in 1977 that Botham had been ignored for a tour, and, with his 34th birthday approaching, many regarded Botham's defiant revivalism as no more than windy rhetoric. As if to emphasise the way he has polarised public opinion, many were glad that cricket's grim reaper appeared to be sharpening the scythe for Botham. Yet his legion of admirers fondly hope that the last hurrah will be delayed before a new era of English utilitarianism and anonymity becomes respectabilised. After all Botham's recent setbacks, was the rejection for the West Indies tour the hardest to bear?*

It was the worst day of my career. I would have given my all on that tour, because I would have owed that to the younger players and to myself. No-one needs to tell me about my poor record against the West Indies. I would have done everything to get a hundred against them. I shall be 37 when they next tour England, and that will be too late for me.

*Have you felt sorry for yourself?*

Well, that just about summed up my season—getting fit again after the back injury, then the fractured cheekbone that put me out of the first two Tests, then the finger injury that prevented me batting properly at Nottingham and kept me out of the Oval Test. I had made my mind up how I would bat against the West Indies out there. Last time I was too loose, because I did not expect to last very long on those dodgy wickets against that class of fast bowling. But this time I was going to play properly and occupy the crease to wear them down. Remember how I batted at Lord's against them in 1984, when I got 80-odd in almost three hours? That was my game plan this time. I know I can still bat at Test level.

*Why do you feel so let down?*

Three years ago I said I would never tour again with England, for family reasons. I did not need any more hassle from the Press. During the Old Trafford Test, Micky Stewart and David Gower kept asking me if I would be available for the West Indies tour. I even rang my wife, who was on holiday in Portugal, and said: "Kath, we've got a big decision to make." I thought about it for a couple more weeks, then decided to make myself available, during the Fifth Test at Nottingham. The prospect of going to the West Indies was also very influential in making me refuse a terrific offer to join Mike Gatting's rebels in South Africa. Yet a month later, I was not in the tour party. I was convinced they wanted me on that tour. Then they turned round and said: "We don't want you!"

*Are you sure you did not misunderstand what the England management was asking of you?*
I have no doubts at all. The fact that David Gower was no longer captain is irrelevant. I was sure they wanted me in the West Indies.

*Ted Dexter said the squad was picked on current form—and you can't argue that by this criterion you were not worth your place in the party.*
Yes, but they picked me for every Test against the Aussies when my form was not all that impressive. By the time the West Indies tour begins, everyone will be starting afresh, and I would have thought that my past England record might have warranted some consideration. If current form was the sole criterion, Graham Gooch would struggle, after averaging twenty against the Aussies. David Gower, on the other hand, scored a century and two fifties against them, and he misses out because of current form. It seems rather strange to me.

*Yet you failed over there in 1986, after a magnificent all-round season in 1985. What makes you think you could turn around your record against the West Indies now?*
If I did not believe I could still do it, I would retire. I have a great drive in me to prove people wrong. I shall decide when to write my cricket obituary, not someone else. I would have given experience to that team—and my own personal pride.

*Does England still mean that much to you, even after this setback?*
I re-arranged the whole of my winter plans as proof that playing for England still means everything to me. I also turned down South Africa. Even after this blow, I still want desperately to come back next summer. I shall be very fit at the start of next season and make them pick me on—now what is the phrase?—"current form". I am sure David Gower feels the same way. I am 33, not 43, and I still have personal ambitions.

*Such as?*
It would be a fair old achievement to be the first to 400 Test wickets and 4,000 runs. Richard Hadlee will probably beat me to 400 wickets, but he will never get near my 14 centuries. Next year my bowling will be faster than last summer, because I was being sensible after my long lay-off. A couple of days before they picked that West Indies tour party, I slipped myself for the first time in the season. I had reached a full year since the surgeon told me I could play again, so I decided to mark the anniversary by bending my back. I was very pleased with those few overs and rang Micky Stewart to tell him so. That call did not do me much good, did it? Anyway, if I am now in decline, why have Worcestershire just offered me a new four-year contract? There is no more dangerous animal than a wounded bear, and that is precisely how I feel. At the moment, no-one has a clue who will be picking the England team next summer. But I shall make them pick me.

*The irony of your comeback in 1989 was that we all thought your sound batting technique would see you through, but that your bowling would let you down. It went the other way, didn't it?*

I decided I would be more use to the team and myself by looking to tie up one end and bowl line and length, trying to swing the ball as well. I reckon I did that. When you have had a bone fusion on your back, it takes time to settle, and I knew that if it went again I was finished. I got stronger as the season went on and put in a lot of long spells. I was disappointed with my batting, but after a year away from the game, I was bound to be scratchy. After fifteen years as a professional, I reckon I have a good idea how to go about my job. The runs will come back.

*When you were lying in that hospital bed, facing the possible end of your career as they reshaped your back, did you ever think negatively?*

Never. You cannot afford to do that in any walk of life. You have to do what you are told when you are pole-axed on a bed, and I simply trusted the surgeon. He has been magnificent to me. I only needed the challenge of being written off to keep me going. The fact that the Aussies were due the following summer was just one more incentive. Games against them are the ultimate, and I am just sorry I failed to repeat my Roy of the Rovers stuff against them. But it was a tremendous boost to my morale to make it back just a year after being flat on my back.

*So is your attitude to pain simply: it isn't there?*

More or less. I tend to float into a particular area of the mind and detach myself from what my body is telling me. When we go on those walks for Leukaemia Research, you have to approach pain with a positive philosophy. I learned so much about that on the first walk—from John O'Groats to Land's End. That lasted five weeks. We walked the length of Great Britain, and I went into uncharted territory there. The secret is to tell yourself that you are not in pain; that it will soon pass—and to think about that warm bath and soothing drink. Accentuate the positive. If someone asks you how you are feeling, always say "Fine". Never start listing your aches and pains.

*But you had that attitude years before you started out on those charity walks, didn't you?*

I was always strong, so that helped. Also, my first captain at Somerset—one Brian Close—would never stand for anyone not being tough enough. You simply got on with the job and ignored pain. He did that at his advanced age. How could we be different?

*When are you off on one of those charity walks again?*

October, 1990, from Aberdeen to Ipswich. It should take about three weeks and we shall be going through territory we did not touch on the John O'Groats to Land's End journey. This time it will be on the eastern side of Scotland and England—untapped territory, lovely generous people. Great fishing area, and top-class Scotch to drink. These walks are hard, but great fun. When you walk into one of those wards and see the kids dying of leukaemia, it soon stops you thinking about sore feet.

*As a cricketer, you have always seemed to enjoy larger slices of luck than other players—apart from this last year. Do you agree?*

You make your own luck in sport, and life. I approach everything in a positive frame of mind, and that often turns in my favour. All the way through my career I have told myself I am better than my immediate opponent, and that has given me the confidence to try things. A bowler is not too keen on being hit out of the ground, and a batsman can

12

be conned out with a bit of imagination. I tell every young player to be positive, to make sure no one psyches them out of it.

*Of all the statistical landmarks you have reached, which one means most to you?*
The record of sixes in a season in 1985 meant I had a lot of fun watching the ball soar out of the ground. I was in good nick all summer. But for consistency, and because it involved Tests, it has to be the first to get to 300 wickets and 3,000 Test runs. Kapil Dev and Imran Khan have done it since, and I admire them both tremendously for their skills and the way they play the game, but I have scored a lot more hundreds than them. It was nice to set records in terms of the fewest Tests in my early days, but 300 wickets and 3,000 runs means you have to be pretty consistent for a long time.

*If you had been older and more established, would you have signed for Kerry Packer in 1977?*
Yes. I reckon he did a lot for the international game. He certainly brought us more money. Top cricketers are still underpaid when you consider how many people they entertain throughout the world. Look at what golfers and tennis players earn. My son, Liam, is developing very well as a cricketer and rugby player—he's only twelve. But if there is one sport I would love to see him play for a living, it would be golf. And I would be his manager!

*Ian, you have slagged off the Press for years, particularly the tabloids. But surely you didn't help yourself by giving your name to a column in* The Sun?
For a start, I was eventually getting £50,000 a year for it, and I would have been dumb to turn that down. Secondly, I was always constructive in my column. I never climbed into other players, and I used to praise a lot of people in the game. It had to be seen by Lord's before it could be published, and I honestly thought it was better reading than a lot of the stuff in *The Sun*. Anyway, it would be wrong to think *The Sun* protected me: they used to run a lot of duff news stories about me elsewhere in the paper. Now I never believe anything I read in the tabloids; I find that much safer. Something should be done about the quality of journalism in this country.

*Will you ever play in South Africa?*
I am more open-minded about South Africa than I used to be. I have talked to a lot of people who have been out there and I would be interested to see what the real situation is. The restriction on reporting is not a very positive idea, but the English guys who have coached out there tell me things have improved greatly since I first turned down an offer in 1982. One day I shall have a look at all that. I have a great deal of sympathy for the cricket people in South Africa. I have met Ali Bacher and believe he has done a fantastic job in making cricket multi-racial—which is what we all want. At the moment, though, playing for England remains my biggest ambition.

*Any idea what you will do when you retire?*
The same as now—enjoy myself. I shall be financially solid and give my family security and comfort. Liam will be twenty when I am 42, and it will be fun to watch how he develops at sport, instead of going off on another England tour as I did when he and my two daughters were younger. In the week I missed out on the tour to West Indies, I had two great consolations from my family: Sarah was made deputy head girl and Liam

13

deputy head boy at their schools. I was really proud of them. Kath has been a fantastic wife to me, and I shall repay all the loyalty she showed during the times when the Press rubbished me. I shall not be at many Tests telling everyone how the game has changed since my day. If I do any commentaries, they will be constructive and supportive of the players, because I know it can be bloody hard out there. I know that some of the ex-players who make a good living out of writing me off in the Press will be lost when I pack up. They will find someone else to knock, I'm sure. And to those who do not know me and yet delight in slagging me off, I say this: Better to *have* been than *never* have been somebody.

# RICHARD HADLEE

**'I shall keep going as long as I am fit enough, but I will know when it is time to bring someone else in ahead of me. '**

GENIUS is an infinite capacity for taking pains. So runs the old saw—and it might have been coined with Richard Hadlee in mind. No other cricketer of his era has maximised all his assets to such a peak of efficiency. In the Seventies he was a talented fast bowler but mentally and physically brittle. Yet he has dominated this last decade by training his mind to concentrate on the job in hand. Hadlee makes everything count by judging the right pitch of performance, in the same way that Lester Piggott upped the tempo as he rounded Tattenham Corner. When Hadlee became the first cricketer in seventeen years to do the "double" of a hundred wickets and a thousand runs in first-class cricket, it came after a season of detailed planning and slide-rule forecasting. He carried around a folder all season in which he numbered his expected runs and wickets for each pitch, with the quality of opposition taken into account. He would enter the results and then re-assess the campaign's progress every day. A calculating machine maybe, but he made himself into a dangerous, late middle-order batsman and a truly great fast-medium bowler. To watch Hadlee's hand action at the bowling crease is illuminating: the wrist is cocked, ready to deliver the ball at deceptive speed. He can get bounce from the most unresponsive surface, because his hand is high at the time of delivery, the arm action whippy and the follow-through vibrant. All this off a short run that is a model of economy and control.

Hadlee has been the main reason for the upsurge in fortunes of both Nottinghamshire and New Zealand. In the Eighties, Nottinghamshire won two county championships, and his country never lost a series at home. Arguably no other player has won so many games in that period. Hadlee's professionalism applies to all aspects of his public life. The only cricketer on the books of Mark MacCormack, his public relations skill satisfies even that demanding agent. Hadlee's ability to conduct himself admirably in public is an

*object lesson to those sporting superstars who bemoan their responsibilities while blithely salting away the banknotes. Is it difficult being such a high-profile figure in a parochial country like New Zealand?*

Well, you are a target, and you have got to be seen to be doing the right thing at the right time. If you give someone your time for just a few seconds to sign an autograph, that is no real problem and you maintain your credibility in the eyes of the public. There are stirrers—those who try to set you up in compromising situations. That is disappointing, because although you are in the limelight and want to set proper standards, you also deserve a bit of privacy. I do not believe anyone has the right to start delving and exposing. It is bad manners and shows a lack of respect.

*Can you find seclusion in New Zealand?*

Yes. We have got a place up in the Marlborough Sands with a boat, and another at Hamlet, about eighty miles away. My wife and I have a good bunch of friends and whenever I go to a pub or a restaurant, they protect me if necessary. I never go to these places on my own.

*You are leading the chase to be the first bowler to reach four hundred Test wickets. How important will that particular record be to you?*

Vitally important for someone like myself, and for New Zealand cricket. I am sure Sunny Gavaskar felt the same on behalf of India after he became the top run-scorer in Tests. You think of most Test records coming from English or Australian players because they play such a lot, so it is unbelievable for someone like myself to get there ahead of others. The barrier of four hundred wickets has yet to be conquered, but someone has to reach Everest and I want it to be me. It is much the same as Roger Bannister breaking the four-minute barrier for the mile. No-one can take that away from him.

*So you are still a target man?*

Sure—that is my inspiration and motivation. I have kept going for eighteen years, and it would have been very easy to go through the motions and pick up the pay cheque. But if you can aim at something specific, then there is pride involved when you do it. That is just me. Others are motivated in different ways. I have slogged away and deserved the things that have come to me.

*Yet others of your quality seem more relaxed. Do you still need to keep worrying away at targets?*

Yes—because I have built up a record comparable to few who have played Tests for any period of time, and I am proud of that. Once you start to dip below your own standards, you are wasting your time in playing. I shall keep going as long as I am fit enough, but I will know when it is time to bring someone else in ahead of me. It is getting that much harder now. I find that if I have a long day in the field, the recovery rate is that much slower. A couple of years ago I had to bowl more than thirty overs on the final day to try to beat Australia at Melbourne. We missed out by just one wicket. I had to bowl the last over at Mike Whitney and he kept me out. But I had to dig so deep that it took me three days to recover. Normally I am fine the following day.

*So will it be fitness rather than inclination that determines how long you continue playing?*

Oh yes—I still *love* playing. I am now having to put more work in than I have ever done before. Twenty-minute runs have been doubled and I am in the gym four days a week, instead of two. I need more net practice now because I do not have the daily match practice I used to get with county cricket. My routines have changed, so I have had to develop a substitute programme because I am not playing cricket for eleven months a year any more. In the past year, I have had three worrying injuries—two strains in achilles tendons and one in a calf muscle. If any of them go again they are obviously telling me something, but I am working hard to build them up.

*I am sure you must have been aware of the irony behind that calf muscle strain early in 1988 when you were all set to beat Ian Botham's Test record of 373 wickets?*

Unbelievable, wasn't it? The first time in my 74 Tests that I had ever broken down, and it came in front of my home crowd at Christchurch with just one wicket needed, and me bowling eighteen overs at my former Nottinghamshire team-mates, Tim Robinson and Chris Broad. Off the fourth ball of an over I knew something was wrong: there was a sharp pain. I bowled two more balls before tea and hobbled off, and that was it for the series. I then decided to go to India later in the year—I had not wanted to visit that country again as a cricketer—and the record came on the twelfth of November rather than on the twelfth of February.

*You were at Nottinghamshire for ten seasons: did you quit at the right time?*

Yes. I went on several years longer than I ever thought I would, and it was a great vote of confidence from the club that they kept wanting me back. There were many magic moments, but the last three years were very hard. Clive Rice and I left at the right time, after the championship and the Nat-West Cup were won in our last season. The club has now gone beyond our influence, and the fact that Nottinghamshire won the Benson and Hedges Cup in 1989 is very satisfying. It suggests the players have become more professional and no longer need to keep looking back at the Rice/Hadlee period.

*When you left English cricket, you had some very strong things to say about the lack of dedication of many players.*

Some of my remarks were distorted, but I do feel strongly that the younger pros should show more respect for their senior colleagues. The youngsters should be seen to be putting in work beyond that which they are expected to do. The perks are there, yet I got the impression that too many of them were happy to get a thousand runs a season or fifty wickets. Why not 1,250 runs or 65 wickets? You should strive to go beyond what you think you are capable of, instead of being satisfied with the bare minimum. There is a lot of talent in English county cricket but at times the attitudes are wrong. If a guy is out of nick and he has a day off, why not go to the nets and practise hard? Why not run an extra two laps when the others have settled for six? Why not spend another five minutes practising catching and throwing? I am a great believer in putting in the work and then being rewarded, so that the bag of three wickets becomes five or six. By the end of the season fifty wickets becomes seventy because of that extra training run and those odd minutes in the nets.

*Did you always have that attitude?*

No. It took English cricket to teach me that. I had to learn the disciplines to get me through the challenge of so many matches. There is no security at all in professional sport, so you have got to approach it just like any other business. You are the managing director and you have got to perform day in and day out. Professionalism can be summed up in one word—consistency. You are an amateur when your performances go up and down. It all comes back to the player and what he wants to achieve.

*Is there more evidence of that in New Zealand, now that the likes of you and Martin Crowe have become an inspiration?*

It took me about five years to develop some sort of plan to my Test cricket, and now I hope that others will come through rather quicker than that. We are investing money in the development of young players. Youngsters have to understand that a dividend is needed on the investment in air fares, coaching clinics and tours that they enjoy. They have to go out there with a sense of purpose and make it happen in a matter of two or three years. These players have to have the right frame of mind; a proper mental and physical preparation, with a deep knowledge of the game and its standards. Players like Chris Cairns and Mark Greatbach have the potential and attitude, and I think they will in time fulful that potential. But they must also be guided by blokes who have been there and know what is involved.

*Players such as Geoff Howarth, Glenn Turner and yourself. Do you see yourself as a cricket administrator, eventually?*

There are a lot of options—selection, management or administration. I am also involved with the media and if you are talking and writing about the game, it is very difficult to be an administrator as well. But when I give the game away, I will not be lost to it.

*What's the relationship these days between Australian and New Zealand cricket?*

It is still a love-hate thing. No problems between the players, but I have had a few run-ins with their crowds and I have been foolish enough to react. There have been times when they motivated me even more than normal, and I have felt like thanking them for it, but some of the personal abuse has been ugly. Ian Chappell and Dennis Lillee have both told me that such abuse is really a compliment to me, but I have found myself thinking: "Why should I stand out here, taking all this? There could be other things I'd rather do." The worst abuse I get comes from Tasmania, simply because I had a spell there in 1979 and did not do very well. They felt I never tried, so whenever I go back, I am greeted by banners calling me "wanker" and "prat" and some that say "Welcome to Hadlee's Holiday Isle". I appreciate good humour, but there are some things that go beyond that. I suppose we have to accept we are actors on a stage and we have an obligation to the paying spectators to grin and bear it.

*Is there still a touch of an inferiority complex towards Australia among New Zealand cricketers?*

It took a long time for them to recognise us. They used to send over their "B" teams, and that was a kick in the butt. We did not play our first official series against them until 1973/4, but since then we have had our fair share of wins and we do not feel inferior. Yet Glenn Turner is still unhappy about their suggestion, a few years back, that our national side should play in their Sheffield Shield competition. He thought that was a huge insult, and that is why he pleased himself when he played against the Aussies.

19

DECLARATIONS

*It seems ridiculous that it took so long to get a full series against them.*

Our international credibility was not all that strong for years and years. We had some talented players, but five-day Tests were ending in four days. Getting experience in English county cricket helped many of us, and, in the last decade, our record has been tremendous—the best in our history. We have beaten all the playing nations at home and lost just two Tests here. We have had a series win in England and another in Australia. It is very difficult to win in other parts of the world.

I think our selectors deserve credit for sticking with players. If you were good enough for one Test, you were good enough for at least three, and possibly a tour. In England, the selectors go through so many players that they cannot play with any confidence of getting a run in the side. I think players should be motivated by desire, not fear. It makes a hell of a difference if you can be told: "Go out there, enjoy yourself; we think you're good enough, and you've got three Tests to prove it."

*Can you point to your best bowling performance?*

It was at Brisbane—nine for 52 against Australia in 1985. I also took six wickets in the second innings. On that day, the climatic conditions were just right: the ball felt good and I moved it around all over the place with complete control. My build-up to the Test had not been good, but I worked hard in practice and bowled for 45 minutes, rather than my usual twenty, to get closer to the wicket. Glenn Turner, our manager, had noticed I was not getting close enough to the stumps, so he placed a drum six feet behind the stumps and told me to imagine that was the umpire. Before that the umpire had always stood about two feet behind and that probably served to push me wider. Since then I have always asked the umpire to stand about six feet back. I bowled wicket to wicket at Brisbane and the nip-backer worked well, as did the one that goes the other way. I took the first eight and then caught the next one. I have never had all ten. . . .

*You have been one of the four great all-rounders who came at the same time. Which one of Ian Botham, Kapil Dev and Imran Khan do you rate the highest?*

Imran Khan. He has been the best batsman. To me, a genuine all-rounder must make the Test team as a batsman or as a bowler, and Imran qualifies better than the rest of us. The other three looked to whack the bowlers around, while Imran would graft and then hit you over the top when it suited him and the needs of his side. Kapil and I would start thrashing it around fairly early on, whereas Both—well you never know with Both, do you?

*Yet all four of you have kept going.*

Yes, but perhaps rather too much of that has been got up by the media. There have probably been other all-rounders of equal stature at other times in cricket history, but today, with the proliferation of tournaments and all the media hype, it has been magnified into "Botham versus Hadlee" and the battle of the all-rounders. It is part of the promotional gimmick, and it is okay if it means the marketing boys get people to watch us. I do not take the historical aspect of it too seriously, though.

*How do you keep calm when batting, if the adrenalin is pumping in something like a run chase?*

By deep breathing. You can get excited, or get a chest pain, or start to feel dizzy, when you are after quick runs and short of puff. So deep breathing is a simple way to relax and get the body back to normal. Talking to your partner helps too. I would always prefer to be out there with a chance of influencing the result than being stuck in the dressing-room without any control. That is when you are really nervous.

*Which batsman did you most respect?*
Definitely Geoffrey Boycott. He was the best, technically. I never felt he was in total control, but he would wear you down. I only got him out twice in my career. I respected Greg Chappell for his fluency and elegance, and Viv Richards for his destructiveness and unorthodox approach. Ian Botham would accept any challenge and try to take you apart. When that worked he could make you look pretty silly. Sunny Gavaskar would be up there too, and Javed Miandad—he works the ball into daft places; he comes down the wicket to you, he's so wristy.

*Who handled you the best among your captains?*
Geoff Howarth. He had an aura about him; he was calm. He gained a lot of respect as captain because he would gamble and a lot of his hunches came off. He used me in short spells, set good fields, let me have what I wanted. Other captains have tended to over-use me, by bringing me back too soon or keeping me on too long. You have got to be fresh.

*As we go into the Nineties, do you think cricket can still compete with all the other leisure options?*
Cricket that drifts on for five days on a featherbed and then ends in a draw will not attract many. That is why one-day cricket is such a hit, even though it is not really a game of skill. We must have pitches that are fair and equal, so that bowlers have some sort of chance. Today's environment cannot cope with Test Match scores of over 600. People want to be entertained more dramatically. The game needs to give more value for money; it must be speeded up. That is why it is so important to have a minimum of ninety overs a day—if the players have to work an extra half-hour, that is their fault—because the public must be given value for money. I have always tried to get on with it. If I get whacked, there is no point in standing in the middle of the pitch, feeling aggrieved. You must get back to your mark, think out your strategy, and run in again.

*Will you be back next year for one final tour of England?*
I hope so, but that will depend on my fitness. I shall not make a decision on that until I have got through what is going to be a very exacting season for me. There are Tests against Australia and India, the usual one-dayers, and three testimonial matches for myself that will take a lot of organising. I will not come to England unless I can be sure of maintaining the standards I set myself. Instead I shall simply set myself new challenges in my life.

# GRAHAM GOOCH

**'I have never had one cross word with any coloured cricketer over playing in South Africa and their governments are perfectly entitled to take whatever stand they wish. But our cricketers are being victimised. '**

PPEARANCES can *be deceptive. Graham Gooch is neither surly nor money-conscious, a man for whom cricket is a chore. He may appear to be in a constant state of vacillation, as he wrestles with the cares of captaincy or the latest England tour itinerary, but that is a superficial assessment, unduly influenced by the rather lugubrious demeanour that matches his moustache. Gooch is no different from any other modern husband who cares about the welfare of his wife and three young daughters. He thinks deeply about the desirability of being parted from them for months. Graham remains drily humorous, at ease with people he can trust, and who are aware of his shy modesty. He does not thrive in the goldfish bowl arena of professional sport, nor make any claims to do so: Graham would rather be en route for a bedtime story with the twins than submit himself to the interminable round of interviews that are* de rigueur *for the England captain. Gooch is an unostentatious team man. Although he broods about his batting, he is no Boycott—inconsolable when the runs are scarce. No other England opener since Boycott has approached Gooch's durability and consistency. He has scored more runs and centuries than any other Englishman currently playing, and his sterling performances over the years against the West Indies—always the litmus test—have reinforced his quality. Those who allege that Gooch has chosen his tours carefully might ponder on the four series in which he has stood foursquare against the West Indian fast bowlers. One wonders whether Gordon Greenidge or Desmond Haynes would have matched Gooch's record if they had had to face Malcolm Marshall, Andy Roberts and the rest of the mean machine.*

*Yet Gooch will be remembered as much for a short tour to South Africa in 1982 as for his majestic batting. The tour, sponsored by South African Breweries, soon became known as "Gooch's rebel tour", with Gooch branded as the ringleader simply because he was captain. Thereafter his name has become synonymous with South Africa, even though he has not set foot in the country since 1984. There were protests about him that almost led to his return form the West Indies in 1986, and the England tour to India in 1988 was cancelled largely because Gooch had been named captain. Now that he has again been named England captain—for the forthcoming tour to West Indies—there will inevitably be flak from some protesters over there. The South African ramifications have brought out the stubborn streak in Gooch, and in recent years he has withdrawn more into his shell—treating the bulk of the media with the wariness a rabbit reserves for both barrels of a shotgun. Is Gooch aware that his image is that of someone not enjoying his chosen career any more?*

I suppose I must appear a bit staid, a bit dour, keeping my emotions in check. Certainly in these image-conscious days, it pays you to blow your own trumpet a little, rather than sit back and let things come your way, like I do. Perhaps my posture has something to do with it. I have inherited my dad's rounded shoulders. My sense of humour is not the back-slapping, bellow-laughter style; I prefer a quite dig without being effervescent. I am still shy, and I feel inhibited that I am now recognised by someone in the street wherever I go.

I do still enjoy my cricket. I am very pleased at the way I came out of the lowest ebb of my career in 1987, when I just could not get a run at the start of the English season. I was so disturbed at the way I was playing—falling over to the offside, playing too much to leg—that it really got to me. I got two "pairs" in just a few days for Essex, and I found myself wondering if I had lost it for good. As a professional sportsman, you must worry when it goes seriously wrong; it affects your enjoyment, you start to wonder whether it is all worth it. It is a mental pressure. You need that enthusiasm that makes you want to get out there and do it. In 1987 I was wondering if it had all caught up on me. Obviously I felt I could still do the things I could ten years earlier, but I had started to notice that I felt exhausted after a hard day's play. I was slowing up and feeling less sharp.

*So how did you snap out of all that? You played so well the following year.*

It started to come back during the World Cup in Pakistan and India. I made one or two technical adjustments and the good wickets gave me confidence. I started the 1988 season determined to do well. I had resigned the Essex captaincy because I felt my form had been affected, and the West Indies were here. For the first time in my career I worked at developing a positive mental attitude. I had always had confidence in my own ability, but now I consciously told myself I was going to play well and score heaps of runs. I kept psyching myself up, telling myself that I was going to dominate the opposition. I forced myself to recall the times when I had done particularly well against the bowlers I was due to face that day. None of this stuff about "Oh, God, It's Malcolm Marshall today—is he going to knock my off-stump out of the ground for the tenth time on the trot?" No more waiting for the worst to happen, no more negative thoughts—even though I knew I would be facing fine bowlers. I got 275 in my first innings for Essex at the start of the 1988 season, and I never looked back. I got my feet moving at the right time, sorted out my pick-up and thought positively. When I went through that awful period, I had so many things on my mind that I had little idea about how I was going to play the ball when the bloke delivered it from the other end. When you are in the right frame of mind, you do not think about the technical side. You just go out there and do it naturally.

*Did the Australians stop you playing naturally in the 1989 series?*

I was disappointed. I had hoped to get a couple of hundreds against them, to get me up to ten Test centuries, but it was not to be. People talked about Terry Alderman having the sign on me, but he got a lot of other players out as well. English conditions helped him, and because he gets so close to the stumps, he has the eye of the umpires and always has a chance of an lbw. When someone like that keeps getting you out, you do not feel all that confident.

*Can you see how your critics would make a lot out of you asking to stand down from the Trent Bridge Test? Did you later feel you ought to have stayed in the side and battled it out?*

If the selectors had really forced the issue, then I would have played. But I just did not merit my place in the side at the time. I said that with the Ashes lost, there was now an opportunity to have a look at another opener, especially as I was not playing well. I cannot see how that should ever suggest I was being selective about when I should play. I believe you have to earn your right to an England place and, at that time, I was not there on merit.

*Yet you are a fusser about your technique; a dedicated practiser?*

Some say I am too critical, too meticulous about my technique. But I have thought more and more about doing myself justice in recent years. I was unhappy about my technique in 1987, yet I still ended up with 1,300 runs, averaging nearly 39, so perhaps I got some of it out of proportion. Basically, it came down to my mental approach.

*And to prosper against the West Indies must have been particularly satisfying.*

I was very happy about maintaining my standards throughout that 1988 series against them. I knew I just had to get my mind right about Malcolm Marshall. He is a very fine bowler and he has got me out a lot in the past. But I just kept telling myself I was going to come out on top. I knew that I had to try to dominate those guys, because they will get you out eventually if you are too tentative. They can also get disenchanted if things do not go their way out on the field. It is a pity that we did not get many chances to prove it. But I can look back with pleasure and some pride on my efforts against the West Indies.

*You must admit, though, that your absorption in your batting has affected your captaincy?*

I suppose that will always be held against me—that I packed in the Essex job for that reason. When you resign the captaincy for whatever reason that goes on your record, doesn't it? I did not want my batting worries to rub off on the rest of the lads in the dressing-room. At one stage, I told Keith Fletcher that I would be better off dropping myself. But he told me I just had to keep playing, that it would come right. I do believe that I am a team man, even though I get absorbed in my batting when it is not right, and I was concerned about what it was doing to the side. Yet people forget that I captained Essex for a lot of the games when we won the county championship the previous season. I have never courted the captaincy of Essex or England. It has not been the be-all and end-all for me, because I have known the limitations of the job. You need good players to put the performances in for you, otherwise it is hard work. There are a lot of hassles involved—it is like being a player-manager in soccer. You have your own problems as a player, yet you have to get the others motivated as well. You have to take on everyone else's problems—like the travelling expenses, the fact that the hotel room is not big enough, who is travelling in which car—and after a time it was draining me. The hardest thing for me was getting to the ground, tossing the coin, organising the practice and then finding myself padding up to open for Essex at ten to eleven, feeling rather frayed at the edges. I am meticulous about taking my time when I am due to bat, and my preparations were being affected. The captaincy on the field is not a problem, if you have been in the first-class game for long enough. It was the bits and pieces away from the middle that meant I was not giving a hundred per cent either to the captaincy or my batting. I have always been very conscious of doing well for the side, not for myself, and I was falling between two stools. So I handed the job back to Keith Fletcher.

*Was it easier to captain England, rather than Essex, because Micky Stewart was around to take care of all the bits and pieces?*
Yes, it was—and I enjoyed it, especially getting the chance to gee up the younger players who were new to Test cricket. All the England captain has to worry about is getting it right on the field. The manager is the confidant, the one who helps take the pressure off the players, sorts out the fielding practice and gives the captain time to think about his own fielding and batting. I need to make everything count at the right time, get myself channelled in the right direction. The England job came my way through accident, rather than design, and it was very rewarding. The highest honour for an England player, of course, and a pleasant surprise, but I knew that for all sorts of reasons, I had it because no one else was available. But we all had something to prove, and although we ended up well beaten at the Oval, we had a couple of good days against the West Indies and made them battle.

*You say you have never coveted the captaincy. Has the job of leading Essex sat more comfortably on your shoulders since it returned to you?*
I have been much more relaxed this time. Keith Fletcher has been around quite a lot, and, as always, his advice and encouragement have been terrific. We appointed Derek Pringle as vice-captain, and that has done him a lot of good. He is a very talented cricketer who needs a boot up the backside at times to squeeze even more talent out of him, but he has taken on the extra responsibility and it has worked well. Above all, I know that if I maintain my form, the captaincy will be no problem. It went well in 1989 and I felt happier about my own captaincy. We could have won four out of the five trophies on offer with a bit of luck.

*When you became England captain in the summer of 1988, you had already agreed to play for Western Province later in the year, thereby ruling you out of the England tour to India. Then the prospect of captaining England on that trip grew stronger and stronger. Can you see why some critics felt you were forcing the hands of the selectors?*
They will put whatever interpretation on it that they like, but I assure you it was not blackmail. Earlier in the summer, after a long look at the Indian itinerary, I realised it just was not feasible to take my family out there. The Western Province offer seemed much more attractive, because I would be based in one place and would see far more of Brenda and the girls than I would in an English season. But having captained England at the Oval, I felt a sense of pride and wanted to carry on. Then came the dilemma over Western Province: I wanted to talk to them out of courtesy and they were fine about releasing me from my contract. I did not hold a gun to anyone's head. There was no

question about me going to India only if I was captain; the circumstances had changed.

*But the England captaincy was the decisive factor?*

Yes. I simply had a change of heart because I had enjoyed leading England so much. You do not hand back that job lightly. I feel the same way a year later. We did not do our best for David Gower and we shall work hard in the West Indies to turn it round.

*Do you think, in retrospect, you ought to have avoided the captaincy of the South African tour party in 1982?*

Perhaps if I had not done that job, we might have toured India under me in 1988. I don't know. Ironically, I emerged as the compromise choice out in South Africa, simply because we did not want Boycott to captain us. It is strange how the figurehead aspect of the captaincy gets out of proportion. It was "Gooch's rebels", as if I was the instigator, rather than just a player. Perhaps if John Emburey had remained England captain in 1988 we might have gone to India, but it is difficult to read the minds of politicians. After all, Embers had been on that South African trip as well. Then again, I was deemed acceptable for the World Cup in India in 1987, so where does all that leave us? It was one of those things that snowballed because of intense media interest. The politicians took notice and felt they had to take action. The initial raising of temperature came from the media—yet they will say that South Africa is now front page news and not to be left to the cricket writers.

*Your South African experience has changed your attitude to the media in general, hasn't it?*

Yes. I have become much more suspicious. They are quite entitled to write or say what they like as long as it is not libellous—and don't forget I won a libel action against *The Sun* for an allegation concerning me and South African cricket—but they cannot expect to turn round and seek co-operation from me after I have been slagged off. Some of them ring up and, without common courtesy—without even saying "sorry to bother you, but . . ."—they dive straight in with daft questions. I take exception to such rudeness, especially as I have never been one to seek big headlines or make silly forecasts. The high media interest in cricket these days means that most things you say can be misinterpreted. For example, take the time when Ted Dexter was appointed the new chairman of the England selectors. A journalist I know and trust rang me up for my reaction, and I said Ted Dexter was perfectly entitled to his opinion about my merits as captain, that I would like to keep the job but, if not, I would be happy to serve under anyone. An hour or so later, up comes this headline on the teletext: Gooch Says He Wants To Step Down As England Captain, backed up by my one quote about Dexter being entitled to his own opinion. I was furious, because it looked as if I was happy to give it away. I rang the agency and told them to put it right, otherwise I would sue for libel. They did correct it, but such incidents would make anyone wary.

*Even though you have not been back to South Africa for a number of years, you will always be associated with that country. What is your feeling about the recent efforts to discourage English cricketers from going there?*

I am disappointed at the new restrictions. The younger players will miss valuable coaching and playing opportunities, and the chance to help coloured cricketers. One section of the sporting community will continue to be punished. At least we all should know where we stand now, but I feel that a citizen of the United Kingdom should be allowed to go there without being punished. Sport is such an easy touch for the politicians. Its high profile commands the headlines, yet it does not really mean a thing materially to governments. When I was last in India, I bought some diamonds for Brenda, and the guy in the shop told me that there was only one country where he could get them. Guess where.

I do not agree at all with Apartheid. It is a terrible system, but the cricketers out there are doing their best to put things right; they are going in the right direction. Yet it seems the South African Cricket Union will continue to get no encouragement for all the effort they have put in.

I have never had one cross word with any coloured cricketer over playing in South Africa and their governments are perfectly entitled to take whatever stand they wish. But our cricketers are being victimised.

*Are you keeping your options open over playing again in South Africa?*

I know that if I went to play there, that would mean the end of my Test career—and at the moment I would like it to continue. My ambitions for England are still strong, and at 36, I still have a few years left in me. Gordon Greenidge and Viv Richards are both older than me, and they still seem to be hungry. I want to be proud of my performances when I retire, and an important part of that concerns an improvement in my Test record. I have thrown away a few centuries by getting out in the seventies and eighties, and I would not want to go out of the game having scored less than double figures in hundreds. I would like to be averaging over forty in Tests, but at the moment my Test record is no better than OK.

*Your views on South Africa underline that you will dig your heels in over issues that concern you strongly. That was particularly evident in the West Indies in 1986, when you incurred the wrath of Lester Bird, the Deputy Premier of Antigua, and you nearly flew home before the final Test in protest. Were you just being stubborn about political mischief-making?*

I tried to be as helpful as I could before the tour began, pointing out that I genuinely do abhor Apartheid. This followed lengthy negotiations to ensure the tour went ahead. I did not want to play in the final Test in Antigua, and it was only out of loyalty to David Gower that I stayed on. At least I remained faithful to my principles.

*When rumours of another unofficial tour to South Africa began to grow, it is fair to say that you and your great friend John Emburey were favourites to be on that tour. Emburey is going—why not you?*

I was never asked. That may have had something to do with the fact that I am sueing the *Daily Mirror* for running a story that I had already signed to go on a tour to South Africa. I had not.

*Has the game become more complicated during your career?*

The complications have arisen *off* the field. The good part is getting on to the field, wondering how I am going to make runs against good bowlers on a pitch that helps them, or how we are to get their best batsmen out. I still get the same pleasure out of cricket; it is a challenge to keep playing well at my age. I know it is only performance that keeps me in the team now, whereas ten years ago, potential might get me the benefit of the doubt. Now I know I cannot live on past efforts. That is not due to any insecurity on my part. I am happy to strive to be at the peak of performance to remain in the team.

*A final word on captaincy. You have had the good fortune to learn your trade under the best two leaders in the English game over the past two decades. How do Mike Brearley and Keith Fletcher compare?*

Tactically they were both excellent—and lucky enough to lead good sides with match-winning bowlers. Mike had Ian Botham at his best when he captained England, plus Bob Willis and other class bowlers. He had the ability to converse with anyone in the team at the right level; he would never patronise someone like me, who lacked his intellectual brilliance. Both he and Fletch never bore grudges, and they could strike that fine balance between staying aloof and being one of the boys. In the Essex line-up, there has always been an open line between me and Fletch, and it will stay that way—even though he has retired from the first team. I always wanted him in the side when I was captain. He is a great man to lean on. Of the two, I would say Fletch was the better player.

# MIKE
# GATTING

**‘We are not traitors; we knew what we were getting ourselves into, and we are taking our punishment. ’**

T HE *vicissitudes in Mike Gatting's life over the past two years have stemmed from the same positive approach that has underpinned the most memorable parts of his career. His strength has in turn been his weakness. That bluff openness which characterises his batting and captaincy led to a series of traumatic events that saw him sign away his England career in favour of South Africa. At the heart of his decision to leave the Test arena at the age of 32 was a deep disenchantment with the English game's ruling body, the Test and County Cricket Board. Gatting's loyalty to his players and fury at being called a cheat led to his public, unsavoury row with Shakoor Rana at Faisalabad in December, 1987. Seven months later, he lost the England captaincy after an alleged nocturnal encounter with a barmaid at the team's hotel during a Test. Gatting's uncomplicated vision of the world could not encompass a decision to relieve him of the captaincy even though the TCCB publicly believed his side of the story rather than the detailed allegations of the barmaid in a tabloid newspaper.*

*With Gatting embroiled at the same time with the TCCB in another dispute (this time over sensitive remarks concerning the Shakoor Rana episode in Gatting's autobiography), it was clear there was a serious breakdown in relations between employer and the employee awarded the OBE a year earlier for his services to English cricket. The breach was never repaired and Gatting retreated into sullen dogmatism. To him, the issue was clear-cut: he had been let down. When Ted Dexter voted for David Gower, Gatting was hurt by the vote of confidence in the new captain for the entire Ashes series. He felt rejected and consigned to the periphery of an England dressing-room he had recently controlled, even though the new regime maintained they wanted a rejuvenated and committed Gatting with them.*

*By the middle of an English season that had promised so much for England and Gatting, he was ripe for plucking by Ali Bacher. It was appropriate that South Africa*

31

*beckoned: he had long retreated into a laager mentality, convinced of the justice behind his various causes and suspicious of any attempts at compromise. Not since Alec Bedser traipsed up and down England's motorways to bring balm to Geoffrey Boycott's ego had there been such wooing of a disgruntled player. So a basically likeable man with a weakness for black and white solutions to complicated issues ended up captaining a side in a country whose constitution has a defined stance on matters black and white. It was a sad way for Gatting to abort an England career that involved so much pride in playing for his country. Gatting's patriotism had always contrasted so graphically with the understated commitment of his contemporaries. Judging by the naivete of his comments on South Africa, he would be bringing to the tour all the gung-ho sophistication of a Sandhurst subaltern on the Somme. Was he concerned at the moral issues involved?*

I know very little about Apartheid, but I do believe in keeping politics out of sport. I understand that the South African Cricket Union are trying to distance themselves from their own government on Apartheid; to try to integrate cricket and break down barriers as much as they can. It seems to me they should be encouraged. I earn my living playing sport, and I should be allowed to do that anywhere else in the world without any comebacks.

*But you are going to face a lot of opposition in various parts of the world.*

I know I shall have to live with my decision. I thought a great deal about not playing again for England—that meant such a lot to me—but I'm sticking to my word to Ali Bacher. I am basically going because of my assessment of what is best for me in cricket and also for my family. I was only prepared to do one more overseas tour anyway, and it would have been unfair to England just to expect to play in home series. In the long run this tour might possibly benefit English cricket because they can start afresh now, with so many experienced players banned.

*How do you feel about headlines calling you a traitor the day after the story broke?*

It hurts to be called that, because anyone who knows me will agree I loved playing for England. But now I have got to do what is best for my family. My home life has been ripped apart recently, and the death of my mother-in-law hit us very hard. I have to put my wife and children first from now on. They have suffered a lot in my absence.

*These are deep waters, Mike. Your tour will pose a major threat to England's participation in the Commonwealth Games, and it might even ruin the Games. Surely it is not just a cricket matter?*

It is difficult for me to say what will happen with other sports, but some members of the Commonwealth are also members of the ICC, and we have done nothing wrong according to recent guidelines laid down by the ICC. All we have done is to decide to go and play in South Africa, while fully aware of the ICC regulation that we would be banned from Test cricket. We are not traitors; we knew what we were getting ourselves into, and we are taking our punishment.

*When did you decide to go?*

Ali Bacher approached me on July 17, between the third and fourth Tests. It was always going to be the major decision of my career, and it took me a fortnight to make up my mind. I did not discuss money with him until another day—after I had communicated my decision.

*Looking back on the events of 1988 that saw you lose the England captaincy, how frustrated were you at that, with the West Indies over here?*

It was particularly disappointing because I felt they were vulnerable at the start of the Test series. In the World Cup in 1987, Graham Gooch had said to me that he was fed up with being smashed off the park by them. We played really well against them out there, and again in the one-dayers in England in May 1988. They were having to bed down some of their younger players, and we were more experienced and in a strong mental state. I was unsure just how fresh some of their senior players were for another tour of England, while we were keyed up. We got an honourable draw in the Trent Bridge Test, and I certainly do not believe we would have lost the series four-nil if subsequent events had been avoided. Despite losing the England captaincy, I wanted to play all summer. But by the time I got to Old Trafford, I was not in the right frame of mind. Too many other things were dogging me, and I realised I had been wrong to get back on the horse again after it had just thrown me off.

*You lost the England captaincy for an alleged dalliance that you have strenuously denied. But do you agree that your preparation for the last day of the Trent Bridge Test could have been better? You were not-out overnight, the captain of the side, and a rearguard was needed the next day to avoid defeat.*

I had not had an excess to drink and I was in bed by half-past midnight. When I got up at 8.30, I had had my full quota of sleep—as much as I get at home—and felt fine. I was in perfect shape to resume my innings, after doing all the hard netting since the start of the Test. The ball from Malcolm Marshall that got me would have finished me off after five minutes on the first morning of a Test. It was a beauty. Do they think that we professionals care nothing about how to prepare for a Test Match? Are we not allowed to relax? If England players get caught drinking at 2.30 in the morning, they ought to be punished, but not for a sensible drink in their own room before midnight. In 1986, when a few of the lads got caught in a wine bar on the eve of a one-day international at Old Trafford, I told them as captain that they were out of order—and I meant it. You do not get caught in public drinking late at night; it just gives the tabloids ammunition.

*How did the loss of the England captaincy affect the family?*

It opened our eyes. Although the phone was taken off the hook, reporters took it in turns to knock on our door. Around midnight one of them actually stuck her foot in the door as it was opened and demanded to speak to me. That was ridiculous. The freedom of the Press allows them to camp outside my door, but where has my family's freedom gone? The idea that by law we should have a right of reply sounds good in theory, but that will only give them a follow-up to breathe fresh life into a dying story. What has happened to my freedom to enjoy a quiet drink in private during a Test?

*But you do agree that some of the media criticism about the events in Pakistan and New Zealand was justified and that as a result England players were bound to be under closer scrutiny after that?*

Yes, but you can only take so much. That was my third tour to Pakistan and nothing had changed in umpiring standards. I agree I went too far with Shakoor Rana, but all the English journalists out there thought I was pushed to the point where even Job might have lost his temper. I know that does not excuse my role in it, but they saw for themselves what was going on.

DECLARATIONS

*Have you played the Shakoor Rana incident over and over in your mind?*

Of course—and it was not a good thing at all for the game of cricket. I had said my piece, and as Bill Athey led me away, I had asked the umpire to get back to square leg and get on with the game. But then he started swearing at me and calling me a cheat. That was the worst thing of all, as anybody who knows me will tell you. I just snapped. I wonder how many would have turned the other cheek? Then we had the situation of an umpire holding us to ransom over the apology. That tour convinced me that English players do not get enough credit for their sportsmanship.

*To compound the felony as it were, the England players were given a £1,000 bonus each soon after Faisalabad. Hardly a public relations coup by the TCCB or your players, was it? Looking back on it, why not give the money to charity?*

With hindsight, you are right. Don't forget that at the time many influential writers were saying we ought to come home early, and there was a lot of confusion around. The cash award just complicated it further. To make matters worse, we showed some dissent during the last Test, just after the Press had been told about the bonus. All I can say about that is that at no stage did I swear at anyone, and the two umpires confirmed that. We were upset by one incident when I knew the ball had carried to Bruce French behind the stumps. There was no question the batsman had touched the ball, but the square leg umpire said he had not seen the ball carry to Frenchy. The batsman would not believe us, and I was amazed that the square leg umpire didn't support us. But all I did was get his ruling as quickly as possible and get on with the game. It just summed up the tour.

*How close were you to giving up the England captaincy at the end of the Pakistan tour?*

I never thought about it; I did not want to be a martyr. I was more concerned that something had to be done to improve the game of cricket.

*Do you think that the events of 1987 might have done some good by the time England go to Pakistan again?*

Only the International Cricket Council can do something about that. The umpires out in Pakistan, India and New Zealand do not have a great deal of first-class cricket, and yet they are in charge of Test matches. I would like umpires out there to work off video tapes; to simulate their work, judge what decision they would give in certain situations. If you like, to stop the action at a particular stage and ask the umpire what is his verdict, and why. It is no different to players looking at videos of the opposition or checking their own techniques. It is just basic professionalism. Overseas umpires never seem to practise, but they are no different to players in their need. That was the gist of my tour report after Pakistan. I understand that umpires are only human; that it is a difficult job. But I tried to be constructive and simply asked for greater attention to detail.

*So 1987 ended on a painful note for you—in stark contrast to the earlier months, when you came back from Australia having won all three competitions, and then you were awarded the OBE. Mike Gatting seemed to be the England captain for years to come, and yet it soon fell apart. Was it a shock?*

34

I never thought it would be plain sailing; my early years as an England player taught me to take nothing for granted. I knew that many hassles attached themselves to the honour of being England captain. Some of the tabloids, for a start. Just before the First Test in Brisbane in 1986 we had heard that one of the Australian papers tried to plant three girls on our tour party to see if any of the players could be compromised. We believe that Micky Stewart managed to head them off, but I had seen all that before on other England tours when others suffered from Press rumour.

*Is that why you were less than euphoric at Melbourne when England retained the Ashes inside three days and everyone bar the England captain seemed to have been swept along on a tide of patriotic fervour? You seemed very low-key at a time which ought to have been a career highlight.*

I was absolutely knackered, mentally and physically. My heart and soul had gone into the task, and a massive wave of anti-climax swept over me. At the start of the tour, we had been written off, and I was still annoyed at that. I had been accused of using the same old cliches at Press conferences. But they kept throwing the same old questions at me: "How do you feel about winning the Ashes, Mike?" How do they expect me to feel? I could write down their questions before the Press conference and they would come up with them. I make no apologies for playing it straight at those Press conferences, because it was a great honour to be captain and I was determined that there would be no misrepresentations.

*So when did the achievements of that Australian tour finally sink in?*

When I sat down at home and thought: "Yes, that was brilliant." Not until then. Even at Sydney, after we had won the World Series Final to make it a clean sweep, I was drained half-an-hour after the celebrations had started. Afterwards, I realised what a great atmosphere we had built up, with guys giving their all—even though strapped up. People said it was not a strong Aussie side. But their best players then are still doing the job now, apart from Bruce Reid. They must have been pretty good. We also beat the West Indies and a strong Pakistan side, as well as undergoing horrendous travel schedules for nearly four months. What really hurts is the way our achievement out there has been minimised by those who were full of it at the time of victory. Since then, it has been a case of "Well, the opposition wasn't very good, was it?"—a classic case of building us up to knock us down again. One day David Gower is a great player, the next they reckon it is time to drop him because he has been caught behind—playing the sort of shot that has brought him stacks of runs at the highest level. You do not become a bad player in a couple of days. Everybody has a bad patch, and then you need encouragement. It saddens me that good cricket writers like Michael Carey and Peter Smith are going out of Test Match Press boxes in unhappy circumstances. There are many contradictions in sports writing these days: editors do not understand that a writer cannot slag off an England team selection just a few days after praising the wisdom of the selectors.

*Unlike some recent England captains, you refused to lend your name to an exclusive column in a tabloid, despite being offered large sums of money for what amounts to a few minutes' work now and again. Why?*

The status of an England captain is too high to get it involved in tabloid exclusives. The rest of the tabloids would have been after me if I had signed a specific contract. I also believe that the captain's views should be for all the papers, not just one. Favouring one paper leads to friction. Also, I do not think that what goes on in the dressing-room should be for public consumption.

*It is ironic that you stayed out of the circulation war between the tabloids, yet one of them brought you down?*

Right. I like to think that people will believe my side of the story against that of such a paper, but I know that it is my word against someone else's. I now believe very little of what I read in the popular Press.

*Let's talk more about cricket matters. You are generally acknowledged as a magnificent player of spin bowling. Did you make a conscious effort to master the spinners, or did it come naturally?*

It came initially by luck and then hard work. When I was about eleven I was lucky enough to spend hours in the nets being bowled at by a leg-spinner called Ted Jackson, who played for my local club. He would bowl me all the variations of leg-spin and I worked hard even then to pick them. When I went to Australia to play grade cricket with Balmain in Sydney at the age of 21, I stayed with a family whose son was a very good leggie. The hard wickets in Australia and a great deal of practice gave me an insight into playing leg-spinners; I think they are the best to bat against because they are quicker and bouncier, and you can use the pace of the ball to play them, rather than force shots. Having said that, you do have to watch the bowling hand a lot more than with other spinners.

On my first England tour to India I spent a long time watching their spinners and talking to my captain, Keith Fletcher, about technique and footwork. I felt it would be a waste to get bogged down by the slow bowlers after weathering the pace attack, so I have always tried to feel relaxed against spin; I am never inhibited by it. If you cannot take the initiative to the spinner, he can trouble you: the ball comes at you much more slowly, and you have to get after him, otherwise you struggle against a class performer and a well-set field. I used to struggle against off-spinners, but now I am more confident because I let the ball do the work rather than play at the ball. With a slow-left-armer the ball is going away from the right-hand bat for most of the time, but when the off-break is coming in at the stumps, you have to sort out your footwork and cut down on a few shots to avoid being bowled, hitting across the line. Against off-spinners it is a case of getting the feet moving to avoid being tucked up. That comes with confidence and experience.

*Do you agree that your dominance of spin bowling as a batsman affects your captaincy; that you could be more sympathetic in your handling of the spinners in the field?*

That is probably fair, although in my defence it must be said that John Emburey and Phil Edmonds usually got what they wanted when I captained them. Perhaps it was more a matter of approach. I like the spinners to attack early on, before the batsman has sorted out his footwork and timing. Embers, for example, likes to get into a groove so that the batsman eventually gets himself out as part of a patient strategy. I prefer to exert pressure right from the start. When I bat against the spinners, I am trying to get them to bowl where I want, so as captain I put myself in their position and try to get them fretting as the spinners attack them. Mike Brearley had a reputation of being more sympathetic than me to our spinners. He was never afraid to ask the advice of Phil and

John and give them the field they wanted. They have both been high-class bowlers, but I do agree that I have expected a high standard from them.

*Back to your batting. You do seem to find some bizarre ways of being dismissed—particularly getting out lbw without playing a shot?*

You mean the "leave-alone shot"? Well, it comes back to haunt me every five years or so, but because it is seen on television people assume I am always making miscalculations. Sometimes a batsman does misjudge the direction of the ball but sometimes so does the bloke at the other end, who did not realise just how much the ball was doing when it hit the pad. I get so cross when I am out that way; you think you are in and you are telling yourself to play positively, then the jinx strikes. On the two occasions when Malcolmn Marshall did me at Lord's in 1984, I had not been in all that long, and when Dennis Lillee got me, I was just thinking about survival with the new ball coming up, instead of getting after him. At Old Trafford in 1988, the same thing happened, but my frame of mind was utterly negative after all the recent traumas. I was in no psychological shape to bat properly. Overall, that particular dismissal does not happen all that often to me, but the cameras play it to death when it crops up. It is like an international goalkeeper letting a soft shot go through his hands. We are all human, after all.

# GEOFF LAWSON

**'There was no mystique about beating England. Terry Alderman bowled a good line wicket to wicket and the English batsmen kept missing the ball. '**

GEOFF LAWSON is one of those fast bowlers who successfully conceal a cerebral light under a fairly thick bushel. He shades Merv Hughes comfortably in the tally of brain cells even though he appears the archetypal Aussie quickie who would remain unperturbed by blood on the pitch. Yet Lawson returns to his work as an optometrist at the University of New South Wales when hostilities cease. For the last decade he has ruffled all the feathers of English batting, from Geoffrey Boycott to Robin Smith. His first encounter with England was at Sydney in 1978, when the raw-boned student disturbed Boycott's amour propre in memorable fashion. With England needing just two runs to beat New South Wales in the second innings, Boycott found himself on the end of four successive bouncers in Lawson's first over. He was warned after the second one, took no notice, and the fourth in a row flew off Boycott's gloves over slips for the winning runs. In the first innings, Lawson had twice dumped Ian Botham on all fours with some selective bouncers, thereby dropping a hint that the natural successor to Lillee and Thomson could be found in the laboratory at the local university.

Since that initial skirmish, Lawson has played a significant role in every Ashes series, apart from that of 1986/87, when he was recovering from a serious back injury. It was that injury which seemed to spark a behavioural metamorphosis. The raw edges appear to have softened as the Damocles' sword of retirement hovered over him, and his bowling acquired greater control and variety while he came to terms with a compromise on physical endeavour. In the 1989 series Lawson proved an able foil to Terry Alderman's unrelenting accuracy, and the Man of the Match award, in the Old Trafford Test that brought the Ashes back to Australia, served as a fitting climax to his career against England. His affable treatment of autograph-hunters and articulate approachability towards the media came as a surprise to those who recalled the times when he carried the fast bowler's natural hostility into less permissible areas. Had Lawson mellowed?—or

39

*was that serenity due to satisfaction at being, at last, part of a successful Australian side?*

When you consider that I might have ended up in a wheelchair after my back injury, I'm bound to treat every day on the cricket field as a bonus. It has helped give me some perspective, so that when I have had a bad day with my bowling, I can look back on the good times and count my blessings. It has also been great to be involved in a squad with such a fantastic team spirit. Bobby Simpson, our coach, deserves credit for that—he has worked us hard, but everyone knew what was needed. We wanted to win every game, because we knew that success breeds success. Our bitter experience of losing a lot in recent years has toughened us and made us appreciate every victory.

*The critics in England have been trying to find reasons for your spectacular success. Were they at fault in under-rating the 1989 Australians from the start?*

They should have taken a closer look at the way we fought back against the West Indies earlier in the year. We lost the series three-one, but it was a lot closer than that. In the first three Tests the conditions really suited the West Indies fast bowlers. At Perth we lasted out until the end of the final day, when I was not allowed to bat because I had a broken jaw. At Adelaide we had the best of the draw. Apart for the first Test, we played well and got battle-hardened against the best team in the world. You get sick of losing, and we were determined to win in England. So there has always been a purpose to our time on tour and we worked hard on the basics. Allan Border's captaincy improved, because we had enough runs to enable him to attack. Before, he used to let the game drift a little. Now he was more imaginative. But there was no mystique about beating England. Terry Alderman bowled seam up on a good line from wicket to wicket and the English batsmen kept missing the ball. If you pitch a ball on the off-stump and a guy misses while trying to hit it through mid-wicket, there is a pretty good chance of an lbw decision. Terry kept saying that we had to be patient on slow, low English wickets, and he was right. Having said all that, I thought it would be a very close series, that a couple of great catches or an inspired piece of bowling would swing a game. I knew we would do well, but not as well as we did.

*You took some time to get into your stride in the series. Did you struggle a little in the first three Tests?*

I lacked rhythm. Like the tempo of a golfer's swing, a fast bowler needs rhythm in his run-up. It is an intangible, but you know when it is not right. It was not until I bowled at Bristol that it felt right and I started to let the ball go at the right time and consistently hit the seam. We went straight to Old Trafford from Bristol and I settled into a consistent, tight groove. Instead of trying to bowl outswingers, inswingers, off-cutters and the whole shebang, I contented myself with a stock delivery. Terry Alderman was right—keep it simple.

*How much homework was done on specific fielding positions for certain English batsmen?*

Obviously men like Border and Alderman had noticed one or two things in previous years they spent in county cricket. But that is just a matter of common sense and I assume the other Test countries do their homework, including England. When I got David Gower caught twice down the legside in the first Test at Leeds, many people thought that was a new plan hatched that summer—but I got Gower out the same way on two occasions in the 1982/3 series. He had not learned to cut out that shot and he was at it again when we played Leicestershire between the fourth and fifth Tests. I had him dropped at leg-slip off the first ball he faced, playing the same wafting shot we had seen so many times before. You would be a pretty dumb bowler if you forgot things like that.

*It must have been particularly satisfying to find England's selectors rooted in a 1981 timewarp, relying on the kind of inspiration Ian Botham provided that year.*

They ignored the fact that some of our team were sixteen or so when that series took place. I lost a lot of sleep about being taken apart by Botham at Leeds in 1981—especially as I hurt my back there and did not play again on the tour. But that was just a one-off. It was a great piece of cricket history, but the game moves on and none of us were worried about facing Botham in 1989. Before the first Test his highest score was 40-odd and he had only taken wickets on dodgy pitches at Worcester. He bowled steadily enough during the series but he was no danger man, and we never believed he would be.

*What did you think of the overall standard of English cricket in 1989?*

I was very disappointed with the lack of fight put up by the counties when we kept rolling them over. Hardly anybody wanted to get their heads down and fight it out. I could not see an Australian State side capitulating in the way the counties did. We approach each Shield game as if it is a Test Match, and the batters know that they could wait a long time before they get another chance if they throw away their wickets. A lot of English batsmen play across the line, and you cannot blame that entirely on too much one-day cricket. We play a lot of it in Australia and yet our top batsmen are correct. Surely you just walk out and bat and then adapt to whatever the length of game.

*It was something of a surprise to see you over here again, bearing in mind the last time I saw you in an Ashes series was at Perth in 1986, where you looked downhearted and unfit.*

I should never have played in that Test. They picked me for the first one, then made me twelfth man, which did not make a lot of sense when you consider I am experienced and did not need any introduction to the atmosphere of a Test. Then at Perth I hurt my ankle stepping over a boundary rope and it came up like a balloon. I should not have played there and took nought for plenty. But I still wanted to play for Australia, and worked hard to get my fitness back. For the last two seasons in the Sheffield Shield I have taken a lot of wickets and been near the top of the bowling averages. I no longer rely on all-out pace—at last using my brain—and now I feel I've got a good idea of where I want to put the ball. The slower one is coming along nicely—perhaps I will take up off-spin!

*How did you injure your back?*

Too much repetitive straining. Fast bowling is a very unnatural activity—it is not made for backs. At one stage during the 1985/86 season I never thought I would walk again. I saw an orthopaedic surgeon who contrived to break two of my vertebrae. Legal correspondence is still in progress about that. I lost two stone and lay on my back for three weeks, doing nothing. To sneeze was the most painful experience ever. Dennis Lillee, who knows all about back injuries, told me it would be a case of two steps forward, then one step back, and he was right. I got through after being happy just to be able to walk, and now I bowl a few less inswingers because that puts a strain on the back. You could say I am happy just to be here. If I am injured I get very down mentally, because you must be fit to do well at this level. At home, when I am not playing, I run five kilometres a day, then do about thirty sprints, plus a lot of sit-ups and push-ups. You have to give yourself the best chance to do well—after that, it is a matter of luck and talent. I know some people think I run too far—it is about twenty paces—but I need that to feel balanced, to be sure I know what I am doing. We are back to rhythm again.

*Were you always aggressive on the field?*

I prefer the word *competitive*. Win, lose or draw, try your very best out there and shake hands after the game. I got a bit of a reputation from that first game against England, but I was unhappy about being bounced by Bob Willis and Ian Botham. Andy Hilditch, my captain, told me I did not have to bowl in the second innings, because only four were needed, but I said "give me that ball" and I let Boycott have it. I have never believed in lying down on the cricket field.

*Nor off the field—you have a reputation of being pretty frank in your views.*

I think the Australian Cricket Board see me as a bit of a stirrer, but all I do is stick up for the rights of all cricketers. I have had many discussions with them over money. I do not think 2,750 dollars is enough when you play a Test, nor is 800 dollars for a one-day international when you consider how many of them we play and how often we pack out the grounds. We need closer liaison between our Board and the players. As far as I can see it is back to the atmosphere of the pre-Packer period. I think we should have a union in Australia and I have had a lot of correspondence about the idea with Geoff Cook, the Cricketers' Association secretary in England. That is something I would like to organise in Australia. There are so many anomalies. You can get picked in the squad for a State, turn up at all the practice sessions and still get paid nothing if you do not make the twelve. Consider the New South Wales set-up: some guys live in the Western Suburbs area of Sydney, and if they travel through the heavy traffic to the cricket ground for practice every Tuesday and Thursday, all expenses come out of their pocket. Yet they might not get a Shield game for the entire season. Therefore they will earn not one dollar, and that is unfair. Financially the game in Australia is in a very healthy condition, but many fringe players put in a lot of hard work for absolutely nothing.

*What about playing in South Africa?*

I have had deep discussions with many of our guys who have toured there and I do not blame anyone for going. The money is good, and maybe the tours help more black people to play cricket. I am a little surprised at the closed minds of some of the rebel tour critics. If an offer came my way in the future, I would have to consider it.

*You are now captain of New South Wales, and by all accounts a successful one. Are the officials in power rather worried you might be encouraging your players to be rebellious?*

I cannot see why. I think I have a fair amount to offer. The job fell into my lap after Greg Dyer was dropped—something I did not agree with. But I had been captain of my club for a fair while and I was keen to see how I would go. Every captain needs good bowlers, and New South Wales had them last season in Mike Whitney, Greg Matthews, Peter Taylor and myself. We beat the Shield winners, Western Australia, twice and I really enjoyed the experience. I made sure we played positively and told the players to stop thinking about getting on the trip to England. About three-quarters of the team were tour candidates, but I told them that if they played well for New South Wales, everything else would take care of itself. I found the physical and mental aspects of captaincy taxing while out on the field, though. I was used to wandering down to fine leg for a breather, but I had to think about field changes and the other bowlers while I walked back to bowl myself. One-day cricket was a real hassle, with no time at all to relax. I can see why few fast bowlers have been captains over the years!

*Has there been a game when it all came right for you and fast bowling seemed absolutely natural?*

Yes, Adelaide in 1982, when I took nine wickets in the match against England. It was a belting wicket and yet I do not think I bowled a bad ball in the game. That was a great series for me, but at Adelaide even the slower ball came out right. All this on the finest cricket ground in the world—a perfect wicket, lovely outfield and beautiful surroundings. For me, Adelaide is the one place where I can look around if I am having a bad day and think: "It's not such a bad life after all."

*Despite a streak of radicalism, I get the impression that you respect many of cricket's traditions.*

If you do not know the history of the game, you are missing out on some of its enjoyment. When we regained the Ashes at Old Trafford, it was a moment to savour on a personal level but also from a historical point of view—the first time Australia had done that to England since 1934. A lot of our guys read up on the game. It is interesting to see how it has evolved. I started off with the history of New South Wales cricket and progressed from there. I have just finished reading about the great Australian side of 1920/21 that won eight games in a row. They had some great players, and I hope one of these days good judges will say some kind things about our 1989 side.

*You seem to take the autograph sessions seriously, too.*

I know what it is like to hang around for them. Where I come from—Wagga Wagga—you do not see too many cricket stars, and I can relate to the kids. My first autograph was Alan Connolly, the Victorian seam bowler, at the Sydney Cricket Ground in 1968 before he played against the West Indies. He was nice to me, and I have tried to be the same to those who have taken the trouble to be patient and polite.

# ALVIN KALLICHARRAN

'**As soon as I got in the West Indies team in the early Seventies it was clear to me that the Asian guys were not going to get fair treatment. It has always been there, but it has just grown and grown.**'

NEAT. Wristy. Nimble. Twinkling. The inevitable, adjectival response to an innings from Alvin Kallicharran. They have been used for nigh on twenty years, as this diminutive left-hander has demonstrated that steely wrists and swift footwork which gets you to the pitch of the ball can happily compensate for a lack of inches. All those years of table tennis and batting with a branch in the sugar plantation area of Berbice in Guyana have helped develop a wristy, keen-eyed resilience, and he has blossomed into one of the most attractive left-handers in world cricket. And prolific: only Roy Marshall and Gordon Greenidge among West Indians scored more first-class runs, and only Viv Richards has exceeded Kallicharran's 87 centuries. Yet his career has been an anti-climax in the past decade. Internal politics and personality clashes meant Kallicharran never played in a Test after 1980. The man who created history in 1977 by becoming the first player to tear up a Kerry Packer contract, caused an even greater furore by playing in South Africa for Transvaal and then for Lawrence Rowe's rebel West Indies side. Kallicharran became a pariah back home in Guyana, and he has not returned there since 1981. Instead, he dedicated himself to scoring runs for Warwickshire, Transvaal and Orange Free State, while his many admirers wondered just how impressively he might have built on his twelve hundreds in 66 Tests.

It may surprise some that such a humorous, cheerful man should become embroiled in various controversies, but Kallicharran enjoys his fair share of grit. Where he grew up, in the bosom of a large, poor family, the game of cricket provided a social passport, a blissful diversion from cutting sugar cane. Slow to anger, but long of memory, Kallicharran has played a marathon mental innings in the face of what he has perceived to be an unfairly hostile attack. His experience as a player of Asian extraction supports the suspicion that the West Indies dressing-room has not been a haven of ethnic harmony in the last couple of decades.

As soon as I got in the West Indies team in the early Seventies, it was clear to me that the Asian guys were not going to get fair treatment. It has always been there, but it has just grown and grown. I scored a hundred on my Test debut, yet I knew that my captain, Gary Sobers, did not rate me and he said little to me. I batted at number six in that first Test, and he said nothing to me about promoting me up the order. Come the next Test and we bat, I was just stepping into the shower when Sobers said to me: "Where are you going? You're batting at three!" By this time our openers were already out in the middle. He spoke very sharply to me, but I just took it and got ready in a hurry. I got another hundred. Still Sobers hardly said a word to me. When Rohan Kanhai took over the West Indies captaincy from Sobers, there were a lot of whispers about him behind his back. Like me, he was of Asian background, and the West Indies Board never really wanted someone like that to be the skipper. When he was passed over as captain for the tour to India in favour of Clive Lloyd, I felt that was because they did not want an Asian leading a West Indies team in India. Rohan never played again for the West Indies, and after that I became more selective about my friends in the dressing-room. In the last two decades, very few have played for West Indies who were not negroes. Kanhai, Bacchus, Bachin, Gomes and myself—no-one else, I think. No wonder the Asians support the opposition whenever the West Indies play one-day internationals in Berbice! More than half the population of Guyana is of Asian descent, and in Trinidad the population is very mixed. Yet the selectors never seem to bother with players from either place.

*Did you also feel that you lost a few points in the eyes of those West Indians who carried on playing for Kerry Packer, rather than tearing up their contracts as you did?*

Very definitely. It lodged in the minds of some influential players that I had dropped out. But they did not have the complications I had. Warwickshire made it clear to me that I had little future with them if I played for Packer, and I did not want to return to live in Guyana with my son just a toddler. I was not sure how long Packer's cricket would last, so I played safe.

*You were under a lot of pressure from both sides at that time, weren't you?*

It all came to a head at Chesterfield, when I announced I was pulling out. I could barely go out of the dressing-room door without being besieged and it was pretty bad indoors as well. There was Dennis Amiss, who had also signed for Packer, telling me that I would face bankruptcy if I tore up the contract, while my captain David Brown—who was chairman of the Cricketers' Association and very anti the whole project—told me to stay with the traditional brand of cricket. To complicate matters, Eddie Barlow, the Derbyshire captain—another Packer capture—was trying to get me into a corner and tell me what a mistake I was making. Then Kerry Packer himself started ringing me up at home, saying he was prepared to pay me anything to keep me, then threatening that I would lose my house if I was in breach of contract. I would not take his money, because that would mean someone owned me. The Cricketers Association lawyers backed me all the way and I got through in the end. But it was a hard time. I am cynical, though, about the reaction in the Caribbean to the South African rebel tour and to Packer. The Packer players were pardoned for playing in a rival brand of cricket, but not Lawrence Rowe's side. And what did both sets of players go to South Africa and Packer for? Money. Nothing else.

*But can't you see how emotive it is for someone of your colour to play in South Africa?*

Yes, but you can only do a certain amount in life. I did not go out there to live in either community; I just went to play cricket. The first person I stayed with was a Jew, and they know all about persecution. It does not just stem from the colour of your skin. I do not believe I was used as a political pawn, and I believe the West Indies rebel tour did a lot to help break down racial barriers. People say we were treated as honorary Whites, but no one ever told us that. Anyway, I live in a nice, quiet estate in Edgbaston, near to the county ground, where there are few coloured residents. Does that not suggest I am an honorary White in Edgbaston as much as in the Transvaal?

*At least you can vote in Birmingham—a basic human right that would be denied you in South Africa.*

And in certain parts of America, and in Australia. Who are we to tell the politicians how to act? I knew what I was letting myself in for by going there. I knew that I would be banned from returning to Guyana, where politics is always a hot issue. I could not even get in there last year for my father's funeral. The money I received will never make up for missing out on Test cricket from the age of 31, but at least it brought me security and independence. And I was driven to South Africa eventually by the West Indies Board.

*What evidence do you have for that?*

Well, I received good reports when I captained West Indies nine times during the time the top players were with Packer. I thought there would be some loyalty when we all appeared together again. I did quite well in Australia in 1979/80 as senior player to Clive Lloyd and Deryck Murray, but when Viv Richards was given the captaincy ahead of me for one game in Perth, I knew the writing was on the wall. Deryck and the manager, Willie Rodrigues, both apologised to me for that, but I knew I was drifting apart from Clive Lloyd. I was not going to win any personality clash with the captain. He then left me out of the tour to Australia in 1981/2, when I was at my peak. From that day onwards, I was not going to have anyone decide my career. I decided to use my own ability to the full to look after my future. So I went to South Africa.

*Your mentor was Rohan Kanhai—a great player of similar extraction and from the same region in Guyana. In fact, you named your son after him. What did he say to you about going to South Africa?*

I have not seen Rohan since I was last in Guyana. We have spoken a couple of times on the phone, and he is obviously hurt that I chose to go there. He is also hurt that no Asians are playing for West Indies any more.

*Did it particularly hit you in 1984 when the West Indies beat England 5/0 and you, a banned player, scored more than 2,300 runs for Warwickshire?*

I blocked it completely out of my mind. I would not even watch them on television. I simply concentrated on my county game. From time to time I think about the years I have missed at Test level, but once I make a decision I stick to it. I still practise and train hard and that gives me a great deal of satisfaction.

*But even your time with Warwickshire has been interrupted by registration problems.*

I missed half the 1986 season and the whole of 1987 because the Test and County

Cricket Board still regarded me as an overseas player and Warwickshire wanted to play other overseas players instead of me. I was fully prepared to take the TCCB to court for a restraint of trade, because I held a British passport and, as a Briton, I could not go to work. They were preventing me from earning a living. In the end I qualified as a non-overseas player for the 1988 season, but I really struggled with injuries and the lack of sharpness that comes from missing a whole season at the age of 38. A back injury then affected my footwork in the 1989 season, but it should be much better next summer. I really mean to bounce back.

*You are now on 87 hundreds—but you are also forty. Can you realistically get the other thirteen?*

That is what keeps me going. I want them badly. Having missed out for so long on Test cricket, that would be a very special landmark for me. I shall get them. I will keep myself fresh for each English season from now on. I shall not go back and play in South Africa.

*Obviously the game is physically harder as you get older—but have you mastered the mental side of batting?*

I think that is one of my strongest points. The top players think more about the game because they have such high standards to maintain. I can pump myself up in a calm way before I go out to bat and, at night, I shall have one drink in the bar, then go home or to the hotel and replay that day's innings in my mind. I cannot learn anything about cricket in a bar, so I must be alone, thinking about how I batted and how I shall play the next day. Top players in all sports spend a lot of time in solitary confinement.

*If you hope to get a century of centuries in your forties, surely the quality of wickets in English county cricket will have to improve?*

That is a very sad state of affairs. They are dreadful. Too many are trying for result wickets, so that in the end, no one will be learning how to play cricket properly. In the last couple of years, the wickets on the county circuit have been the worst I have experienced anywhere in the world. Even the ones that turn square on the first morning in Pakistan and India were never dangerous and they often led to a fascinating contest with the spinners. In England, you have to cope with a couple of quick bowlers, then a good medium-pacer. They are made to look dangerous—and world-beaters. What is the point of playing that type of cricket when nobody really enjoys it? I think Michael Holding was absolutely right to refuse to play on at Trent Bridge when the wicket was so diabolical. The Cricketers' Association should threaten to take the players out on strike unless our working conditions improve. We are talking about our livelihoods here.

# DAVID GOWER

**'People say I am too casual, but there are ambitions, fears, trials and tribulations all whirling around in there. '**

OF all recent England cricketers, David Gower has managed best to square the circle of aesthetic appeal with the pragmatism of solid achievement. His detractors may rail at his self-destructiveness, but even they must admit that an hour of Gower comes with beguiling guarantees. The cavalier's plumes cannot top off the roundhead's breastplate; what you see, you get. Unlike many fey stroke players, Gower has turned in major performances against all the Test-playing countries. His statistical record ought to be more than enough for those who claim he has under-achieved, and his physical bravery is the more impressive for the absence of bravado. The West Indies, those implacable barometers of Test cricket's highest standards, rate Gower alongside Graham Gooch as the only Englishman worthy of a place in their side. That only served to make his omission from the 1990 tour to the Caribbean the more bizarre.

Gower's ability to treat Rudyard Kipling's two imposters, truimph and disaster, in the same manner, has been an object lesson to a sport that has become increasingly strident during his career. His dignified bearing as captain throughout the two "blackwash" series against the West Indies was only surpassed by his urbanity during a strange Press conference at Lord's in 1986 when the chairman of selectors left his sacked captain to fend for himself. He did. Admirably.

Under Peter May's chairmanship, Gower's whimsical, self-contained persona was always likely to prove his undoing, especially as his players lacked class in depth. Gower has never been one to be swept along on a tide of exenophobic myopia, as Peter West discovered in a TV interview immediately after England had clinched a three-one series victory over a disintegrating Australian team in 1985. Amid the cork-popping euphoria, the captain's sardonic observation that "the West Indies will be quaking in their boots now" was vintage Gower. Such realism may have diluted his dedication to the task, but

*it also confirmed his attractiveness as a human being. He was also dead right about the West Indies.*

*When Ted Dexter took over from Peter May as chairman of the England selectors, Gower was re-appointed captain for the entire Ashes series. It was a popular dream ticket, but it ushered in a nightmare summer for England and Gower. Australia outplayed them from day one at Leeds, when Gower put them in and saw them make over six hundred. Gower's public show of insouciance cracked once—at the Saturday night Press conference during the Lord's Test—but that apart, he conducted himself with maturity under such intense media villification. He refused to offer an horrendous crop of injuries as excuse, as England slipped to a four-nil defeat in the series. Most observers felt that England were lucky to get nil, and Gower would not disagree. Worse was to come. Amid yet another own goal of man-management, Gower lost both the captaincy, then his place on the Caribbean tour, inside 24 hours. At this low ebb in Gower's fortunes, Noel Coward's dictum that "the secret of success is how you cope with failure" applied pertinently. He handled all the media enquiries with calmness and tactful humour, declining to make capital out of the widespread astonishment in the game that such a fine player of fast bowling would find himself a few months hence on the Cresta Run rather than at Sabina Park. Was that 24-hour period the worst time of his career?*

No. My worst period came in Australia at the start of the 1986/87 tour, when I was coming to terms with the atmosphere under new England management and with my own poor form with the bat. People ask me if I am shocked by the decision to leave me out of the tour. I think that is a rather extreme word that you use to describe your feelings after something like a car crash. A little shocked might be a preferable description. We are, after all, talking about sport rather than a matter of life and death. It was a new experience—the first time I have been scratched from an England tour. But Graham Gooch remains a good friend. As a former England captain myself—sadly, not a terriby exclusive club any more—I know what it is like to disappoint players who were banking on an overseas tour and expected the call. Some people have to be disappointed, and this time I was one of them.

*The official reason was that you had an inconsistent season. Do you agree?*

A return of a hundred and two fifties in eleven Test innings in a series is not the kind of standard to which I aspire. But I was pleased with my hundred at Lord's because of all the extra pressures (with a few newshounds after my blood following my celebrated walkout from that Press conference), and when I made 79 in the last Test at the Oval, I played almost as well as I could have played.

*After all the early summer euphoria and optimism, how awful was it for you as the season wore on and things just got worse?*

Things are never as bad in reality as they seem at the time. A lot that was written and spoken in the media was exaggerated, and that tends to alter one's perceptions. I have seen how the pressure has affected other captains when England keep losing, so I was not surprised at the intensity of the vitriol. What I do know is that much of the vitriol is crap. I know that one cannot lump all the media together. Some are constrained by the nature of their job to be unreasonable, while a good many others are constructive and reasonable. It was a shame that relations got strained for a time, but we could have avoided all that by winning a few Tests. I thought about resigning during the Old

51

Trafford Test when it was clear we were about to lose the Ashes, but that was more a case of responding to outside pressures. That feeling was nipped in the bud by Ted Dexter's support and the way I felt about the job. I did not want to feel hounded out of it, because the England captaincy is an honour worth attaining and keeping, whatever the traumas.

*On that first morning at Leeds in the First Test, you put Australia in after winning the toss—and they played well to get through an awkward day. How significant was that first day for the series as a whole?*

They were worried about playing at Leeds and going one down at the start of the series. Recent experiences had made them uptight about the ascendancy likely to be enjoyed there by bowlers who could swing the ball and bowl tightly. Yet by the end of their first innings, they had wiped away all those misgivings. Now if I had been absolutely sure of the favourable batting conditions, I would have batted first. But then we might have been well and truly Aldermaned and the headlines would have said I was "Captain Cock-up". We should have escaped with a draw on that final afternoon, but they exerted pressure on us and we lost too many wickets between lunch and tea. We ought to have drawn, then gone on to Lord's thinking we had simply had a nightmare and done well to avoid a defeat. When I took the side to India in 1984, we lost the First Test, but rallied to win the series. There was still no reason why, in a six-Test series, we could not turn things around against Australia, but they kept playing very well indeed. They got large totals on the board every first innings, then attacked us in the field with confidence and typical Aussie aggression.

*For all sorts of reasons, Allan Border outshone you as captain in the series. Did you really want the England job back again after losing it once?*

It is another incentive to do well and, at this stage in my career, that is important. I have always said that the extra responsibility forces you to pull out that little extra in your own performance, whether in the field or with the bat. There is a degree of honour and pride involved in captaincy.

*You are not a demonstrative captain. Do you think you are as good as other leaders who* seem *to make things happen out there in the middle?*

There is a lot more going on inside my head than people may realise. In many cases, you are dictated to by situations. For me, it is a bit like batting—when it is right everything seems to click and good things happen instinctively. All of us at some stage resort to standard captaincy—keeping it simple, pegging back the batsmen, waiting for mistakes by them. Sometimes you just have to wear them down in the field, even though it does not look particularly exciting.

*Nevertheless, it appears that you have twice lost the England job because you had become fatalistic, letting things drift.*

People have this impression of me being permanently "laid back", and apparently they would appreciate a bit more obvious fire to be shown on the field. I believe that a lot of good work is done in the dressing-room, which is the place to deliver any harsh words. Out on the field one has to try to maintain control in all senses! Similarly, it is fruitless trying to deliver long, rousing speeches at the start of each session of every game—your words soon become worthless and repetitive. Many a time I will just say:

"Right, let's go and get on with it" and feel that is enough. You are dealing with experienced professionals playing for their country, not schoolboys, and they would soon get rather bored with hearing the same old rhetoric, as I would. I agree that now and again we all need a kick up the backside, especially as much of Test cricket is played on flat wickets and you can be batted out of the game, but you have to choose the right moment to say the right things. As for my work out there in the middle, I see no reason why I should behave unnaturally by waving my arms about, just for cosmetic reasons.

*Your sense of humour showed itself when you wore a T-shirt with the legend "I'm in charge" printed on the chest in the last few days of your tenure under Peter May in 1986. Do you now regret that? Did it count against you?*

I have no idea, but I thought the T-shirt was a good joke. There had been a lot of criticism about my attitude to the hammering in the Caribbean, and I thought that some of it was unjustified. The stuff about "optional nets" was rubbish; you should have seen some of the nets we were supposed to use. They were dangerous, and a complete waste of time. If ever I told the players to go to the nets, they would all go. But if it was left to them and they did not attend, I had no complaints. It was simply a matter of consistency and treating players like adults. Believe me, we practised hard out there whenever the nets were satisfactory. We got hammered because the Test wickets were largely under-prepared and their fast bowlers were just too good for us.

*So you lost the job because of the prevailing view that something had to be done, that action had to be taken for cosmetic reasons?*

To a certain extent, yes. When Peter May came out to Barbados for his fortnight's holiday, we had a half-hour chat and all he offered were the criticisms he had read in the Press. We then had a chat at Lord's in mid-April along similar lines. Perhaps I did not do enough forelock-tugging, but I stood by my players and my conduct of the tour. Anyway, I just hoped that my one Test on trial would settle things down—after all, we should have been good enough for India. There was a general malaise in the England dressing-room for that Lord's Test; too many players were looking over their shoulders, expecting to be dropped if they made a mistake. They did not have complete concentration on the job in hand.

*Both your sackings could have been handled better, couldn't they?*

Both were rather interesting. In 1986, while I was telling Peter West on TV that I had no clue about my captaincy prospects, Peter May was offering the job to Mike Gatting. Then I got the call into the physio's room and by the time I returned to our dressing-room, it was common knowledge. It was a pretty low moment and I was grateful for the support in the Press conference. The media seemed actually embarrassed for me.

Then after we lost to the Australians this year, we had the "change in direction", in Ted Dexter's phraseology. Now I knew what that meant when I met up with Ted—time for a new leader, thanks for everything, etc, etc. We even discussed a suitable resignation statement, which I rejected in favour of simply giving the bald facts. By the time I had slipped off to Portugal for a short break and to taste some of that country's delightful ports, the phrase "change in direction" had become more ambiguous. According to the Test and County Cricket Board, I was still in the frame. For a day or so it was a good running story, with the popular Press trying to find me in

Portugal. But I had resigned myself to losing the job by the time I came home.

*In 1986, after your first sacking, how soon did you start to feel you would like the job back again some day?*

Initially, I was in a decent frame of mind. I had rationalised it—no point in moping around; out to graze at cover again. I still wanted to enjoy the game and to do myself justice, but later on in the summer of 1986 I started to feel sorry for myself. I actually missed out on the last couple of weeks of that season—quite rightly the subject of some ribald leg-pulling after I had just scored a hundred in the Oval Test—and I was rather down. By the time I got to Australia that October, just being there was not enough for me.

*During that first month on England's tour to Australia in 1986 there were strong rumours that you thought of retirement.*

It crossed my mind, but only fleetingly. Again, I was grateful to those that showed concern, but in effect all I was suffering was a crisis in confidence. I arrived in Australia with no official status for the first time in four tours and I felt slightly left out. After all, we had a captain going on his first Australian tour, with the tour manager and cricket manager in the same position. I had captained England in 26 Tests, had played in more Tests than anyone else in the party, and I was on my third full tour of Australia. I was entitled to think that I might have contributed something to the pre-tour discussions and the early weeks out there, but I was never asked my opinions. In that first month, it was becoming obvious there were factions developing in the party—one involving myself, Allan Lamb and Ian Botham (who both also felt left out of things) and one involving the rest. I spent a lot of time with Ian and Allan, and that is not a pace I can keep up for very long! One night, at Bundaberg, I went on a self-destruct mission and was severely ill from over-indulgence in rum. It took some while to get the gloom out of my system. Dropping down the order to accommodate Mike Gatting at three took some of the pressure off me. I scraped a few runs in the first Test and, before the second, I took a long train journey out to Kalgoorlie in the company of a few soul-mates and I talked it out of my system. I got a good hundred in the next Text at Perth and thoughts of retirement were put on the back burner. I knew that once you have given it up, you cannot get it back. My life could easily be an anti-climax once I retire: it is not easy to combine a job that gives all the attractions of touring the world, plus the earning potential of an international cricketer. I am glad I snapped out of it when I did and I was pleased that the lobbying by the Press got me on to the selection committee after a month in Australia.

*Another low period for you was May, 1985. You could not get a run—you were out for nought in the one-day international at Edgbaston, chasing a wide one, and that night you actually discussed batting at number eight at Lord's in the next game. There was talk that you were going to be dropped. How was your morale that weekend?*

Again, I was at a slightly low ebb, I suppose. I had not scored many runs on the India tour, although I was pleased with my captaincy, and a combination of bad luck and indifferent batting left me short of confidence when we started to play the Australians in the one-dayers. That night at Edgbaston I admitted that I was seriously thinking of batting at number eight to give a chance to the in-form batsmen. But next day I changed my mind; the selectors did not want it and neither did I. It would look like I was running away from a problem I had created. I was not going to think like a number eight batter, I was going out there to bat to think like a number three—whatever happened. I decided to play as if I was in great nick and block nothing. As luck would have it, I took a good, swirling catch in the deep to get David Boon in their innings and I drew confidence from that. As far as I was concerned it was going to be my day and when I had some luck early on in my innings with a few flying edges, I knew I would get some runs. I got a hundred. I was set up for the summer, and the rest is history. That catch helped—every little notch of confidence contributes when you are down.

*At that stage you had not enjoyed a good twelve months as a Test batsman. Were you beginning to wonder if you had lost it?*

It *was* a long period. The obvious excuse might be the cares of captaincy, but they had not affected me in Pakistan, when I got two big hundreds as soon as I took over from Bob Willis. Nor was it a problem in the Test series of 1985 against the Aussies. I admit a lot had been weighing on my mind as we were hammered into the ground every day by the West Indies. They are not a side against whom you can expect to regain form. Perhaps there was a reaction from my bout of blood poisoning earlier in the 1984 season. That took some time to get out of my system. I am told it was serious and that 25 years ago, I would have pegged out. Whatever the reasons, it was a bleak twelve months for my batting.

*Are you aware of the frustrations many feel about your batting—the fact that you can make it look so easy one day and then you suddenly look as if you have picked up a bat for the first time in weeks?*

The hard part is that when you have achieved a certain standard on a particular day, that is accepted as your norm. I cannot maintain sublime standards every day. Everything has to be right—getting out of bed, feeling good, enjoying a bit of luck, finding my timing early on. However long I play there will be days to remember, but more often, there will be days to forget. Somewhere along the line, something can go wrong, and it is not always my fault. There are some decent bowlers around. One of the best bits of earthy Yorkshire advice I got early on at Leicester came from Jack Birkenshaw, who told me that there are many more bad days than good in the game and to savour the good ones. When I have been dropped by England, I have gone back to the county circuit and tried to concentrate on the pluses—that I am just below the best eleven English players available and that I am a good deal better than the two hundred-odd who are available to the selectors.

Sometimes I look at myself batting on video just to encourage myself. Somehow it always seems easier when it is on TV! There are days when it all seems in slow motion: minor matters, like where you are looking when the ball is on its way, and the actual time it takes to adjust. Sometimes it all happens too quickly and you struggle; sometimes it all happens in its own good time and that is when I bat well.

*Do you think there is realistic chance that you will be a better player as you approach your mid-thirties?*

I suppose we are talking about consistency here. It is not about technical limitations, or whether I can still engineer the eyes into the right place. A lot depends on the mental state—how desperately you want to score stacks of runs when you walk out to bat. There is no way I am going to be in exactly the right mental shape every time I go out there. Part of my character whispers "Oh, I've done that, what a relief, that was nice". I am not as driven as someone like Graeme Hick, who scores runs remorselessly. I wish I loved the whole process of batting as he does, but that was not meant to be. Strangely enough, on the occasions when I have grafted away for seven hours or so and made a big hundred, it has been more satisfying to me because it is not a common occurrence.

*So can you get hungrier and meaner as you get older?*
We all need a bit of a rocket sometimes. I know I am going to have to drive myself more. I do not want to coast along. I shall probably have to work harder in the nets—something I have avoided in the past, because I did not want to lose even more confidence if the facilities were poor, or because I did not want to mess anything up if I was in good nick. I agree that it is wrong to believe that it will come right as soon as I step on to the field. I will have to accelerate the process.

It is nice to have good things written about me, and the public have by and large been very supportive over the years, but I would like more impressive figures to look back on. Look at Allan Border—there is solid consistency for you. We have played more or less the same number of Tests, yet he has scored a lot more hundreds than me. I ought to have scored more Test centuries when you consider that I average over forty.

*So, this failure to turn fifties into hundreds. Is that a failure of concentration rather than technique?*
There are technical defects. I rely a lot on a good eye, timing and the pace of the wicket. But there cannot be all that many if I can get past thirty against Test bowlers over the first half-hour or so. I tend to lapse in concentration after telling myself "this is good stuff, I'm going well". I come down a shade from that plateau and start thinking about scoring runs, rather than playing each ball on its merits. I find myself thinking about the next scoring stroke before the ball is delivered. The adrenalin gets to me. When you are on song, you make your decision that fraction earlier.

*Are these concentration lapses typical of a dilettante approach to life in general?*
They are probably a fair reflection. I do try to be relaxed because I do not believe in shouting it from the top of the pavilion if I have had a good day. I like to savour it quietly, to set alongside the memories of the bad times. When I have had a really bad day, I come back to the sanctuary of my home with the cartoon-style black cloud over my head, and it does take time for it to go away. I cannot say "it matters not", because it does. I do not linger in too many depressive states, but I am not totally horizontal about the knock-backs. People say I am too casual, but there are ambitions, fears, trials and tribulations all whirling around in there. Success does make you feel better, and your ups and downs are analysed so much that you have to draw strength from the achievements when you are low.

*At the end of your first tour with England in 1979, the captain Mike Brearley described you as "a minor genius who might yet become a major genius". What is your verdict on your career after more than a decade as an England player?*
I was flattered at the time by Brears' comment, but all he was really saying was that I was a promising lad and I had started well. At my best I would say I had been somewhere near the "major genius" standard, but for most of the time I have been bumbling along in a minor key, or even below that. When I got that seventy-odd in the

Perth Test of 1982, I do not believe I could have played better at any time—hands, feet, eyes all came together at the right time. There was the 150 against the New Zealanders in a one-day international on the same tour. That was fluent and productive. I was pleased with the ninety I got against the West Indies in the final Test at Antigua in 1986, against fine bowlers at the end of an arduous tour. On the previous tour to the West Indies, I grafted long and hard for a not-out 150 at Jamaica: I just had to stay in for us to avoid defeat. I had a bit of luck early on, but I felt I deserved that because I had played well throughout the series but could not get a big score. This was my last chance, and I just kept on going.

*What personal ambitions are left to you?*
To get back in the England side, to improve my Test record, and to appreciate the quality of life. I am only 32. I reckon I could play for England until I am at least 33!

# DENNIS LILLEE

**'I was like a bull terrier if I had a batsman by the throat. I liked him to know that he should not really be out there, stealing runs from my team. '**

DENNIS Lillee is just like one of the those ageing vaudevillians who break into a favoured song-and-dance routine whenever the fridge door happens to open ... Lillee was, and remains, a performer. A great fast bowler, unquestionably—probably the greatest of all time. But he also managed to engage the attention of cricket fans and the wider world with a personality and charisma rivalled only by Fred Trueman and Keith Miller among post-war fast bowlers. Lillee could suffuse the dullest day with a sense of theatre. His example spawned a whole generation of youngsters who turned and bellowed out an appeal to the umpire from a squatting position, with the right index finger pointing at the official. Yet there was only one Lillee. Even in his fortieth year, with many parts of his formidable physique begging for mercy, his bowling action remained pure. When he appeared in a charity match at Edgbaston last summer, in the company of many world-class cricketers, it was instructive to hear the admiring comments about Lillee's matchless technique from such luminaries. The general feeling was that no one of their time had managed to merge all the thunderous and aesthetic elements of fast bowling so successfully. Underpinning that wonderful action was a psychological supremacy over batsmen, an unquenchable spirit, an enviable knowledge of batsmen's foibles and an unmatched technical mastery. Dennis Lillee never allowed an easy passage, whatever the conditions.

Lillee has always known his financial worth, and it was inevitable that he should play a crucial role in selling World Series Cricket to a public that preferred drama to technical dissertation. He made his pile from cricket, but no one can begrudge him that. Anyone who has ever dealt with Dennis Lillee on a business footing will acknowledge that he gives good value for money: watching him charm the cricket bores at personal appearances in England confirmed the notion that Lillee is still a professional to his fingertips, even though his greatest cricket contributions now belong to the video library.

59

*He made a deep impression on the players and officials at Northampton, where he spent the last two English summers. Not only did he manage to impart his views on fast bowling to an admiring crop of novitiates, but he brought a whole new dimension to the social life of a county side that has long been in the vanguard of conviviality. When we talked, Lillee was bemoaning the fact that his fortieth birthday celebrations had lasted five days, and expressing relief that he would leave England just before his great mate Rod Marsh flew in to plunge him further into the social whirl. Mention of Marsh reminded him of the flight to England in 1981 when the craggy wicket-keeper set up the record for consumption of lager on a cricketers' flight from Australia. . . .*

Doug Walters had set the record on the previous tour to England with 44 cans of lager and Marshy set out to beat him in 1981. I acted as pacemaker on the first leg—from Melbourne to Honolulu—then others helped out on the last two stretches as I enjoyed a good sleep. When we got to London, Graeme Wood and I were fresh enough to help him off the plane. The man needed some help after 45 cans! Typical Marshy. He played hard, gave everything to the side, and he was never one to lock himself away when we were having fun. A great mate.

*This feeling of "mateship" seemed to run through that great Australian side under Ian Chappell in the mid-Seventies.*

That's right, and Ian Chappell deserves much of the credit. He took a young, inexperienced side and moulded them into a terrific unit. Somehow he managed to stay one of the lads, yet we all knew who was in charge. I never saw him have a go at one of the players on the field. He would wait until he had the chance of a quiet beer. No one else knew about it, so the player was not embarrassed, but he soon knew he was in the wrong. That is where Ian gained a lot of respect, because he never made a fuss about being in charge. He had a quiet control, none of this clapping of hands stuff. We always felt that he had something up his sleeve as the game rolled on. He was like the good umpire—you were unaware of his presence until it was necessary. And he fought for us, too. Chappell was totally loyal to his team. He was easily the best captain I knew in the game. I would put Ray Illingworth next—he made a big impression on me as a youngster in my first Test series, in 1970/71. After those two, I would put Mike Brearley. A fine record, but he did not always come up against the strongest sides. He also had a brilliant performer in Ian Botham, a great fast bowler in Bob Willis, and some pretty useful batsmen.

*So that Aussie side had a great captain, but also some top-class bowlers and a group of great fielders.*

In some six years, I do not recall our close catchers dropping more than a handful. They were amazing—the Chappell brothers and Redpath at slip, Mallett and Walters in the gully. And do not forget Ross Edwards saving us stacks of runs in the covers. He was so good we could afford to take a man from there and put him in a catching position. I would be happy to have him patrolling all that cover area and go for seven men in the slips and gully positions: usually a man at bat/pad and a fine leg if necessary; occasionally a mid-off if I was concentrating on a full length, and sometimes a third man if they were looking to flick me over the top. But usually I wanted as many in for the catch as I could spare—and they rarely let me down. We also had bowlers of contrast. I really rated Ashley Mallett as an off-spinner, a very underrated performer. Max Walker was just the best kind of third seamer—what a man to come after me and Thommo. And

Thommo! When we were at our peak, he was a great foil for me. I would pitch it up more than him, as I tried for the kill with the late outswinger, while Thommo's lethal pace meant he would be devastating with his steep lift off the pitch. A great heart as well. He never gave in. If I did not get five wickets, invariably Thommo would nip in with a bunch.

*During that period, you seemed to have a psychological hold over so many batsmen. Were you aware of that and how much did you try to play on their nerves?*

I was lucky because I had a good memory for the weaknesses of batters. I could pick them up by watching their reactions after a few balls. I then had a basis for where I would try to get them. I was like a bull terrier—I would not let go if I had a batsman by the throat. I made sure he knew that as well. I liked him to know that he should not really be out there, stealing runs from my team. It was also a case of knowing what I was doing, and that came with experience. I never went into an over without a plan; it was never a case of just sending down the ball. You cannot just think: "I'm a fast bowler, that's all I'm going to do and if that fails, tough luck." If it was not working at full speed, I would throttle back, try to work the seam, try a few leg-cutters, see if it would swing much.

*Were you always so confident of your ability?*

No. I sometimes thought I could not bowl, especially in my younger days. But I never gave in, always sought advice, while trying to make sure I did not take in so much advice that it complicated things. The most important thing to realise is that cricket is a very basic game that we try to complicate. It is the theories that get you into trouble. When you are struggling, remember that cricket is a sideways-on game: never give in, and you will not go far wrong.

*Did you ever give in on the cricket field?*

Once—at the Oval in 1975, when England batted for days and days. I bowled a stack of overs in their second dig, but when it was clear that they were safe, I said that if I was called on to bowl again, it would be off-spin. I was not used again!

*Your action was one of the glories of the game in the last two decades. But you had to change it after your serious back injury in 1973.*

Yes. I was very open-chested early in my first-class career. We always imagine we are fluent like Ray Lindwall or Michael Holding, but reality soon sets in. My alteration was born of necessity, to take the pressure off my back after the stress fractures I picked up in the West Indies. I had to ease the pressure off my back foot by putting it at forty-five degrees to the crease, instead of getting it all the way round. Then I had to work at bowling across my body, to get more side-on to ease the pressure off my back foot. As a result, I could control my bowling, and master the outswinger.

*As far as I can recall, you were the first fast bowler to take a scientific interest in the art.*

That was partly because I desperately wanted to play again, and as I started to recover I learned a lot about the human body and the endurance factor. When I came back from the West Indies in 1973, I was put in a plaster cast for six weeks, then a brace for another six weeks. I then did absolutely nothing for six months. After that, a gradual introduction to the lightest of exercise, then a huge build-up at the University of Western Australia under Dr Frank Pike. Everything was scientifically monitored and I became very interested in the scientific approach to fast bowling. At that time, no one knew what to do with stress fractures among athletes. There must have been so many that struck down fast bowlers—they should have been treated more sympathetically by those who wrote them off as head-cases because they complained about their back every time they were asked to bowl. Things have changed so dramatically since then. When I heard Ian Botham had a stress fracture of the back, I was certain he would pull through and play again, not just because of the kind of guy he is, but also because of the advanced surgery now available.

*Did you ever despair during that comeback?*

A couple of times. I did so much strengthening and flexibility work on the spine that I strained all the ligaments down the base of my back. I simply pushed myself too far. I was really down, I thought I had messed it all up again. Fortunately the doctor reassured me, told me it was just a strain that would sort itself out within three weeks, and he was right. But it was a test of faith at the time.

*You have spent the last two English summers advising fast bowlers on their techniques. Is there anyone coming through that might be the new Willis or the new Snow?*

Not until you change the kind of cricket played in England. You have got to play four-day cricket as soon as possible, not least to protect the fast bowler. I feel sorry for them—I could never play five or six days a week, with all the travelling involved, then be expected to blast out sides. After a time English fast bowlers learn to protect their bodies, rather than be fresh and strike hard. For the big games in other countries, there is a gradual build-up. You train hard, then taper off as the big day arrives. I never looked to contain myself because I never played too much cricket, so I was always flat out, looking to burst through the batting. You cannot do that in England. Until four-day cricket arrives, the only way out of it for the fast bowler is to have a rotation system, whereby he has one game on and the next one off. Fast bowling is the hardest part of cricket, and bowlers have to be nurtured.

*Surely the wickets in England and Australia are little help these days to the fast bowler?*

Everything stems from the wicket, and groundsmen do not seem to put in that tender loving care they used to. I wish there were more around like John Mailey, who produced some great tracks during World Series Cricket. He came up with the best wicket I ever saw—at the Sydney Showground, when we played eight days in a row on it, and it was as good as ever at the end. He produced some phenomenal wickets out of nothing, but he got fed up of all the hassles when World Series Cricket ended and he is now working at a school. A great shame. John Mailey was tremendously talented.

In the 1974/75 series, when we hammered England, the wickets were fast and bouncy, apart from Adelaide and Melbourne. Mind you, the English quicks did not get what we managed to extract from the pitches! But some of our wickets in Australia have deteriorated. Perth has been a nightmare in recent years, Melbourne has had cracks and uneven bounce, and that is no use to a good game of cricket.

*Talking of World Series Cricket, how much flak did you take in Australia over the secrecy and timing of the project?*

It was an unbelievable situation. Some people did not know whether to look at me in the street. I felt like a leper at times. But I believed very much in what I was doing, and I was not going to let any of those blokes deter me. As top cricketers we were close to child labour in earning power. Look at the Centenary Test in Melbourne in 1977—a great occasion, the ground packed for five days, TV rights bringing in endless cash for the game. Yet the players were getting around fifty dollars a day, less tax. It was criminal. It really bugged me when our critics said that we ought to have come clean. Does anyone show his hand in business dealings until the last moment? Many tried to slag off WSC, but it contained some of the hardest cricket I have ever played. If you lost form, there was no chance to return to a lower standard and work your way back, because nothing else was available. So you battled away against a full-strength West Indies or the Rest of the World, and there were no easy pickings there. Because we had to play away from the Test grounds, the run-ups on the park grounds were very sandy, so a fast bowler never had a good footing. But you just had to get out there and play.

*On to that remarkable 1981 series in England, when Ian Botham turned the series around, starting at Leeds. Why didn't the captain, Kim Hughes, bowl Ray Bright's spin at Botham when he was smashing you pace bowlers all over the place?*

Search me. I could not believe that he bowled us in such long spells. It was remarkable that he did not try to tempt Botham with prolonged spin. Sure, the ball was seaming around, and he could have been out ten times to the fast bowlers. But Botham is the kind of batsmen who gets himself out against the spinners. Having said that, it was a remarkable innings, although the hundred at Old Trafford was a better one technically. He kept hooking me then, taking his eye off the ball. I was sure I would get him with the bouncer, but the more I fed him with it, the further the ball disappeared.

*Did the Australians lose that series as much through their lack of fight as through Botham's heroics?*

A bit of both. Luck favours the brave and all that, and certainly England proved the bolder side. If you look at our performances at Edgbaston and Leeds, when we lost chasing small scores, they followed a similar pattern—a good start, a middle order collapse and nothing from the tail. We folded under pressure. The guys in our dressing-room were worried about failing in search of a low target, rather than thinking about the people we were playing—guys who had not played well earlier in the series. That shows how important it is to have mental strength.

*That is something Ian Botham rarely lacks. He has long been a mate of yours and you have had a few scrapes together. Putting aside your friendship, where does he stand as a cricketer in your time?*

I rate him super-highly, as one of the game's great characters and all-rounders. His presence is so positive, his never-say-die attitude can lift a team. A huge amount of natural ability as well—and do not forget his wonderful catching. I cannot believe how the Press hound him in England. There are a few rubbishy papers in Australia, but nothing like the amount in England. Botham is news and people do want to know what he gets up to. The papers say "That's a good one on Botham—that's another 40,000 on the circulation," and yet it could be garbage, a pack of lies. Why can't a person be judged for his cricket alone and go back to normality when the day's play is over? If someone thumped you in a pub as they have done to Both—would you say "Oh that's nice, someone's hit me"? Or would you hit him back—or at least have him put in jail? Why does Both have to put up with all that?

*Botham did not make much impression on the 1989 Ashes series. Are you surprised at how easily Australia clinched the series?*

Yes I am, although England did not play very intelligently. Their batters played too many one-day shots and the bowlers did not bowl straight enough. That is all that Australia did, apart from batting positively. Allan Border has suddenly become a great leader, but often it is about the players, rather than the captain, and he now has some fine players. If you are a good captain of a bad side, you can still look a poor captain; but if you are a mediocre captain of a very good side, you can look a bloody great captain. Players count above all.

*Looking back, Dennis, is there any performance that you particularly cherished?*

You often remember a game for the number of wickets you took, rather than the actual quality of the performance. I remember once I knocked over the first four West Indian batsmen one evening, when we desperately needed a breakthrough after being bowled out cheaply earlier in the day. I bowled very fast, everything worked and we got out of jail. It was an inspired spell and the performance matched the tally of wickets for once.

*And the best innings played against you?*

Gary Sobers at Melbourne in 1972 for the Rest of the World against Australia. A fabulous double hundred after I got him out first ball in the first innings. When he came in second time around, he half-fended a ball that he tried to hook and it dropped just over Kerry O'Keefe's head at short leg. After that he murdered me. I took the new ball when he had passed a hundred, and the first ball—a good yorker—was smashed straight past me. By the time I looked around, it had come back towards me off the fence. Then I posted three guys square on the offside boundary—no more then twenty yards apart—yet he kept piercing those small gaps. What can you do against that sort of talent?

*What does the future hold for Dennis Lillee?*

I will tell you what it does not hold—any of this fast bowling stuff. I have done enough of that, I reckon! I might come back to England and Northants if it can be tied up, but I am going to be very busy back home over the next year with all sorts of business interests. I will do some cricket coaching, but the body has told me that playing the game is not feasible. My wife is going back to college to get her degree, so I shall be a house-husband, staying at home, looking after our two kids, and doing business from home.

*I understand your home is no shrine to your deeds on the cricket field?*

I have got just one photo hanging up from cricket and that is the one of me asking the Queen for an autograph at the 1977 Centenary Test. It is signed by her, too. I suppose I breached all the protocol rules by asking for her autograph at the match, but she seemed amused enough. Her aide sent me the signed photo and as an ardent monarchist, I am very proud of that. I hope she does not remember the first time I was introduced to her—at Lord's in 1972, when I said: "G'day, howya going?" Bob Massie cracked up as he stood beside me, but I was very young and nervous. You do not really know what you are saying at those times, do you?

# GRAEME HICK

**'I have no real complaints about waiting seven years for my qualification. I do not think people should just be able to walk into a national side. '**

IT is impossible to consider Graeme Hick without disappearing under a Niagara of statistics. At 23, his career record of a hundred every five innings is surpassed only by the phenomenal Bradman. He may appear fallible on the erratic Worcester pitches, but his mastery on a good wicket is now taken for granted. The opposition would happily grant him a hundred if a swift dismissal could then be guaranteed. The euphoric effect on the fielders when he fails is as graphic as the frisson of uncertainty that sweeps through Worcestershire's dressing-room. Homer has nodded: they must be bowling superbly out there.

Although bowlers usually win championships, Hick's contribution of more than 4,500 runs in the last two seasons for his county was the decisive factor. He looms large in the consciousness of every captain who decides to set Worcestershire a fourth-innings target. A batsman who blocks the ball to the boundary with a defensive stroke has a habit of moulding a match to his own will. Around the county circuit, the word is that Hick is vulnerable in the off-stump area. But which batsman isn't? Apart from that, he has no discernible weakness. His impeccable technique, honed on shirt-front wickets in Zimbabwe, is a tacit admonition to groundsmen and county committees who sanction rogue English pitches that are stifling the art of batsmanship.

Graeme Hick will stride out to bat for England for the first time early in the 1991 season, once his seven-year qualification period is over. There seems no reason why he will not handle the elevation. His England cap will not need to be an extra-large size, because he is a popular team man, genuinely supportive of lesser talents. Already he is a mature cricketer, possessed of the requisite steel needed by every great player. But is he worried that too much will be expected of him when he finally qualifies for England?

I will just have to live with that. It is something you must learn to handle. This season so many people have been asking me what is wrong with the England team and who should be playing. It is not something I can really comment on, although I believe they started off the Australian series with just about the best players available. I have been on the outside, really, yet at the same time I have wondered what it would be like for me in that kind of situation. I am not crossing any bridges yet, but I know that I shall not feel fulfilled unless I play for England. If I do not make the grade, that is fair enough. But I have to feel I have done my best. I am hungry for the chance. Guys like Allan Lamb, Graham Gooch, David Gower and Ian Botham have been great players, and I would love to walk out alongside them in an England team.

*Did you always want it to be England?*

Yes, there was talk about me playing for New Zealand—the qualification period would be less—but since I was a kid, I have been reading about the great England players. To represent England at Lord's would be the highlight for me. I have no real complaints about waiting seven years for my qualification, because I do not think people should just be able to walk into a national side.

*Surely you will feel some sort of pressure as you sit with your pads on for the first time in an England sweater?*

I will be keyed up, but I always am when I am about to bat. Otherwise you cannot give of your best. The plus part of having to wait so long to qualify is that I will be fairly experienced by then, yet I will still be only 25. It is not a bad time to start an international career. With a bit of luck, I will have scored about fifty first-class hundreds and played against some fine bowlers around the world. I should be able to handle all the media attention better than if I was just twenty. I will not be bewildered by all the interest, because I have had a fair amount of that in the past few years. Basically, it is something I want to achieve and if I am lucky I will get the chance. Then it is up to me. I do not see myself as English cricket's Great White Hope—especially as there have been some great players in the team over the years. I just want to be able to see if I can step up a gear.

*How much notice do you take of your Press coverage?*

If I have had a good day I glance at the tabloids, then move swiftly on to the more interesting bits in those papers! I usually read the serious ones and send the cuttings back home to my parents. They have always kept scrapbooks about me. One day I will sit down and read them!

*By your standards the 1989 season was a lean one. Why?*

I scored just under 2,000 first-class runs, and only Jimmy Cook got more in the English season, so it was not too bad an effort. But it was a little disappointing after last year, when I got that 405 not out and a thousand runs in May. I fancied repeating that this season, after I started so well with 173 not out in April against the MCC. But things went wrong for a time. To begin with, I was a little mixed up because I had to give serious consideration to a generous offer to play for Queensland in the Sheffield Shield. I handle my own cricket contracts, so it was basically a decision I had to make. Although I knew that the extra competitive element out there would be good for me, I just did not feel right about the deal. I was unsure how much they really wanted me at Queensland. In the end, I turned it down. I would like to play out there at some stage in my career, but for the moment that is shelved. Anyway, that decision occupied my thoughts for some time. Also, the wickets were poor early in the season and I could not get going. I like to occupy the crease for long periods, and the pitches were so unreliable that you were never really in. My feet were not moving properly; they were not carrying me to the areas where I could judge the length of the delivery. I was crouching too much at the crease, subconsciously expecting an unplayable ball, and I was never really sure where I should be playing it. My mother noticed my crouched stance when she came over with dad early in July. As soon as she saw me at the wicket, she said I was far too low in my stance. When I began to pick things up in July with a few hundreds, I stood up taller and felt more comfortable. It is difficult to take your good form in the nets out on to the pitch when you are not sure if you can play forward happily without getting one in the face.

*How do you prepare for your innings as first wicket down?*
I watch the first couple of overs and see how our openers are doing against the fast bowlers. But I do not want to get absorbed too much in the play. If a guy is bowling magnificently, you do not really want to know that. Our captain, Phil Neale, watches about 95 per cent of the play, but I cannot. I would get too tired. I have a chat with someone in the dressing-room, read a paper, keep one eye on the play and have a closer look if it is a bowler I have not seen. But I try not to get too tense. Basically, I like to go out and just play. Batting all stems from the head and the eyes. You are looking to keep your head still and watch the ball all the time. Then it is a case of timing—and you cannot do anything about that until you actually get out there. When you love batting as much as I do, you do not want to over-prepare. You want to make it all count at the right time.

*You scored your first hundred at the age of six. You have never been dismissed in a first-class game for 99. How do you approach the target of three figures?*
It is funny, isn't it, that a hundred is the target—not 75 or 150? Anyway, I never freeze when I am on the brink. I'll tighten up if the ball is seaming around or the wicket is unreliable, but I still play my shots if the ball is there for it. Generally, I like to get through it as quickly as I can. When I get there and I know I have had a bit of luck, I will wave my bat rather sheepishly to the crowd, with a grin on my face. But there are times when I have played well. Then it feels terrific. Either way, there is always a sense of achievement for me in getting a hundred, because that is what I am in the team for. And that is the time when I tell myself to press on and get a big score. I get very annoyed with myself if I get out through a lapse of concentration after just reaching a hundred, when both my inclinations and the team's needs are geared towards building on the situation.

*Your coach at Worcester, Basil D'Oliveira, also came from Southern Africa and he went on to a great career with England. Obviously, Basil hopes for something similar for you. Is there a special affinity between the two of you?*
All I know is that I admire and respect him tremendously. I always want to get praise from Basil, because it is rare and you know you have to work for it. A couple of years ago, some people at the club were putting the rumour around that Basil and I did not get on very well. That was because I respected him so much, and I felt that I had to earn his respect. We would talk a little about cricket during the day, but I could not go up to him in the evening in the bar and start a conversation with him, because he was on a pedestal

for me. I remember at the end of the 1986 season I needed another 103 to become the youngest to score 2,000 runs in a first-class season. I got 107, and we also won the match in a run chase. That night in the bar I plucked up courage to stand alongside Basil, and he just looked at me and said simply: "Well played." Coming from him, that meant a lot. Sometimes he never said a word to me when I got hundreds in the second team. That was very clever of him, because I would then go out and try to do something special to get a "well played" from him. Now that I am established in the first team, he knows exactly how to handle me. If I have got myself out and I am sitting in the dressing-room, furious with myself, he will just look at me and I know what he is thinking. I will be so embarrassed, because he knows what I am feeling. I look away and go and do something else. He makes you really want to perform well for him. His son, Damian, is my best friend in the team. We room together and stand at slip. We often have an affectionate laugh about Damian's dad, but we both know how much he has helped me. When I was offered terms to play for Western Province a few years back, Basil was very sensible. He told me I did not need the hassle of a South African stamp on my passport if I managed to get in the England team and we were due to go somewhere like the West Indies. He said it was vital to get it right, out there in the middle—forget about the noughts on the contracts—and that money would come through eventually from various sources, as long as I did myself justice as a cricketer. And with someone like Basil in the background, you never forget the importance of the team's interests, rather than your own. I think what he achieved twenty years ago was fantastic. He must have been a tremendous player to do so much at an age when many are thinking of retirement.

*Everyone is convinced you will be in the England side as soon as you are eligible. But I don't suppose you are taking anything for granted.*

Certainly not. What if I have a bad season in 1990 and start poorly the following year? I am intrigued to know what it is like when the best players in the country gather at a Test Match ground: it will be different from Worcester! I have watched the Tests more and more on television in the last couple of years, and I do find myself wondering about the pressures and the extra challenge. One thing is certain—I will have a lot of friends in the crowd. So many relatives and friends back in Zimbabwe have told me they will be there for my first England game, and I am sure they will be. It will be nice to think I shall have that kind of support.

*So you are not playing State cricket in Australia this winter. Where will you play before reporting back to Worcester?*

I am going back home to Zimbabwe. My parents have a tobacco farm about fifty miles from Harare, and I want to have a rest for a few months. I have worked out that if all goes well I should be pretty busy with cricket for the next few years, so it seems sensible just to take stock and step off the roundabout for a time. A lot has happened to me in three or four years and I do not want to get burned out. I will play a little club cricket and keep fit, with weight training and aerobics to keep me flexible and supple. Besides, I am an uncle for the first time and I want to enjoy that new experience! All this will help me get freshened up for the 1990 season, when I want to play very well. Hopefully the wickets will be better than this year, and give us a fairer contest between bat and ball.

*So far, what have been your most memorable innings?*

They all came in the 1988 season with Worcestershire. The most satisfying was the 212 early on at Old Trafford, where the ball turned sharply. The most enjoyable was the 405 not out at Taunton. And the most important was the 197 against Glamorgan right at the end of the season, when we needed all four batting points. We got them with just a few balls to spare, and I knew that I had a lot to do with that. And we won the championship by just one point from Kent.

# GRAHAM DILLEY

**'I have become disillusioned with the England set-up. I believe Mike Gatting has been harshly treated. '**

BODY language can be a useful guide when assessing the personalities of cricketers. A minimalist like Allan Border bats in gritty character while a noisy, bustling extrovert such as Mike Gatting is hardly a blushing violet when he twiddles his bat at the crease. Graham Dilley has foxed us over the years. He has never really given the impression that cricket occupies every one of his waking hours. The ability to bowl fast marked him out as an England prospect while still a teenager and, for a time, it appeared that Dilley was taking his talent for granted. His heart and determination were less obvious than his knack of blasting out top batsmen by sheer speed. The early period of Graham Dilley's England career seemed to consist of occasional devastating spells against the background of a sustained campaign to win the Chris Old Memorial Trophy for tweaked hamstrings and prolonged occupation of the physio's couch.

That changed after Dilley was forced to spend a year out of the game with a serious neck injury. He went to South Africa to prove his fitness and remodel his action under John Lever's sympathetic coaching. He returned a better bowler: slower, more controlled, closer to the stumps. And with the priceless new asset of an outswinger. When England triumphed in Australia in 1987, Dilley was the best bowler on either side, pinning the batsmen with late swing at a brisk pace. At last, he appeared to know exactly what he was doing with the ball. A move from Kent to Worcestershire brought him further peace of mind and, despite persistent knee trouble, the old days of pulling up the ladder have gone.

Dilley is not exactly his best advocate. Laconic and self-contained, he does not cultivate the media to ensure favourable mentions; he prefers to puff quietly at his filter tip and keep his own counsel. Yet those close to the Worcestershire dressing-room acknowledge his dry wit and the professional, unselfish part played by Dilley in securing *two successive championships. He has gone on the field for them carrying injuries that would have seen him limping around the golf course in earlier times. Dilley has been happier with Worcestershire than with England in recent years, a fact influencing his decision to end his Test career by going on the unofficial tour to South Africa under Mike Gatting. He may have played just 41 Tests in a decade, and never managed to last an entire series, but Dilley leaves the Test arena as England's best fast bowler since Bob Willis. So why end his Test career now?*

Various reasons, that all went into the pot. I have become disillusioned with the England set-up. I believe Mike Gatting has been harshly treated over the past couple of years, and my own experience in New Zealand, when I was fined for swearing on the field, did nothing to help. I was so annoyed at the rumpus over that incident that I asked for my passport so I could come home early, but I was refused. After all, I had not sworn directly at the umpire. I came out with the kind of frustrated curse every fast bowler offers at some stage, and the television microphone picked it up. You will find that most of the lads who went to Pakistan and New Zealand with Gatt became as disillusioned as me, and a fair amount of them are going to South Africa. I am also running out of time as a strike bowler. I am thirty, my right knee has had two operations in the past year and I have not exactly got a great record in the fitness department over the years, have I? I am unlikely to have too many years left in me as England's main fast bowler.

Then there is the money. I am not naive enough to believe that this tour will break down racial barriers, although at least I have been out there, and have more first-hand experience than those who wave placards at college. Ali Bacher is an impressive man, and he has done everything to make cricket in South Africa multi-racial, which is how it should be. But the money was a very important consideration; it gives me security.

*You agreed to go to South Africa at the end of May, a week before the Test series against Australia started, and you then went on to play two Tests. How can you justify taking your Test fees when you knew you were on the way out, by your own choice?*

It was never certain that there would be a tour to South Africa, until the story broke on August 1. Even now, it is not definitely on until we get there. If I had dipped out of England consideration, people would have wanted to know why, and we had been sworn to secrecy.

*Surely all the uncertainty must have affected morale in the England dressing-room this summer.*

Those of us who had agreed to go only ever talked about it when we were alone and it was then along the lines of "have you heard anything? Is it still on?" There were no huddled groups of whispering rebels. We all wanted to do our very best for England against the Aussies—not just for the sake of the team, but because it would help our own image in South Africa if we came there with good individual performances behind us.

*So why did England play so badly against Australia?*

They had the luck that we had over there in 1986/87. Now, I agree you make your own luck, but it is astonishing how often the team that is on top gets the bigger slice. Then their confidence just snowballs. What about the times Steve Waugh got an inside edge that went past leg-stump when our batters would play on in the same situation? What about losing half the first day at Leeds, when conditions were absolutely right to

74

put them in and expect the ball to swing around? I think David Gower made the correct decision. But that first day proved the most decisive of the series, because the Aussies grew in stature after half-expecting to get bowled out cheaply. They did not fancy playing the first Test at Leeds, and I thought they would struggle in the series, because they are not good players of swing bowling. I believed that Phil Newport would be our trump card against them, and I also hoped that I would get a few of them out as they played across the line to mid-wicket. But we both got injured. Even when we went two down at Lord's, I still thought we would pull it round. In May, I would not have given you any odds on them beating us in the series; I was so confident they would not bat well. Too many blame David Gower, but I do not see what else he could have done. It is not his fault he never had the eleven he wanted, due to terrible luck with injuries. Far too much was made about him being laid-back and all that, but I share David's view that if you are good enough to get a place in the England team, then you must have a fair idea of how to play the game. I like his relaxed air; it helps to defuse the tension that is never far away when you are on England duty.

*You mentioned that last tour of Australia, when you finally broke through and took five wickets in an innings after? Tests. Had that comparative failure got to you by then?*

I had begun to despair of getting there. As a strike bowler, my job was to nip out the first two or three, then clean up the tail. But although I always seemed to be able to get among the best batters, I never put it all together. Before then, I had been a four an over man, dangerous but expensive. After John Lever worked so hard on me in Natal, I was a much better bowler. Confidence is so important, and after doing so well in Australia, I knew that I could bowl sides out in Tests. That is not to say that I am going to have a succession of good days, because fast bowling is not like that: rhythm is so elusive, and you have to know exactly what you are trying to do. But in recent years I have been more confident of my own ability.

*How much have you worried about the responsibility of being the side's strike bowler?*

The biggest worry is when you are expected to take a hatful in favourable conditions. You start to strain too much, you over-step the crease and get called for no-balling. The crowd love it when the fast bowler gets taken apart, because he is built up as the lion. The batsman is the Christian, if you like. When the tail gets twisted, they love to see the bully get his comeuppance.

Experience is vital here. When I first started, I expected a wicket every ball. Now I know that the combination of speed and swing should get you a stack of wickets every day—but that is not possible, because it is such an exact science. The ball can come out of your hand at the wrong speed, your line might be astray, the wicket too slow, the ball too soft, you are too tired, you are at the wrong end, the wind is in the wrong direction and the batters are pretty good players. You settle for hoping for the best and telling yourself to remain confident. It is not the batsman's fault that he keeps playing and missing, so there is no real point in pumping yourself up and giving him the verbals. I sometimes say something like: "Bloody hell, this is a good game isn't it? Nick, four, miss it, nick four." But that is all. It is up to the bowler to put the ball in the right place.

*I remember when you first came into the England team, in 1979, the grapevine reckoned you threw the occasional ball. Did you ever wonder about that?*

On that 1979/80 tour to Australia it was mentioned in some of their papers, and I must admit I sometimes used to think they could be right. The odd delivery used to be so quick I thought: "I wonder if I chucked that?" There is always a chance of that with a faster bowler. We wondered about Terry Alderman when he first came over here in 1987 and took all those wickets after deciding to bowl faster. He was filmed, examined frame by frame, and cleared. In my case, I am around 85 per cent of the speed I was in my early days with England, and now that I am more controlled in my action, I am sure that every delivery is now legal.

*Do you always know where the ball is going when you release it?*

I have a rough idea, but I reckon that if I don't know, then neither does the batter. For variation, I rely on getting it wrong. Unless you are a Dennis Lillee, who could swing it either way, you have to hope the batsman makes a mistake. I cannot bowl the inswinger any more, and the good players know that, so they are expecting the outswinger as my stock delivery. I am experimenting with the slower ball and sometimes it comes out fine, but as yet I am not exactly a Franklyn Stephenson in that department. I sometimes fool them when I get my action wrong, and the ball does not come out as they expected. It goes straight on, or even dips in. If you bowl perfection all the time, the batsman gets used to you. The deliveries they leave now are totally different from when I first started. Then I used to angle it in at the right-hander from wide of the crease. If I pitched a foot outside the off-stump they would have to play at me, because it was on its way in. Now, if it pitches a foot outside off-stump or starts on off-stump, they are looking to leave it, because I swing it so much away from the right-hander. So as a variation I rely on not being good enough to bowl what I want all the time.

*Do you have hang-ups about particular batsmen?*

It is funny, this one. I would rather bowl at world-class batters like Allan Border or David Gower, because I know what they will try to do. But stroke-players like Paul Johnson or Paul Parker and the Wells brothers at Sussex have often caused me trouble. They put the ball in areas you had not bargained for; they have enough strokes to mess up your line.

*Do you agree with the criticism about lacking stomach for the fight and not giving everything on the field?*

That used to be fair comment. I used to look for excuses and an easy way out. I could never really be relied on in a tight situation consistently. But after that neck injury in 1984 I had a lot of time on my hands to ponder. Eventually it was discovered that a disc was trapped against the spinal cord, and that a piece of reshaped bone from my hip would be used to replace the disc. If the operation failed I could easily have ended up a cripple. I was also tested for cancer and multiple sclerosis before they found exactly what caused the numbness down my side. It took a year before I was ready to test myself out in first-class cricket—a year in which I took a long, hard look at myself. Now I cannot help it if I do not look too effervescent. I am not the type who runs around all over the place, looking over-enthusiastic. I have always been fairly quiet and low-key. Why try to change your nature? But since that injury I reckon I have shown a greater determination to get on to the park. I know there have been times in recent years when I have played through injuries that would have kept me in the dressing-room when I was younger.

76

*How much is that to do with your change of county?*

In the last few years at Kent I was very unhappy, particularly when Chris Tavaré was removed from the captaincy after two very good seasons. I am a total Tavaré man and things were never the same there for me afterwards. I have really enjoyed my time at Worcester, they are a well-run club and the committee are very supportive of the players. Phil Neale has captained us excellently and I have the utmost respect for him. I know that many people said that Ian Botham and I were trouble-makers and that we would upset the dressing-room. But although we both knew that was rubbish, it was up to Phil to prove that we could be blended into the team. There was never any problem about that, and I like to think that our big-match experience has helped the lads as we began to pick up trophies after a few near-misses. I think we have been good for each other. A championsip side takes twenty wickets regularly to win games, rather than getting home now and again in a run chase on the final afternoon after a declaration. In the last couple of years, we have shown what can be done with a happy dressing-room and a positive attitude. The captain is intelligent enough to allow free expression from the players on tactics, and it has been terrific to be part of a group that speaks frankly and then goes out and pulls for one another. We even go into the members' bar for drinks and don't get earbashed! That would never happen at Kent. We would be off to a pub to avoid all that. At Worcester, the bulk of the members seem genuinely on our side and want us to do well. To a player, with all the tensions and frustrations in a season, that is very reassuring.

*Yet you never really look as if you are enjoying your cricket, Graham.*

That is all image rubbish. I do not care what the Press write about me; I am perfectly happy to be in the background. All I know is that playing cricket is what I do best, and that I shall miss it when it when I pack up. I cannot help it if I plod back to my mark slowly, trying to get my breath back and concentrate on the next ball. I suppose I am a bit like Chris Waddle in soccer; people say he is lazy and looks disinterested, but he can play the game. All this stuff about body language is a waste of time. You just have to be yourself and keep putting in the performances. There are certain things about playing cricket I dislike—we play too many games, we do far too much travelling and our privacy is too often invaded—but I am glad that I have made it to some sort of standard. I do not see why I should walk around with a stupid grin on my face to prove it.

# TONY
# GREIG

**'The African does not have the right to vote ... why the hell should he condone a game of cricket just because the barriers are down at a cricket ground?'**

**M**ORE *than a decade after world cricket's most profound revolution, one of its architects remains a stimulating character. Tony Greig's ability to polarise opinion has always amused him; a man who has divided his life between the varying social climes of South Africa, England and Australia has never felt the need to bow the knee to considerations of class. Tony Greig wanted to get on in the world and he was honest enough to admit it. Along the way, he has alienated many by his eye for the main chance, and his defection to Kerry Packer outraged even more whose own business ethics hardly embraced the creed of St Francis of Assisi. Judging by the hysteria generated by Greig in the summer of 1977, absolute secrecy in setting up a vital business deal began with an Australian media tycoon and his persuasive headhunter. One man's disloyalty is another's prudence. No one can be surprised that today Greig works for Channel 9 television and as marketing director for an insurance company—he was always very keen on image, communication and aggressive salesmanship. An enviable lifestyle in Sydney is no more than Greig feels he deserved; yet many ought to be grateful to his iconoclastic streak. All international cricketers have benefited financially from the mould-breaking, while Greig's talismanic qualities as England captain inspired the men under his command. Those who were led by Greig in his two years in the job still speak warmly of his loyalty and capacity to inspire. The media also had good cause to bemoan his demise. No other England captain has enjoyed a better relationship with the scribes and the men with microphones. Greig positively relished such jousts, and his charm, articulacy and massive self-confidence ensured few longueurs at his press conferences. Greig was the ideal cricketer to front the public relations campaign demanded by Packer—a large enough personality to withstand the character assassinations with rather more humour and dignity than some of his detractors. Yet he was never really a radical firebrand, a tilter at every windmill in the manner of a Phil Edmonds. Cricket* *was just a signpost in the avenue of his life and it would never consume him. Today his opinions on some aspects of the game could almost come straight off the production line marked Disgusted of Tunbridge Wells. . . .*

I have a problem with the basic philosophy of one-day cricket. It's like the fast food chains—you know, McDonalds or Kentucky Fried Chicken. The eating habits for cricket have changed to accommodate those tastes. I prefer a decent restaurant and I'm no different from the older ones who prefer the traditional brand of cricket. We need the one-day stuff to finance the game, but how do we market it properly so people realise it is just McDonalds rather than gourmet food? Test cricket must not be gazumped by the one-day stuff. We play too much of it in Australia, but that is a legacy from Packer. I suspect he lost a fair amount of money early on with World Series Cricket so that he had to strike a favourable deal in 1979 when peace broke out. No doubt that involved a great deal of covering one-day cricket, and so it has proved.

*During the Packer period, you kept saying it was a crusade to improve the financial lot of cricketers. Do you now think the players are earning too much money?*

When I re-read some of my statements now, I know I got some of the emphasis wrong. In the players' minds at that time, Packer meant a lot more money: I didn't want to be an umpire, thank you very much, and I wanted to end up in the business environment. But I was wrong about giving everyone a fair crack of the whip financially. It has gone too far now—blokes are being put on long-term contracts that they do not really deserve and I am sure the various Boards do not want that either. If you pay players too much money you create a situation where no one can dip in and out of the professional game and the programme never gets slimmed down, which I believe is vital. There used to be a marvellous mix of characters in the English game who were not steeped in cricket as a full-time career. We had a cross-section of society and it worked. In England the philosophy is that the educated should lead and I agree with that—you do not go to war with dummies in charge of the battalions, you get men who lead naturally. To a certain extent the same used to happen in Australia, although they picked the best man to captain out of the best eleven players available. I do not agree with the coach idea; the captain should be able to lead. Now I believe these guys should be paid damned well because in many cases they are giving up the chance of movement in another profession, but they should not be allowed to live off all their money from cricket—it should be put in a trust. The game should be freed of total professionalism and "professional" should simply equal "very good" rather than "very well paid". When I captained Sussex there were two guys down in Brighton good enough to play for England but they would not give up being a banker and a solicitor to go for it. I thought they were right, but the system of first-class cricket ought to have accommodated them. Make sure that a man holding down a good job can still play for his county or state side without sacrificing his other profession. Defer the payments to the English and Australian players and put more money back into the game so that there is a proper environment to breed better cricketers. I want to see a situation where a man good enough to play for his country does not have the money worries I had while building my career. Intelligent guys should be able to combine two careers to solve that problem.

*Surely that's asking too much of English cricket. It sounds as if you want to turn the clock back many years.*

At the moment the English game is archaic. I am saying that a social change could easily be ushered in over the next twenty years. Every county in England has financial worries and I am simply coming to terms with reality. The days of having forty fuddy-duddies on each county committee who look after a geographical area have long gone. Some pretty bold initiatives are needed to kill off the diehards but it is clear to me that a lot of the potential in England is not being tapped. I would like to walk down an English street, ask a youngster what cricket he plays and get an answer that reassures me—that he has good facilities, a caring schoolmaster to guide him and a club interested in his abilities. But the supply of those marvellous masters is drying up now and the public schools and Oxbridge aren't turning out good enough players. Every time I see that ridiculous Kwik Cricket on a Test Match ground at lunchtime, I want to die. I thank God I was lucky enough to play proper cricket with a hard ball and adults when I was a kid. The situation is better in Australia—you can go down to the Waverley Club in Sydney at the age of twelve, get to the fifth grade at fifteen, then if you start making hundreds you have a chance of making first grade, then into the State side. At least there is some sort of infrastructure there, whereas the club scene in England needs to be strengthened.

*What about the structure at the top, at Lord's?*

This will surprise a few people, but I have always had a lot of respect for some of those guys. I think Gubby Allen was one of the smartest administrators that cricket has ever had, but the problem of getting the structure right is now too big for one man. It needs an inner group of dedicated, far-sighted men. I believe Ted Dexter is a good choice to reshape English cricket; he has got some refreshing ideas. He will stand back and let the captain do it his way. The captaincy of England is still one of the game's great honours: it is more creative and challenging than in soccer and I do not like to see the post devalued by the presence of a coach. I cannot relate to Micky Stewart having such a high profile, because the only one who will be sacked is the captain and he should be the one making the public comments, not someone who is safe with a contract. I cannot remember how much I got paid for being England captain, but that never bothered me. It was a great honour.

*And yet you were ready to give it away by signing for Packer?*

The truth of the matter is that I had given everything I had to English cricket. I had an offer I could not refuse and after three days of hard thinking, I took it. With hindsight, I wish I had made myself unavailable for England in the 1977 summer for personal reasons. I could not go to the chairman of selectors, Alec Bedser, and tell him what was about to happen. He had been very good to me, and if I had shared that dynamite story with him, Alec would have been placed in a dreadful position. He and the other selectors were not as lucky as me. They did not have a lucrative alternative.

*It is amazing that the story did not leak out sooner. After all, many players were involved and some of them must have talked.*

It was a very big story, but the bigger they are, the better the secret is kept. The Press and the cricket Establishment were so busy preening themselves behind their gin and tonics after the success of the Centenary Test that they did not know what was going on. Some pretty good journalists were caught out and that is one of the reasons why the initial reaction was so hostile. When I flew from Melbourne to Sydney to meet Packer—at my instigation, incidentally—I knew nothing about his plans. I just wanted to explore any commercial possibilities. After I had signed, I flew off to the West Indies, where they were playing Pakistan, and signed up the necessary players in two days. Viv Richards was the only one who wanted to look at the contract for a day. The South Africans were then flown to London and they did not need much persuading! After that, the boys who had played under me for England were lined up and there were few problems there.

*When the story broke, one of the most interesting observations from the Establishment was that it was only to be expected. After all, Greig was not an Englishman through and through. In other words, you were a bit of a bounder. Did that amuse you or anger you?*

I just laughed at it. Anyone with half a brain knows that those making such statements have got problems; they do not live in the real world. I would love to have been more open about the deal but getting the thing off the ground demanded absolute secrecy. We also had that great commentator, Henry Blofeld, writing in one of his books that my judgement had been impaired because I was an epileptic. Well, I am proud to have cracked my epilepsy and carried on playing at the highest level. That slur was an example of the Establishment resorting to anything to discredit me. Everyone else in the cricket media knew about my epilepsy but they and the players had the integrity to keep quiet about it. I do not recall too many remarks about my judgement when I was doing well as England captain. Anyway, that same Blofeld is now the biggest media commodity you have ever seen in Australia, taking advantage of all the things that Kerry Packer created. If you wait long enough, you will find inconsistencies in everyone's behaviour. You do not have to be a colonial upstart to be criticised.

*Surely one of the legacies of Packer is that the game has become more aggressive—less sporting, more ruthless.*

I do not think so: Ian Chappell and the others were just as aggressive before Packer came along, you know. I agree that we have gone through a period when there has been a fair amount of snarling, but I have a lot of faith in modern youth and I do not think it is as bad as it was. There are a lot of top players now who are pretty cool out there. When we look back on it all in twenty years' time, I reckon it will appear as a little phase that got out of hand for just a short period. I think the game is now more intimidatory because of the poor wickets, not due to Packer. Not enough research has been done into the question of wickets. They are a disgrace. We must get back to good, hard white wickets so that we get rid of the boring medium-pacers and select spin bowlers to back up the speed merchants. The West Indies have got the pace bowlers that the rest of the world lacks. They have been able to dominate world cricket because the pitches have been so inconsistent in bounce. I still cannot forget Old Trafford in 1976 when I picked Brian Close and John Edrich to open against the West Indies. I knew what I was doing. I wanted two of the toughest cricketers of all time to go out there and battle away on a dreadful wicket. Well, I was criticised for choosing them and when I spoke the truth about that dreadful wicket, I was fined and warned about future statements. I was simply speaking the truth and yet Cedric Rhoades, the king of Old Trafford at the time, never spoke to me again because I had dared to criticise his pitch. Until the wickets improve, there is going to be a big problem. It is going to get harder and harder to keep cricket in the forefront in Australia and England, because in this space age there are just too many things for kids to do. We are going to need all the help we can get. I would like to see top-class cricket go the same way as rugby union, a sport that still gives a lot of fun while embracing well-rounded characters. It will help if they can play on proper surfaces.

*You were born and reared in South Africa. Do you see any hope of resuming Test cricket with them? Do they deserve it?*

No to both questions. I can see no chance unless Apartheid is dismantled. I can honestly say that I am now a better South African for the exposure to the likes of Sunil Gavaskar, Imran Khan and Clive Lloyd. One should never lose sight of the fact that the African does not have the right to vote and if he is not a free man in that context, why the hell should he condone a game of cricket just because the barriers are down at a cricket ground? I admit that I did not think that way as a youngster in South Africa, but since then I have thought a lot harder about a system where guys could not have the vote in South Africa yet they have played cricket with and against me in other parts of the world. I still go back there and I am sure that many South Africans are now beginning to understand that a normal society is a requirement. The papers will say that they have been serious about that for many years, but believe me, they have only been working at it since the mid-eighties.

*Yet because of South Africa's isolation, there will still be unofficial tours out there that make a lot of money.*

Funny thing about money, whether it's Packer, South Africa, television or business—it does talk. I'm glad I didn't have to rely on little old ladies putting a few pence into my benefit kitty when I played in England.

# MICHAEL HOLDING

**'We have a saying in the West Indies—if you want a drive, go and rent a car. I've never believed in letting anyone drive me. '**

IT may have been Friday the thirteenth but Michael Holding felt lucky. That morning, at Headingley in 1984, he had taken his 200th Test wicket; late in the day he smashed the tiring English bowlers out of sight. Bob Willis, at the end of a distinguished career, was the principal sufferer, as five sixes soared away from Holding's bat to land amid the jeering imbibers of Tetley's bitter. As Willis plodded off the field, contemplating figures that screamed out for a phone call to the Samaritans, Holding put a consoling arm round him and said: "Don't worry about it, Bob, it was my day. I got four winners in a Yankee as well!" That just about sums up Michael Holding's attitude to life and cricket: he could contemplate cricketing success with the same equanimity as his frequent failures on the horses. An occasional victory over the men with the bottomless satchels and sharp suits would elicit a slow, toothy smile and a philosophical shrug of those slim shoulders. Michael Holding invariably appeared at peace with himself, once he had banished some early behavioural excesses from his make-up. As a cricketer, he had great cause for satisfaction, both practically and aesthetically. Not only his notable fast bowling impressed: the man had style by the bucketful. He invested all his deeds on the cricket field with a grace and liquidity of movement possessed by a handful. Even those who carped about the slow West Indian over-rate suspended criticism when Holding was mentioned. That long, flowing run-up and smooth, economical delivery transcended any suggestions that the batsman had time to sprout stubble around the chin during one of his overs. Watching Holding bowl has been one of the great sights of recent Test cricket, on a par with the felicitous stroke play of David Gower and the splendour of Roger Harper's fielding. "Whispering Death" they called Holding, and although the years finally blunted his explosiveness, the umpire at his end still couldn't be sure when he was nearing the stumps. Such a thoroughbred never needed to strain, snort and stiffen every sinew like the shire horses

85

*who ran from the sightscreen.*

*As well as adorning Test cricket, Michael Holding proved to be the perfect ambassador for the overseas player when he joined Derbyshire. He was unlucky to play for a side that turned under-achievement into an art form, but he never compromised his own high standards, gave an immense amount of his spare time to colleagues of lesser talent, and offered unstinting loyalty and advice to his young captain, Kim Barnett. When Holding ended his first-class career at Derby in 1989, he left behind warm memories of a dignified, altruistic man. Meanwhile a spokesman for local bookmakers reported that trade would suffer, holidays to the Seychelles were off the agenda, but that life had to go on. We would be lucky to see such an elegant destroyer again, although the video age ensures the artistry of Michael Holding will survive. When did he first become aware that his bowling style was out of the ordinary?*

I've never really thought about it in technical terms, although I like to look back on good performances on the video machine. When I was a youngster, no one told me that I had a particularly good style; in fact some told me that my left arm should be higher. My father got someone to coach me at one stage, but the way I bowled felt comfortable and I stuck with it. That is the thing all budding fast bowlers should remember: does it feel natural? If so, stick to it. I was lucky enough to be athletic, although not to the standard that many journalists have suggested. For the record, I was never a 400 metre runner to Commonwealth Games standards, as I've read so many times. I think the Press got confused with a fellow called Seymour Newman who opened the bowling with me in youth cricket. He was a fine runner. I couldn't even represent my school as a runner; I had to make do with the field events.

I always had a long run from my schooldays. It measured around 25 steps, but I only worked out the length after it felt comfortable. It takes a lot of energy to bowl fast so you have to feel right as you run in. It is all about rhythm and I needed a long run to help me gather pace. One of the secrets is the timing of releasing the ball to get the maximum force behind it. Also a fast arm action to send the ball down as fast as you can. As for the length of my stock ball, I always tried to get the batsmen in "no man's land", so that they were never quite there for the drive or the cut and pull. We have a saying in the West Indies—if you want a drive, go and rent a car. I've never believed in letting anyone drive me.

In England the coaches are obsessed with fast bowlers bowling line and length rather than naturally. The one-day stuff does not help, but a club that is genuinely interested in the welfare of a young fast bowler ought to leave him out of those games, where accuracy is more important than raw speed. At least Derbyshire have done that. Devon Malcolm has genuine pace and he only bowls in the Nat-West games, where he can steam in off his long run. The wickets in England do not help, because you do not have to be a very good bowler to bowl sides out. Good, strong fellows are not interested in bowling fast, because they do not need to. All they do is put the ball on the spot and the wicket will do the rest for them. Back home, speed still gets wickets because the pitches are rock-hard. The shine has gone after about 25 overs and you need to put a lot into your bowling to dismiss good players.

*Is it true that you Caribbean fast bowlers all bowl bouncers at each other in your domestic cricket?*

Yes, it's all part of the game and no one takes it personally. Don't forget, the wickets are truer over there, so there is less danger of uneven bounce. Anyway the fast bowlers all fancy themselves with the bat! There has been a lot of bleating about bouncers in Test cricket over the years but that only comes from those who can't dish it out themselves. Lillee and Thomson didn't squeal about too many bouncers because they could return them.

*Why can't England produce fast bowlers in the way of the West Indies?*

We are fitter for a start. That only began when Dennis Waight joined the West Indies team during the Packer period. Before then we would just jog a few laps and think we were fit, but Dennis took us on 45 minute runs and we soon knew we had to toughen up. Then I started weight training to build up my muscles. I may be slim but I have muscle definition and that is more important than just looking muscular. Most English fast bowlers don't have muscles in proportion to their bodies: you can't see where their biceps begin and end, nor their pectorals. Fast bowling is hard work. You need strength and rhythm, but you must not be muscle-bound. Diet is important as well. Too many English county cricketers live on junk food like fish and chips and hamburgers. They should eat pasta and sweet things, so that they can burn off the carbohydrates. Lots of proteins as well—plenty of vegetables. Keep them out of the fast food places!

*What about the natural athleticism of the black man. Does he have an essential suppleness that white fast bowlers lack?*

Possibly, but the fact that we can spend so much of the time outdoors is more relevant. We like to be doing sports in the sunshine and that helps to build up muscle definition. We are also hungry for success. In England you can make a reasonably good living from playing county cricket and perhaps some of the good players are not committed enough. In the West Indies, competition to get into the Test side is fierce. There is no professional cricket other than with the Test team. You also make headway socially and professionally if you represent the West Indies. Some used to be waiters or golf caddies, but once you are acknowledged as a Test player, you can go to places you only dreamed about. They just take cricket more seriously in the West Indies.

*How crucial was World Series Cricket to the West Indies?*

Kerry Packer did a lot for us. He gave us the chance of extra professionalism. He signed us as a team and that brought great self-respect. That feeling of pride has never disappeared. We perform well because we know that millions of people back home are depending on us to be the best. We never have any problems on the pitch as a team, but we have had a few upsets off the field in our time together. When you tour for so many months in the year, you are bound to have some personality clashes. I remember one occasion, on the eve of the Lord's Test against England in 1984. The night before, two fellows in the team almost came to blows and someone had to part them. Next day, one of them got a wicket and the guy who had argued with him was the first to run up and congratulate him. No, I won't tell you their names!

*Apart from having better players and superior fast bowling, isn't it a fact that the West Indies have out-selected England in recent years?*

Certainly England have chopped and changed too much. We have been fortunate in that we have kept winning. In the early Seventies, the West Indies used too many players in series that we lost, but we learned a lesson from that. We tend to give young players a chance and persevere with them if they show enough talent. The England selectors should believe in their young players and back them if they fail initially. Look at Rob Bailey. He seems a good batsman to me but he is out after just one Test against us in 1988. The West Indian Press is also less destructive. They are not interested in the off-the-field stuff. If someone drops a catch they will say it was a dolly, but they won't suggest that was because the guy had five ladies the night before.

*How is the production line of West Indian fast bowlers coming along?*

It is going to last a little longer, but it is not like the Japanese car industry, not a constant thing. These things come in cycles. We have a few good spinners coming through—Perry, the Jamaican, looks good—but we are bound to start losing some time. The game is like that. Ian Bishop, my colleague at Derbyshire, has got what it takes—a very good action, strong and fit and he is prepared to listen. But it is too soon to say if he is going to be a great fast bowler.

*What about the turgid over-rates whenever the West Indies play. Do you think the public has been cheated over the years?*

This stems from the fact that we have dominated world cricket through fast bowling since 1976 and our critics are jealous that they do not have the resources. It is a red herring to detract from the quality of the West Indies team. The over-rate from both sides was the same in the 1984 series in England—and what about 1976? I have a tape of the Oval Test, and the captions point out that the over-rate didn't go above twelve an hour, whichever team was bowling. I do not remember many complaints then.

*What about intimidation—is there too much of it now from fast bowlers?*

I never wanted to hurt anyone at any time. When I hit Dennis Amiss on the head during the M.C.C. match in 1976, he ducked into the ball. When I hit Derek Randall in the face at Launceston in 1982, the pitch was responsible. It was a killer—which is why I pitched the ball up after that. If it is a tail-ender who can't really defend himself, I would not bowl it above shoulder height. But I would try to get him caught at bat/pad by aiming at his rib cage. Apart from that, against top-line batsmen in a Test Match, I did not worry about bowling bouncers. It was my country against theirs, and although I hoped they would not get hurt, that was their problem.

*The Oval, 1976. Fourteen England wickets on a flat pitch, nine of them clean bowled. Is that still your supreme performance?*

I have bowled as well in Australia and got fewer wickets, but I can't imagine I've done better. I was young—just 22—and more than a thousand runs had been scored in the first innings alone. You could only get the ball above the waist with the new ball and with most of the batsmen coming forward, I had to pitch it up and beat them through the air with pace. Along with the other West Indies fast bowlers that summer, I had been spurred on by Tony Greig's "grovel" remark. I can see him now, on the balcony at Hove at the start of the season, saying: "When West Indies are down they grovel, and I intend to make them grovel." He then hurriedly substituted "we" for "I" but he was too late to cover himself. Nobody forgot that, and whenever he came in to bat, we found an extra two yards of pace for him.

*Did that have anything to do with the fact that he was a white South African and that the word "grovel" might have possessed racialist undertones?*

Not at all. Greigy was a good sportsman and he accepted defeat well at the Oval. We didn't like the way that he had placed himself in the forefront at the start of the season. He seemed to have forgotten it is a team game.

*There were two incidents early in your career that seemed uncharacteristic. The first was at Sydney in 1976 when you sat down on the pitch and cried because the umpire had ruled against you. Does that now embarrass you?*

I was very young and had no experience of such dreadful umpiring. I remember it vividly. I got Ian Redpath first ball after tea, and off the next delivery Ian Chappell was caught behind. Everyone thought so except the umpire. It was an unbelievable decision and I just broke down. I was ready to pick up stumps and go home immediately. I wanted no more part of Test cricket. But Clive Lloyd and Lance Gibbs pulled me up onto my feet and told me that was an element of the game and to get on with it.

*Then there is that famous photograph of you kicking down a stump in 1980 during a Test in New Zealand, with the batsman, John Parker, seemingly oblivious. That photo went all round the world. You can't have been pleased with yourself that day.*

At that stage in my career I was still a little hot-headed. Later I learned to control my emotions. You can never excuse bad behaviour, but the background is important. This was a very close Test and they needed just over 100 to win in the final innings. The day before, on the rest day, all the guys on the radio had been crowing about New Zealand's first victory over the West Indies, the world champions. They were gloating, and that fired us up. Well, Parker gloved the ball to our keeper, the most obvious dismissal you have ever seen. I was right beside the batsman as he started to take off his gloves and started to walk. I was so confident I didn't even look at the umpire and I was about to congratulate Deryck Murray, our keeper. Then I noticed Parker putting his gloves back on, so I said "howzat" and the umpire replied "not out". It was so blatant. I was furious and I lashed out at the stump alongside me. I never did anything like that again, but you have to understand the context. There was a lot of bad feeling in that series. In the Christchurch Test we all sat in the dressing-room as the umpires walked out for the resumption of play, and we said we wouldn't go back out there because the umpiring was so terrible. So Clive Lloyd and their captain Geoff Howath had a quiet chat and agreed to help the umpires as much as they could. Soon after we resumed, Howarth stood his ground after nicking one to the keeper! It was ridiculous. We only continued that tour under duress.

*On to happier times and the day when you suddenly decided to come off your long run again at the Oval in 1984—with disastrous consequences for England. What made you do that all of a sudden?*

I give the credit to an Englishman whose name I never knew. He was a Surrey member and he mentioned how much he had enjoyed my fourteen wickets there in 1976. After tea on the fourth day in 1984, I was coming out on to the field again when he stopped me and said: "What about a repeat of 1976?" I thought "why not?" I had felt good, I had been conserving my energy off my short run, so I switched to the full version. I got Broad, Gower and Lamb in seventeen balls and ended up with five in the innings—thanks to that Surrey member. I could not have done that every day, though. I was too old!

*Why have you hung around at Derby, playing so many years in county cricket?*

It did not kill me because I could share playing duties with John Wright, the other overseas player. Apart from that, Derbyshire have been a good team to play for and I have enjoyed Kim Barnett's positive captaincy. It has been frustrating because we have not made enough use of our talents. In my first summer with them, I was in tears in the dressing-room after we lost an important one-day game against Middlesex that we ought to have won. Since then I have become more used to defeat after winning so much with the West Indies—but you never really like it if you are a professional. Apart from the lads in our dressing-room I have also enjoyed the quality of horse racing in England. Much better than in America—the racetracks each have a different character. Gambling is my only vice, and although I rarely finish up on the bookies, it gives me great pleasure. I will keep coming back to England for a couple of months each summer but not to play serious cricket. The cold and wind really bring pain to my shoulder, knees and back.

*Your outstanding performance for Derbyshire came near the end, in 1988, when you took eight for 21 against Sussex in the Nat-West?*

The figures flattered me. It was partly good bowling on a pitch with extra bounce, but mainly bad batting. Many of the Sussex batsmen did not want to know when they saw the ball bouncing around. Imran Khan and Paul Parker got out to good deliveries but most of the others did not get behind the line of the ball. It may have looked impressive but I am conscious that I have not performed to my fullest potential for Derbyshire. That will be a big regret I take into retirement, because they have been very good to me.

*How do you see your future?*

I will go home to Jamaica and see more of my three children. My father is a building contractor and he is building a house for me. I will open a sports goods store and ponder an offer to become a partner in a fast foods restaurant—but I won't encourage cricketers to eat there!

*Finally, Michael, who was the most difficult batsmen you have bowled at and why?*

There are two—Geoffrey Boycott and Ian Chappell. People keep telling me it was a great over I bowled at Boycott in the Barbados Test of 1981, but I do not really remember much about it. But if Boycott rates it, that is fine by me because he was a great technician. He had the shots for the bad balls but otherwise he grafted and accumulated. You had to bowl very well to get Boycott's wicket, his defence was immaculate. I rated Chappell for entirely different reasons. You could never predict what shot he would play to a particular ball. You always had to think one step ahead of him because he was so unorthodox. Both players were great challenges and they were also very strong mentally.

# STEVE WAUGH

**'Some of the England batsmen told me that the pitches were so bad for county games that they would nick one soon enough if they played straight. '**

T HE *eyes have it with Steve Waugh. They burn straight through the interviewer. A man with such an inscrutable gaze is not someone to take on at poker. The fact that he speaks rapidly suggests that the reserve in those eyes is based on shyness, but he never buckles in any contest on the cricket field. A bowler who greets Viv Richards with three bouncers off the first deliveries he faced in a Test series has a pretty shrewd idea what lies in store for him when it is his turn to face the Caribbean music. Steve Waugh's inner confidence does not feature anything more than a cold stare when he is on batting duty. Merv Hughes has never been his role model. Waugh just gets on with the job, chewing gum methodically under the baggy green cap, giving the bowler no encouragement.*

*A technique as pure as Waugh's marks the best insurance against self-doubt, yet there is a chink or two. Extreme pace has discomfited him at times. He does not play the hook shot with any great control, and extra bounce has occasionally undone him on the back foot as he goes for that devastating cut, which is his trademark. In other words, he was far too good for the England bowlers in 1989, whose idea of line and length often seemed to be avoiding hitting the square leg umpire on the shoulder. When he reached his first Test hundred at Leeds, the wonder was that it had taken him 27 games. Another glittering unbeaten hundred at Lord's ushered him nearer to the pantheon of great Australian batsmen. By the time Angus Fraser first breached his defence at Edgbaston, after 13 hours four minutes in the series, Waugh was being saddled with the Antipodean kiss-of-death: comparisons with the insatiable Bradman.*

*Steve Waugh can cope with such distortions. He has learned to handle the premature praise of the golden boy, that turns into the calumny Australians reserve for a player from another state who fails to deliver the goods at once. The fact that the great but splenetic Bill O'Reilly saw immortality in the young man from Sydney made no*

*impression on the sages from Bay thirteen at the Melbourne Cricket Ground. Waugh's dominant batting for Somerset was dismissed as cashing in on inferior Pommie trundlers. He had to battle through the West Indies series to clinch his place for the England tour; at one stage his twin brother Mark seemed a likelier proposition. But Steve's quality got him through, after he began the series padding up to Malcolm Marshall for an ignominious dismissal. Since then he has always appeared to know the exact location of his stumps. Was that earlier campaign against the West Indies the one which really attuned him to Test cricket?*

I was pleased to get through against the West Indies by being positive. After playing no stroke against Marshall at Brisbane, I decided there was no point just hanging in there at the crease, because sooner or later you will get an impossible one. Apart from Marshall, Curtley Ambrose bowled magnificently in that series and he was often coming up with the unplayable ball. So I tried to get after them. They give you nothing to drive off the front foot, and it is hard to score when they bowl straight, just short of a length at a fair old pace. So I had to rely on backfoot drives and cuts. I got two nineties in the series, and although I was annoyed at missing out on a century, I felt they were important innings. At Brisbane, I was unlucky to be caught off a full-blooded shot that went straight to a fielder. At Perth I cracked under the pressure—thinking about my first Test hundred—and I played a bad shot. I thought we did very well to last out until the last afternoon at Perth on a poor track, and we did brilliantly to get into the fifth day at Melbourne on the worst Test wicket I have played on. We did not get enough credit for the courage we had shown on difficult pitches. We had every right to be confident against England after the character we had shown against the best team in the world a few months earlier. We had also grown up together over the previous four years; we had been on a lot of tours and our team spirit was very high.

*You made it clear that Australia would not buckle easily to the West Indies when you bowled three bouncers in a row at Viv. Was that deliberately symbolic?*

I thought he would not expect one as soon as he came in, so why not give him a few? He was not happy about it, but I wanted him to know that we were out there trying. They seemed to think we would not bowl any bouncers at all, yet they were happy to hand them out. You have got to stand up for yourself and the team in cricket.

*Did your victory in the World Cup Final of 1987 also start Australia on a bit of a roll?*

Yes. A lot of people put down one-day cricket, but we have been happy to take consolation from our successes, while doing badly in Tests. Confidence in the one-dayers can eventually spill over into the five-day stuff, and you get into the habit of winning. We have built on that World Cup experience. You cannot measure the importance of confidence, but when you have stuck together in the bad times and you come through that to start winning, your confidence soars because you know what it is like to be losing consistently. So you appreciate your great team spirit even more, and you enjoy playing aggressively and winning.

*Were you happy to be seen as underdogs when you came to England?*

It suited us, just like it did England when they came to us in 1986 and beat us deservedly. At the start of the 1989 tour, Bobby Simpson told us he wanted at least 350 runs a day and then to bowl out the opposition twice, to get into the habit of winning and not bother whether the counties were putting out weak sides or not. We trained as hard as anyone in world cricket, so we were super-fit and battle-hardened after the West Indies experience. Allan Border had learned a lot from Keith Fletcher at Essex about field-placings to the top English batsmen. We knew that Graham Gooch had to have a man in short on the leg-side, that Mike Gatting does not like someone on the off-side at bat/pad, that David Gower should have a leg-slip, that Allan Lamb is a candidate for the bat/pad catch because he plays a long way forward, with bat away from the pad. There was a lot of commonsense involved, and we bowled straight and to a pattern. We applied pressure on them at Leeds, and it worked. We knew that some of your blokes play across the line and that Terry Alderman's changes of pace would trouble them.

*And soon England seemed to be on trial and the confidence just drained out of them. Were you surprised that they were so vulnerable so early in the series?*

That is a sign of a good opposition team. It meant we were doing the basics right and we had them there for the taking. Give us credit for that, rather than concentrating on their defects.

*You know all about the pressures of being on trial at Test level without really delivering the goods, don't you?*

I have been lucky. Any other Test side would have dropped me at least a couple of times, because I kept failing to go on to centuries after passing fifty. My bowling helped, otherwise I am sure I would have been sidelined. Twice in twenty Tests I have taken five wickets in an innings, and a lot of specialist bowlers cannot say that. Yet they did not get the grilling I got because I did not get a hundred until 27 Tests.

*When you finally broke through you got another hundred for good measure at Lord's. What made the difference?*

All the various bits and pieces of batting just came together. I cut out technical defects, like failing to put my body properly into the shot because I was not bending my knee enough when striking the ball. As a result, the ball was going in the air too often. It is amazing how simple it all feels when it works and you are organised.

*Do you remember, exactly, the circumstances at Leeds when you got off 99?*

I remember that I was having trouble getting some saliva into my mouth! I was chewing gum so hard to make me concentrate that my throat went completely dry and I could not swallow when I was on 99. But a little dab to deep point off Phil Newport did the trick. After a difficult start, when my first ten runs were a bit dicey, the ball went where I wanted it to go. That is the best I have ever hit the ball. It was not a great wicket on the first day, and Mark Taylor and Geoff Marsh deserve credit for sticking it out in conditions that favoured their bowlers. I think our batting then was more crucial than England's collapse on the last afternoon, because we could have been easily out for 200. But our batting set the standard for the series, and they never recovered from the disappointment of winning the toss in a situation that should have aided their attack.

*After your second hundred in a row at Lord's, you seemed certain to get a third in four Tests at Old Trafford. But Tim Curtis caught you at mid-wicket for 92. You looked furious. Was that because you got yourself out?*

I should have let the bouncer go; I rarely hook. It was a very good bouncer by Angus Fraser—a yard quicker than I thought it would be, and I didn't play the shot very well.

There were just two wickets left, it was the last ball of the over, and I knew that Fraser would want to keep me off the strike. A bouncer was on the cards. One to the bowler!— but after missing out so often on a Test hundred, I wanted to get every one possible from Leeds onwards.

*During the Ashes summer, much has been made about the supposed technical defects of the English batsmen, and you have suggested that your side was well aware of them. Do you feel that the poor standards of pitches in England had something to do with that?*

Some of their batsmen told me that the pitches were so bad for the county games that they knew they would nick one soon enough if they played straight. So they set out to get quick runs by playing across the line. They knew they would not last very long. That seems a funny way to go about batting, but if they also think they will get out to a good ball, they cannot be very confident.

*You played at Somerset in the 1988 season, when the wickets were bad up and down the country. Did you feel the need to alter your technique?*

In my experience, the county wickets were possibly poorer in my year in county cricket than in 1989. But of course I did not change the way I wanted to bat. You have to stay with a technique that gives you confidence. Four-day cricket and flatter wickets is the answer for English batters. They were bound to struggle on flat Test tracks after trying to combat unreliable county wickets.

*Have you finished with county cricket?*

I shall not play next year. I need a break. I have a few niggles, and shin soreness has affected my bowling this season. Playing against quality opposition for Somerset definitely helped my game, and the different conditions improved my approach. I enjoyed the county circuit, but you definitely lose your competitive edge when you play so much cricket. If you took a poll of all the English county players, around 80 per cent would be against the Sunday League, and if you are not enjoying the game, you cannot play well. In county games, everybody seems to get on fairly well. They have a laugh; but in Australia the State games are played very seriously. I can understand the English attitude: if you were tough every day of the summer, you would go round the twist.

*You have the reputation of being very tough on the field. It has been said that you often advise a bowler to stick one on a batsman's face. I believe the phrase you use is "hit him on the melon."*

I never like to see anyone badly hurt on the cricket field, but I admit I like to get fired up when I am out there. When I am bowling, I do not give out much mouth. I am not quick enough to get away with it.

*You are one of four brothers, all talented batsmen. Mark, who is four minutes younger than you, is already on the way. There is another, Dean, who has broken all records in the Bolton League, and a fourteen-year-old who I understand looks the genuine article. What chance of a Waugh dynasty in the Australian side?*

Mark has already made it to the one-day side and his experience with Essex in county cricket will make him a better player. He scored his first championship hundred when I got my century in the Lord's Test, which was nice. Dean has a lot of potential. He is four years younger than us and he has just broken into first grade back home. If he shows the dedication to go with his talent, he could make the State side and go even higher. He is a lot bigger than Mark and I, and he loves to play his shots. But we all have that in common. Dean will be put under a lot of pressure because of his elder brothers, but I reckon he can handle it. As for our kid brother, let us leave him out of it until he gets a little older.

*Has the achievement of this Australian tour sunk in yet, with the series just over?*
I do not think the players really understand what they have done. The feedback from home has been great, but we will only appreciate it when we get back home, relax and let it all sink in. It is hard for the English Press to give us too much praise, after giving us such a bagging at the start of the tour. So they are just concentrating on bagging Gower and his team now, and saying we had nothing to beat. Can't win, can we?

# JOHN EMBUREY

## 'When the ban ends I will be 44. There is no reason why I cannot play for England again if I keep fit. '

O VER the last decade, *John Emburey has been one of the most likeable and approachable of international cricketers. No modern England player can emulate his deep knowledge of the game or its historical context, and few rival his articulate exposition of its complexities. Emburey is happy to talk cricket in the bar with the humblest practitioner, and he stands in the Bob Taylor class for endurance in the face of ear-bashing monologists. A cool, undemonstrative cricketer, Emburey eschews the clenched-fist histrionics spawned by the age of Kerry Packer: he is the thinking cricketer par excellence. Even his idiosyncratic batting style is the product of rational analysis. His attitude to cricket's current obsession with fitness training is equally clear-headed: "It's funny how the thoroughbreds keep breaking down, while carthorses like me keep on going. I reckon you can't pull a muscle if you haven't got any, so I steer clear of all that stuff if I can."*

*When John Emburey took over as England captain from Mike Gatting, those who knew him well were delighted for a man who had been thwarted in his keen ambition to lead a county for the rest of his career. For the media, the contrast between Emburey's expansiveness and Gatting's taciturnity was graphic. Press conferences were packed, notebooks full. Yet Emburey's decline as an off-spinner meant he was no longer worth his place in England's side. At the time he agreed with his critics, and harboured no ill-feelings. The self-deception and obscurantism of many major sportsmen have never appealed to Emburey.*

*He was equally forthright in his attitude to another rebel tour of South Africa. When the identities of the tour party broke, his was the most unsurprising name on the list. Was it just the money, or had playing for England lost its appeal?*

I did not enjoy my Test cricket last summer. When you play under the pressure of so much criticism—and I agree I have not bowled well for England in recent years—you

cannot say you are at your best. It makes you wonder if it is all worthwhile. As soon as I went back and played for Middlesex I bowled slower and looked the part again. The wickets for the Tests were too slow for a spinner, so I had to push it through in the vain hope of getting bat/pad catches, or getting one to carry to slip. Yet I was criticised for bowling flat and negatively: no spinner could do well on those pitches, unless he pushed it through. You read and hear all the criticism about the England boys and you feel sorry for them. We were very unlucky with injuries, but we were expected to turn in the performances of a settled team. In the end, I was happy to get out.

*What about the morality of playing for England some time after you had agreed to go to South Africa. Were you serving two masters and getting two pay packets?*

All we did this time was make ourselves unavailable for the England winter tours; we are still available for England next summer. I have never gone out to do anything other than my best. I played my hardest from day one of the series to the afternoon when I batted so long with Jack Russell at Old Trafford.

*What were your feelings as you left Old Trafford that evening, with your Test career over?*

I only saw it as the end of seven years of my Test career—and I still do. When the ban ends, I shall be 44. Fred Titmus, another off-spinner, went to Australia when he was 42. There is no reason why I cannot play for England again if I keep fit and perform well. It is an incentive for the younger players on the South African tour to carry on doing well for their counties. Matthew Maynard will be a better batsman at thirty than he is now. After we were banned in 1982, people like Arnie Sidebottom, Les Taylor and John Lever played for England when the ban was over. As a bowler I am bound to get slower as I get older, and that will be good for me. I shall want Middlesex to stay in the frame for the big games—the one-day finals at Lord's, and the run-in to the championship. They will now be the biggest moments in a domestic season for me, and I want to be a part of that for a long time.

*Yet you have declined in influence in the last few years, John. Does that decline mirror the lot of all modern spinners?*

We talk about the eclipse of the spinner every year, don't we? The best ones in England are all well into their thirties. I remember when Rajesh Maru came on our staff at Middlesex. He looked a class slow left-hander and it was great to watch his loop and flight. Then Mike Gatting, a superb player of spinners, got after him in the nets, smashed him out of sight. Maru's flight got lower and lower, and his confidence dwindled. He ended up at Hampshire, sadder and wiser, after realising that in first-class cricket, good players can get down the pitch and murder you if you give it too much air. If you are a very slow bowler, you cannot vary your pace so much, and that is an important thing for a spinner at the top level.

*So you have bowled flatter and flatter as the years have gone by.*

I have had to. The one-day game and its emphasis on economy has not helped. I was a much better bowler when I first came into the county side than I am now. By the time I was 23, I had learned how to bowl and everything came naturally to me. I was confident, having come up through the ranks with the other players, and I hardly seemed to bowl a bad ball. My loop was there for all to see.

*Will you ever get that back, or are you just going to remain a modern spinner?*

Fred Titmus tells me that all the spinners in his day bowled flat, but started to give it more air in their late thirties. The body slows down, you are not as fit as you were, you do not attack the crease as powerfully as before, and you end up bowling slower naturally. Certainly Derek Underwood bowled a lot slower towards the end and Jack Simmons has used more variety in his forties. I just hope I will be able to get there before I am too old and that I will do it consciously. My confidence has suffered in the past couple of years and I have tended to fire it in more as a result. Yet when I was dropped by England during 1988, I suddenly started to bowl better for Middlesex. Geoff Boycott rang me up and said he had been watching me on television. All I had to do, he claimed, was use the crease more. He said if I bowled wider, it would create a different angle and the ball would turn in more sharply and get between bat and pad like it used to. I had been trying to do that all season, but Boycott gave me the confidence to vary my line of attack. And it worked. Until then I had got into a rut; I was not using my body enough. I was lobbing the ball, not bowling it.

*When do you know if you are going to bowl well?*

It is all to do with timing and co-ordination. You know when you are bowling well if you spot something a fraction early, such as the batsman altering his movement just before you release the ball. You adjust your trajectory, hold the ball back and beat him in the air. It is just natural. Nothing gives me more pleasure in cricket than beating someone in the air and hitting off-stump with a little drift as he tries to drive the ball. That is a classic dismissal in my book.

*Surely for a spinner, so much depends on captaincy and sympathetic field-placing?*

That is right, and Mike Gatting and I often disagree about field-placings. Mike Brearley was better for me in this respect, because he was an orthodox batsman and, like me, he used to want fielders in orthodox positions for my bowling. But Gatt is such a marvellous player of the spinners that he can hit them anywhere, even cutting balls off his middle stump. So he tends to think everyone might hit me in certain places and forgets that not everyone can bat like him. He will want a man at square cover for me and no extra cover, whereas Brearley would dispense with a man behind square on the off-side and give me an extra cover and mid-off. Then I could encourage the batsman to drive the ball. With a square cover, your length has to be that fraction shorter and I find myself being cut—something that should never happen to an off-spinner. Under Gatt, my length has definitely got shorter to accommodate that extra man behind square. We do compromise as the innings progresses, but my bowling has been affected by things like that.

*Can you regain your confidence then—and hang on to it for any significant length of time?*

I am confident in my ability, but things have stagnated for me in terms of taking wickets. When I am not putting in the performances I have felt I should not be playing for England; that I am there under false pretences. I was really looking forward to touring India again, because with so many spinners available to them, the wickets would have favoured slow bowlers. I would have loved the chance to prove I could still take twenty wickets in a series, instead of about seven on flat wickets—just filling in while the seamers had a rest. But the politicians had their say and the tour was called off.

I do not like the fact that I have played more Tests than Fred Titmus and taken fewer wickets. When I started, I wanted to aim at his level because he was a great off-spinner, and I still want to do myself justice.

*More generally, what can be done to get the spinner back into the mainstream of cricket?*

In England, it has to be about the pitches. Somehow they must be drier. There is no reason why the same pitch cannot be used three times a season to help the spinner. Watching good players combat spinners on turning pitches is one of the charms of cricket. It should not be about hitting through the line on flat pitches; the balls should be turning halfway through the allotted time span, and that way, everyone gets involved. I also think we should go back to uncovered pitches in England—not least because all the batsmen want them covered. What is the point in having a pitch that turns on the third or fourth day of a Test against the West Indies when their fast bowlers have decided the game on the first two days? They get it right at Sydney, where the ball turns on the first day and the Tests are always exciting. It was right in Pakistan on our last tour. The cricket was also gripping, even though our batsmen did not think so against Abdul Qadir. For my part, it was a lot more interesting than watching our lads get their heads knocked off by the West Indies.

*You have always been interested in the nuts and bolts of cricket. What changes in its structure would you want to see?*

In England, we play six different types of cricket at county and Test level, and that is too much. I would like to see sixteen games of four days each for the county championship and, in a few years time, three new sides—making the total twenty. The first division would comprise the top ten sides from the previous season in the championship, and the second would be made up of the bottom seven, plus the three newcomers. You would play a side home and away, ending up with eighteen games lasting four days each. That makes 72 days of first-class cricket—precisely the number we play now—with promotion and relegation adding spice. At the moment, most sides are just playing through the last month of the season, longing for a rest. But this way, most of the teams involved will still be playing positive cricket—some striving for promotion, others desperate to avoid relegation. Traditionalists will say that Yorkshire and Lancashire might be in separate divisions and the Roses Match would be no more. Well, put them together in the same Benson and Hedges zone. And they can still play each other in the Sunday League.

The Sunday League has to be revitalised, because the crowds are bored with it and so are many of the players. We should have coloured clothing and a white ball. All the players I know fancy that; they recognise it is a different game on a Sunday. All our one-day games should be of fifty-over duration, to bring us in line with overseas cricket. Do you know, we are the only country that plays one-day matches of sixty overs duration? You can be more flexible with fifty overs and still get in a full match on a rain-interrupted day. I also believe we play too many Tests in England in a summer. Money seems to be the main consideration.

*You mentioned financial considerations there. Are you saying that the Test and County Cricket Board in England has concentrated on money to the detriment of cricket's standards?*

I think more ought to have been done in recent years to safeguard the interests of the game. Look at coloured clothing on Sundays—it's going to happen, so why not get on with it, rather than wait for younger men to come onto the Board? We must do more to get people through the gates, get youngsters interested by handing out free passes to schools. Cricket is dying in so many schools; local authorities should be putting in more artificial wickets and creating a climate that gives teachers the desire to coach at cricket, rather than go abroad as I'm going to do. When the Indian tour was called off that was a great chance to get the England players involved in grassroots coaching, but nothing came from the TCCB, the Sports Council, the National Cricket Association or even the Government.

Clubs should be more inclined to consider wearing the larger sponsors' logos on their shirt. Professional soccer has shown it can be tastefully done, and something like a six inch by four inch logo on the heart of the cricket shirt would not be intrusive.

*Were you surprised at a three-year Test ban in 1982?*
Disappointed. I thought a year would be enough, but we had been warned of the consequences a few months earlier, so that was it. When England played the First Test against India in the summer of 1982, I really missed being part of the scene, knowing I would be out of it for the next three years. But I just knew I would have to buckle down and produce the kind of performances that would get me picked again when my time was up.

*And yet you would have made as much money if you had turned down the offer and played for England for the next three years.*
I did not know that then—and besides, the South African money was up-front. It enabled us to buy a house, rather than a flat. The timing was also perfect, because I had not enjoyed the cricket in India in 1981/2. If we had been in Australia at the time the offer came up, I doubt if I would have gone. But in life, timing is often crucial. We were tempted when feeling very down, and bored with Test cricket. I enjoyed the tour to South Africa and the next two years with Western Province. My only real regret is that I lost the vice-captaincy of Middlesex as a result. I was due to fly out to South Africa a couple of days after I attended a Middlesex committee meeting. They took it very seriously that I had not informed them of my intentions. With the cloak-and-dagger nature of the trip, I could not see how I could break cover; perhaps I should have pleaded jet-lag and stayed away! It was the biggest blow of my career, because no other member of the tour party was disciplined by his club. With Mike Brearley retiring at the end of the 1982 season, I am sure I would have been the captain of Middlesex—an ambition realised. Perhaps I might then have been England captain ahead of Mike Gatting, because of my county experience. Who can say? In 1989, at least the players knew what to expect. There is no reason why anyone should jump on the backs of players going to South Africa, because in so doing, they will have sacrificed the chance of playing Test cricket. The TCCB in effect has backed down in the face of the black countries.

*Perhaps that's over-stating the case. Don't forget that New Zealand and Australia proved less than friendly to South Africa when it came to the vote at the crucial ICC meeting. But surely English county cricketers can still go to South Africa, earn money, gain experience, help the cause of multi-racialism if they wish. All they are giving up is the chance to play for England, and in most cases, they would never sniff that anyway.*

You try telling that to a young player. When they are young, all players have that ambition, and it is a shame to see them robbed of it. You only need one good season to get a winter trip with England; they always take one young hopeful.

No sensible person likes Apartheid, and I accept that politics and sport cannot be separated. Now England players can sit down, work out what they will lose from a Test ban and say to South Africa: "That's my price." The South African issue is here to stay. The counties in England will benefit two-fold—Test cricket has been saved, money will still roll in from those receipts, and the members will see more of the banned players, instead of losing them to England duty for half the season. It is now perfectly straightforward and a matter for the individual.

*On to more amusing matters—your style of batting. Are you aware what fun it gives us?*

Yes—and that gives me a lot of satisfaction. As a bowler, I work and work at a batter and get him out with a strategy. That is usually lost on a spectator, and if I can entertain them with my batting for a few minutes, that is fine. I am pleased that I can now go on to get fifties when I have reached thirty, because I used to be happy with just a few runs. I started off my county career at number eleven, worked my way up and then, after the ban from Test cricket, I changed my approach. I decided to go down the wicket and play shots—even to the quicker bowlers. I enjoyed shovelling them away with a short backlift, and I got a hundred against Northants the first time I tried the new method. Soon I was batting at six, ahead of more technically accomplished batsmen like Paul Downton and Phil Edmonds. In the summer I do not bother with a net, because I know I will play exactly the same way as I do out in the middle and I believe that nets are for those who want to play correctly. I don't.

*It appears that your batting has kept you in the England side when your bowling has declined.*

I agree. I wish I had been been as consistent with the ball as with the bat in recent years. Finger spinners are not match-winners in Tests in England—they need the harder, drier wickets abroad. But that is no real excuse. I am glad I have got a few runs.

*Do you miss Phil Edmonds at the other end?*

Of course. Philip Tufnel has it in him to be a fine slow left-arm spinner, but he is learning his trade, and that puts more pressure on me, as the senior partner, to get wickets, Edmonds and I worked well together, because we were different types of bowlers. On basic ability he shaded me, with his knack of coming up with an unplayable delivery, whereas I liked to work out a strategy and plan a dismissal. Together I feel we exerted a lot of pressure, kept it tight and helped control the game. For England we did not go for much more than two runs an over. At county level, we were good enough to play on green pitches because we knew where to put the ball, and our batting was useful as well. I remember that Phil once said to me that we did not bowl enough bad balls. He was right. A bad ball from a spinner often gets someone out. They pin back their ears and pull a long-hop to mid-wicket. But we were played with a lot of respect for most of the time. We created pressure that was capitalised on by our seamers.

*Yet you and Phil Edmonds under-achieved at Test level.*

103

Yes. You cannot argue with the statistics that in more than a hundred Tests between us, we only managed around 250 wickets. But don't forget that we have played in an age of covered wickets, so it is unfair to compare our figures with those of Laker, Lock, Wardle, Titmus or Underwood, who had more favourable conditions. And good players work you out after a time. When you bowl line and length like we did, a batsman knows the ball is going to be pitched in an area of around two feet. So if the ball that is pitched just outside off-stump, he can hit you over the top, while a bowler less accurate is likely to get someone out by the element of surprise. Against us, the class batsmen would just wait for the occasional bad ball and pick us off. That is when variation in flight and line becomes important—and you can only do that when you are feeling confident.

*Which batsmen have you particularly rated in your time?*

I suppose Viv Richards has to be the man who can slaughter you when in the mood, although he is not the most compact of players. I have always felt I had a chance of getting him out because he likes to impose himself on me right away. I like to think that is a mark of respect. It was not until the West Indies' tour of 1988 that he really got after me, but then I was not bowling well at the time. First he tries to get rid of my silly mid-off and short leg, then he takes the mickey by stretching forward a long way and playing defensively, when there is no-one around the bat. He smiles at you, knowing that he has pushed the field back. I stare back, yet he knows that is round one to him. Then he hits you for six, runs all the way up to your end, pats the crease with his bat, taps you on the backside as if to say "well bowled". Then you stare back again and tell him to get stuffed. I have never really got him out, and I need to do that to be confident of dismissing someone, as I am now with Richie Richardson. I have to admit that Viv has the psychological upper hand over me. But I still love bowling at him; he gives you a chance because of his arrogance. Having said that, the spinners should not bowl at Viv, it should be seamers like Neil Foster and Gladstone Small who have the accuracy to bowl just a foot outside his off-stump on a good length. Have you noticed how often Viv chops on to his stumps against this kind of bowler when he is trying that little guide down to third man? He doesn't go all the way forward or back when playing it, and it gets him out.

Allan Border is a very good player of the spinners. I bowl over the wicket to him, to try to get a different line to the left-hander and tuck him up. He used to hit me through the offside by giving himself room when I bowled round the wicket. You rarely get him playing half-cock; he goes all the way back or forward. Because he is a small man, his reach is not very long and sometimes you can get him caught off bat and pad because he has not smothered the spin. He sweeps very well, but early, and occasionally he gets a top edge if he is not quite there. Apart from that, he is a top batsman; a great fighter.

Javed Miandad is a high class batsman. Brilliant footwork. He can play right back on his stumps and manipulate the ball into the most frustrating areas. A big innings man—a great player.

*Turning to your two matches as England captain in 1988. They involved a lot of "If onlys", didn't they?*

The first two of those were "if only I could be captain against another country" and "if only I could be the England captain to beat them for the first time since 1974". Then, after a great first day at Lord's, it was case of "if only we had held Gus Logie in the slips" and "if only he had nicked his first ball on to the stumps rather than just past the off-peg." It is all ifs and buts, and I was thrilled to be the England captain for the first time on my home ground at Lord's. But I was very disappointed with our abject batting in my two Tests—first on a flat one, then at Old Trafford, when we lost seven wickets on the final morning. With rain about, we should have held out for a draw. Our techniques let us down and I said so both to players and the media.

To be honest, I was a little embarrassed at being made England captain at a time when I did not deserve to be in the side. I was not bowling well enough and getting the job on a one-match basis did not exactly instil me with confidence. Overall, I thoroughly enjoyed the experience, but with the next Test scheduled for Leeds—a ground that favours the fast bowlers, I was obviously destined for the chop and another England captain was needed. No complaints from me about that decision.

*You were very frank in your Press conferences as England captain. How did that go down with the hierarchy?*

When I took over, I told Micky Stewart I would speak my mind to the media and he let me get on with it. Besides, I think we England players all needed a kick up the backside at times. It can be too cliquey, and I agree that sometimes it seems harder to get out of the England side rather than into it. Some of the senior players—including me—needed to be dropped at times to get us performing properly again. I have never had any trouble with the cricket media. I would rather guide them on certain lines than say "no comment" and leave the more unscrupulous reporters to make up something.

*At least you have captained England, yet it looks as if your ambition to captain a county side regularly has gone.*

I nearly moved from Middlesex a couple of years ago because I felt that the captaincy would raise my game and get me thinking again. With Mike Gatting in charge at Middlesex, I knew I would have to move, and I was gratified that nine counties came in for me. One offered me the captaincy, but insisted that I stopped playing for England—with appropriate compensation. I was tempted by another one from Warwickshire, but I did not really want to uproot the children. If Surrey had come in for me, I would have gone to the Oval. But Ian Greig was doing a good enough job there. So I have stayed put.

*So you remain unfulfilled on two levels—as a spin bowler and estwhile captain?*

That is why I want to stay in the game; to keep aiming for things. I want to remain vice-captain of Middlesex, because at least I will lead the side on occasions. Ironic, isn't it? I never expected to captain England, and yet it came at the most unexpected time, when I could have been a county captain somewhere else!

# MARTIN CROWE

**'Before a Test I sit down and visualise how I am going to play. I visualise positively, so that I come out on top . . . I never read the papers if I fail. '**

IN attempting to forecast the world's best batsman of the Nineties, the smart money has to be on one of two players separated by three-and-a-half years and joined by a common experience of New Zealand cricket. One is Graeme Hick, for the last few years a prodigious run-scorer for Worcestershire and Northern Districts. The other is Martin Crowe. Hick's Bradmanesque tally of a century around every five innings in first-class cricket is only threatened by Crowe's one in six among current players. Yet through no fault of his own, Hick is untried at the highest level, while Crowe has been churning out Test hundreds since he was 21. A century every seven innings for his country puts Crowe in the Border/Richards class, up there with the greats. He also takes guard again after getting to three figures, as scores of 188 (twice) and 174 would suggest. His technique is so exemplary, his stroke play so classical that it will be a major surprise if he fails to follow Glenn Turner to a century of centuries. He would be only the second New Zealander to do so.

Crowe also has character in abundance. At 21, he was filling the position of Viv Richards for Somerset in the 1984 season, and although suffering from the effects of food poisoning and a broken thumb after a tour of Sri Lanka, he impressed everyone at Taunton with his maturity and leadership qualities. A lesser man than Martin Crowe would have buckled under the weight of the passions aroused when Somerset decided to engage his youthful talent, rather than the ageing, spasmodic brilliance of Viv Richards and Joel Garner. Many a stand-in overseas player would not have made the kind of impression that galvanised the club to an historic decision, and which also led to the departure of Ian Botham. Next season, Crowe showed his mettle by catching the first available flight from Colombo when the tour to Sri Lanka was abandoned for political unrest, then travelling for thirty-six hours and arriving at the wicket at midday with no sleep behind him and Somerset 24 for two. He made 65. He scored more than 2,000 runs *in all competitions for Somerset in that 1987 season, despite missing a month through a broken thumb. Sadly his days were numbered at Taunton. A serious back injury forced him to take a complete rest and he is unlikely to offer himself again to the county grind. He may be a team man, but Martin Crowe knows the tunnel vision of all great players. Sport is in his blood: his mother has been a fine all-rounder, his father played first-class cricket and his elder brother Jeff captained New Zealand. A batsman who scored more than 4,000 first-class runs in one calendar year at the age of 25 could be said to be rather exceptional, but Crowe is an ambitious perfectionist.*

I suppose when I look at my batting I have answered the question about how I want to play in terms of style and technique, but I would like to be a little more natural, to let things go a little bit. My technique is probably too tight—there are times when I have batted for ten hours in a Test and scored 170-odd and never really stepped up a gear. There are times when I feel so much in control of myself—elbow high and straight down the line—that I cannot find that little extra to take me up higher. I now know that my technique and patience will allow me to bat for ten hours in a Test Match, but I want to be like the great players who can raise the tempo when they like. That is my main ambition.

*How do you make yourself concentrate in an innings?*

I keep telling myself to play straight, watch the ball, keep my feet moving. These affirmations keep ticking over and I do not allow negative thoughts to enter. Bowlers like Merv Hughes may try me with verbals, but I do not see the face of the bowler nor the fielder's face when I am playing well. I scored a hundred in the Lord's Test of 1986, and apart from a couple of deliveries, every one hit the middle of the bat. It was just me, the ball, the bat, and the arm of the bowler. Just tunnel vision. I did not notice anybody else. I would switch off from the last ball and turn on to the next. Relax and breathe deeply between deliveries, and switch on again to batting with an affirmation about feet, head and watching the ball.

*How do you prepare yourself before a Test Match?*

They are the pinnacle for me now, and I have got to continue succeeding at that level. The big thing is to know your game plan and strategy—what you can do and what is beyond your capabilities. Before a Test, I sit down and visualise how I am going to play. The pictures are clear in my mind—the bowler will be in the picture, the fields he will set for me and how I should play him. I visualise positively, so that I come out on top. I try to make the visualising as clear as possible, so that when I finally go out to bat, nothing is strange or disconcerting. I never read the papers if I fail, but I do if I bat well. I also want to be around people who are positive, who will not entertain negative thoughts. I am pretty controlled now in my approach to batting, so the next step is to make it more instinctive.

*Have there been times when it really worked—when you switched on and off at the crease?*

Glenn Turner explained the process to me and it started to come good in Australia in 1985/6. It worked beautifully against South Australia when I scored 242 not out; I felt so fresh at close of play because I had been switching on and off. Yet when I turned on, my concentration was so intense—and it enabled me to bat for a long time. It then rolled over to the next week, when I got 188 in the Brisbane Test. It could easily have been around 220: Allan Border put everyone back on the boundary because I was batting with a tail-ender, and I tried one shot too many after refusing lots of runs and I got out. The other time it really worked was at Lord's in 1986, when I never felt I was going to get out. According to my father, I had dreamed of getting a Test hundred at Lord's since I was eight, so nobody was going to stop me!

*Which bowlers have you respected?*
Richard Hadlee is the best I have faced; he is the complete all-round bowler. And he has never got me out yet! The faster ones like Andy Roberts, Michael Holding and Jeff Thomson have tended to get the heart pumping a little. And I have always enjoyed the challenge of Abdul Qadir, because I have made some big scores against him.

*You had a tremendous duel with Andy Roberts when you first started at Somerset in 1984.*
That was the turning-point for me. Somerset versus Leicestershire at Taunton. Before that innings, I felt flat, tight, too tense, I was not moving my feet. I was getting found out technically—and there I was in the place usually occupied by the great Viv Richards. I decided to take on the challenge of competing daily against the best bowler, and I came up against Andy Roberts bowling magnificently. It came at the end of our fourth game in a row. I never played more than four or five days in succession, but here I was, after about fifteen days on the trot, facing Roberts with his tail up. I took a few on the shoulder, a couple in the guts and he whizzed a few past my nose. In between all that, he was bowling beautiful outswingers. It was classic stuff. I was really enjoying the challenge. Then once the short-pitched stuff started in earnest, I thought "stuff this, I'm not getting hit any more," so I took out a lighter bat after lunch. I started to pop him down to fine leg. That got him going again and it was an even contest. Mind you, he was taking a few wickets as well. Towards the end of our innings he started bowling short at me again, and when he came into bowl I ducked before he delivered the ball. He knew that I knew he was going to bowl me a bouncer. Then he bowled me another bouncer and I ducked out of the way again. I thought "next one he'll pitch up at me, he can't keep bowling short." By that stage I had made three of four strides down the pitch and hit him back over his head. You can imagine the next two balls—they just flew past my ear. He was now trying to pin me, and I got very pumped up. He soon wrapped up the innings, and I walked off, shaking and white. Roberts had really got to me and I had lost control, which was unlike me. But I had made 70 not out, and in the second innings Roberts did not get a wicket as I scored 190 and we chased a big total to win by six wickets. That first innings was good experience for me when I played against the West Indies in Tests.

*You made a great impact in that first season with Somerset. Were you aware of your powers of leadership before that summer?*
I was the youngest of three, and my brother and sister fostered a competitive element in me that led to a forceful attitude. At Somerset, I spoke forcefully about what I believed, and I suppose I stood out, compared to others who were less positive. I was intrigued and fascinated by the game. I wanted to learn, and I could not understand why some of the younger Somerset players did not share my thirst for knowledge. I told them that if you want to succeed, you should try to fulfil your potential, because it sure feels good when you get the best out of yourself. I identified my skill at an early age—it

happened to be cricket, so I have always wanted to make the most of it.

*Then in 1986 you were portrayed as the great white hope for Somerset in the future. You were dragged into the personality issues that were not of your making. How difficult was all that for you, bearing in mind that you were on tour with New Zealand in this country at the time?*

That was a tough one to take on. In 1984 I had felt privileged to be given the chance to play county cricket and it was a memorable experience for me. I felt loyal to Somerset and wanted to come back and do it again. But I did not think it would happen, because Viv and Joel were still there and an extra overseas player was not possible. The execution of Somerset's decision was poor. The story broke in the middle of the Oval Test and I was hassled for quotes. I was seriously misquoted as well, and I am sure that Viv, Joel and Ian must have thought: "Who is this guy? How can he say that sort of thing?" All I wanted was to play for Somerset. I felt they had to look to the future and could not rely on the fact that they had won trophies in previous years. It was a case of getting Somerset up and running. I do not think enough quality players have come through yet, but it is a far happier club now. There is an environment for players to develop their skills, but they still do tend to rely on the overseas player and one or two senior players.

*So how did the expectations of the 1987 season affect you after the great exodus of three world-class players?*

There was pressure of course—not least at the start, when all I wanted was to get out of Sri Lanka and get to Taunton! The spotlight was on me, but at least I had already played with most of the guys and I knew what we had to do. I had a great season on a personal note, but it became harder each week because the expectations among the supporters for a trophy were so high. Despite the momentous decisions of the winter we were not near to a trophy. It was a case of building for the future, looking to 1990 or 1991 and picking up experience.

*But you won't be there for that, will you?*

I am 99 per cent certain I shall not play county cricket again. My priorities are in New Zealand, to prepare myself to peak for the Tests. If I need to take three months off for that, I shall do so. When you simplify it that way, there is just no room for county cricket. It was a great experience and if I kept playing there, I would learn even more, but now it is a case of ploughing what I have learned into Test performances.

*So you can hammer our bowlers all over the place! Does your own example with Somerset confirm that overseas players do nothing for the good of England's Test prospects?*

If there were no overseas players, the focus of responsibility would be back on the English guys and they would benefit eventually. But that would be a slow process, because you would have to undo all the old attitudes that these young players have, which are not positive or geared to consistency. If you take the overseas cricketers out, will people still come and watch? You have got to seek a balance. There is nothing better for an international player than to have six months in England, because if you then tour here with your national side later, you will feel comfortable. Steve Waugh is a classic example. By taking my place at Somerset he gained the experience to do well against

England the following year. That is obviously to the detriment of the English national side. In terms of the quality and development of players who would represent England, it probably is best for the English game to get rid of overseas players. This summer I played in the Lancashire League and it was simply a matter of overseas player pitted against overseas player. The amateurs were just a waste of time. That is no good for pushing your youngsters through the nurseries towards the top.

*You have had problems with your back and also an illness that affected you for some time. What is the situation now regarding your back and that salmonella poisoning which was in your body for so many years?*

The back will be fine, as long as I look after it and maintain fitness and flexibility by daily exercise. I have an inflammation in the fifth lumbar vertebrae that should not get any worse. The salmonella goes back to 1984, when I had a really bad dose. No general practitioner could solve the problem when I came to Somerset—I was listless and suffered from constant diarrhoea. Wherever I travelled in the world I would pick up viruses. Four years later, I tried homeopathic medicine and it worked after eight months treatment. I was off alcohol and caffeine for all that time, and the self-discipline made me want to carry on looking after my body, once I felt so much better. So a beer with the lads is out—just an occasional glass of wine these days.

*Your experiences with the salmonella poisoning prompted you to write a book on how to live more healthily.*

Yes. It is called *Winning Ways* and I wrote it with my best mate, Graham Fox, the All-Black. We helped each other with our rugby and cricket at school, and our careers have run along parallel lines. In the book we compare the two sports and look at how performance can be improved by attention to the mind, body and nutrition. The mind involves the attitudes we adopt, our body language, our behaviour in public and how we control ourselves. The body section features how we prepare for the coming season and how to maintain fitness throughout. In my case, I do a lot of yoga to develop my back muscles: it is fantastic for the flexibility all cricketers need. We talk about building up upper and lower body strength, circuit training, how to avoid getting stale, and how to peak at just the right time. There is advice on roadwork and how to build up oxygen intake that affects your stamina. Then there is the diet and the need for nutrition. While I was coming out of my salmonella poisoning I discovered that my body suits a set routine of eating. I now avoid eating after seven o'clock at night, and by eating more in the morning and at lunchtime I can work off the energy during the day. I look for a balanced diet—mainly fish and chicken, a lot of vegetables and fibre, yoghurt and fruit juice at breakfast. It is all based around eating early in the day. I want to train in the afternoon, so I usually have fish for lunch. All that is what suits me. It makes me feel better, and I hope it will make me a better cricketer.

# IMRAN
# KHAN

**‘I have often felt cheated when teams lose in Pakistan and then blame the umpires. Whenever we had similar problems abroad we would be accused of whingeing. 9**

*I*T does seem unfair that one cricketer should possess as many gifts as Imran Khan. A magnificent all-rounder, he has also kept a few gossip columnists in a job as they detail his alleged dalliances. Patrick Eagar, that brilliant cricketer photographer, has good cause to raise the occasional glass in Imran's direction. One day in Australia he caught Imran in just the right sultry pose—and the subsequent orders from all over the world were due testimony to the heady brew of a gold chain resting on the dark, hairy chest, accompanied by the haughty stare and tousled hairstyle that must have taken ages to organise. Imran was the original designer cricketer, long before the yuppies discovered designer stubble and Ray-Bans. But most males who dwell on Imran's charisma suffer the influence of the green-eyed monster. He does have an enviable ability to breeze through life. One cannot imagine Imran Khan ever being disconcerted by the latest rise in the retail price index, the worrying emergence of a bald spot, or getting stuck in a traffic jam. Only Imran now plays Test Matches without appearing in other first-class games; he knows the extent of his capabilities better than anyone, and he sees no reason for a facade.

Imran has always known his own mind, much to the distaste of certain Blimpish westerners who see the role of Asians in England as compliant purveyors of groceries from the corner shop on a Sunday. It is a considerable mind, a challenging mind, one that thrives on iconoclasm. On the one hand, a boon to the cricket media (who always like trenchant observations from a great player), while at the same time an uncomfortable presence amid county colleagues who preferred to discuss the charms on Page Three to economic sanctions against South Africa. By the end of his days at Sussex, many at the club had grown tired of Imran's preference for Stringfellow's and the pages of Tatler to a session at the Hove nets or the sponsors' tent. Thus the parting was inevitable. Yet Sussex, like every other team graced by Imran, were better for his *presence. From his first-class debut at the age of 16-and-a-half he was destined for greatness. A privileged background in Lahore equipped him for golden days at Oxford University, where he thrived amid excellent sporting facilities and the intellectual hothouse. He was rarely deflected after that, apart from injury and a spat with Lord's. For some reason the powers that be failed to understand why Imran preferred the social whirl of London to the grind of county cricket up at Worcester.*

*Even by the Byzantine standards of Pakistan cricket, it seems odd that Imran had to wait until he was thirty before he captained his country. Since then he has been the only man to keep the side's anarchic tendencies under some degree of control. He will never be well-loved in the game, but his stature cannot be denied. A magnificent fast bowler, of resource and courage, his orthodox, masterful batting was good enough to keep him in the side whenever injury hampered his bowling. An inspirational leader, he averages over forty with the bat as captain. He is, in short, a thoroughbred. His detractors say he is arrogant, with a highly-developed sense of his own importance, while his friends aver to his reserve and desire for intellectual stimulus. Does he feel he is too outspoken for his own good?*

I believe there are two sides to every argument, that you should toss ideas around and open up people's minds. I never worry about what they say about me behind my back, because whenever you hold strong views you must expect people to react. I started a cricket magazine this year—which I edit—as a challenge to established viewpoints. I want to put forward the views of the players, not the Establishment, and I am finding it very stimulating. Take the question of neutral umpires. I did a survey for the magazine and every international player I contacted was in favour of the idea. Yet that is one subject which has not been properly aired in England.

*You have been very critical of certain aspects of English cricket. As an overseas player, do you feel you are entitled to climb into a structure that has helped you become a world-class player?*

Surely after seventeen years in county cricket, my opinions have some validity. Eventually I found it hard to play county cricket because of its organisation. I was not enjoying it any more. Too many treat it as a nine-to-five job, whereas for me it must be fun. My relationship with the Sussex players was always good, I believe. If they spoke badly about me—well, it was not to my face.

*So what is wrong with English cricket?*

Seven days a week is a joke. No player can be competitive playing that number of days. There is also far too much one-day cricket. England are now one of the best teams in the world at that, but you only defend in one-day cricket, instead of having to take wickets. A Test batsman has to learn to occupy the crease, but he has to play shots in the one-day game. Also, three-day cricket is an anachronism. Unless you under-prepare a wicket you cannot have a positive result in these type of matches. When you under-prepare wickets, you get bowlers prospering who are not good enough to perform on good wickets in Tests. You cannot just run up, bowl line and length, and expect to get wickets. You have got to bowl batsmen out with skill and technique. All over the world we play four-day cricket—except in England. There are seventeen county sides of a high standard in England—much higher than anywhere else—and something is wrong if they cannot produce a good Test eleven out of all that.

114

*You watched this year's Ashes contest after being out in Australia earlier in the year to observe the Australians at close hand. Were you surprised that England lost so heavily?*

Yes, I was. No one expected England to perform so far below their potential. It is a question of pressure—not individual, but team pressure. Once a team is under pressure early in the series—as England were after Leeds—it is very difficult to come back. Australia were no better on paper, but they just grew more and more confident.

*This summer the England team has been affected by the departures of various players to South Africa. I don't suppose you have any sympathy for those who decided to go there.*

If someone wants to go, because his place in the team is insecure or he feels he has to secure his family's future, that is up to him—as long as he is not troubled by his conscience. I cannot understand why the England regulars have chosen to go there. England players make more money than any other Test players, and, for me, playing for your country still holds the greatest attraction. I have had my problems with the Pakistan cricket authorities, but at no stage have I ever wished to drop out of playing for my country. After I signed for Kerry Packer, I realised that I could not play for Pakistan, and I would have given up World Series cricket in favour of Test cricket if the authorities had not struck a deal. Why are the England players so disillusioned? Is it because they are not playing very well? Have they been treated badly? If they are opting for an easy pay-day after failing at Test level, then England are well rid of them. You need players with a great desire to represent their country. England should now follow the lead of Australia and persevere with younger players. From a personal standpoint, I shall never go to South Africa while someone of my colour is judged a second-class, inferior person. I was offered a fortune to play there in 1981, but I refused. Imran Khan an honorary white? That is an insult. The Boards of Control are powerless to alter the status quo in world cricket over South Africa; the politicians decide the course of action. There will be no change in the attitude of the black members of the I.C.C. until the political structure of South Africa changes. Too many think that everything will fall apart in South Africa if the non-whites get a say in that country's decision-making. That is very patronising. All that the influential non-whites need is the chance to develop skills and participate in the running of South Africa. Equality of opportunity is the key.

*You have advocated neutral umpires in Tests for years now. Are we any nearer to it?*

I believe that pressure from the players is mounting and that they will eventually have to bow to that. None of the players want the aggro; they want to win fairly and do not want an umpire to be accused of bias when he makes a mistake. Away from England it is a major crisis now, with almost every series affected by serious complaints about the umpiring. So far, in my experience, there have been no real problems when the umpires come from a third country. When home umpires make mistakes, the touring side takes it as bias. What you must remember is that all cricketers at Test level are professionals, and yet the umpires—apart from the English ones—are not. So the incompetent ones are being exposed by television replays. That affects morale in the dressing-room, when you come back and see the replay and know you have been badly done by.

*But is it fair to say that Pakistan have caused more problems for umpires than any other Test team?*

It is not just a matter of concentrating on one country. After the Shakoor Rana/Gatting incident, people in England at last woke up to the fact that there are

115

regular umpiring difficulties. I have often felt cheated when teams lose in Pakistan and then blame the umpires. Whenever we had similar problems abroad we would be accused of whingeing and being bad sports. There is no doubt that the cricket umpire has the hardest job in sport, and he should be helped, so that accusations of bias can be eliminated.

*Assuming that you believe English umpires are still the most competent, would the neutral umpires' panel consist mainly of Englishmen?*

They do make fewer mistakes than the others, but the rest of the Test nations will not accept a panel mainly made up of English umpires. The only fair way is to provide two from each Test-playing country and ensure that members of that panel are highly paid and given the full backing of the I.C.C. So umpires the world over would have a real incentive to get on the panel and many top cricketers would be tempted to go into umpiring when they retire. It is time we stopped shielding inadequate umpires.

*Turning to your career; how much longer can you carry on?*

Since I fractured my shin in 1983, I have only looked one series ahead at a time. If I continue to feel fit enough, and happy with my form, I shall continue to play for Pakistan. It is much harder to keep fit when you are not playing first-class cricket, but at this stage in my life there are more important things to do than play too much cricket. I still enjoy captaining Pakistan, despite the inevitable power struggles and the bickering. In recent years we are the only team to have played two series against the West Indies and held our own. In fact, we dominated the last series in the West Indies, only to hear that they had declined. A month or so later, they came to England and won the series four-nil, so I suggest that we did not do too badly out there. We have some good young players coming through, and they will be thrown in at the deep end to see if they can respond to the pressure. At the age of eighteen English players are still struggling in the county second team, but we put them in the first team to assess them. The English also get tired because they play so much cricket. The Australian bowlers have been able to rest before a Test Match while the English guys have been up and down motorways, playing one-day games and championship matches. I think the England hierarchy should now organise a squad system, where the fast bowlers are protected from too much cricket and are kept fresh for the Tests. The counties will still want these bowlers to run in for them in all sorts of games, but it is the England team which suffers if the fast bowlers are not fresh. Whose interests are more important?

*Apart from your cricket magazine, what else are you doing?*

I am trying to raise funds for a cancer hospital in Pakistan. It will be in memory of my mother, who died of cancer. That experience brought me in touch with the medical services in Pakistan and made me realise how poor the facilities are. In a population of a hundred million, there is not one specialist cancer hospital. A poor person has little chance of surviving cancer. We are trying to get a feasibility study going. It is a massive project—one that is taking up a lot of my time—but it is worth it. My life will always involve many interests away from cricket.

# ALLAN LAMB

**'The English are a bit soft. I like the way people like Ian Chappell and Tony Greig captained their sides. '**

ONE-DAY *cricket may have a few defects for the purists, but when it is played the Allan Lamb way, the blood is stirred. Lamb is one of the greatest batsmen in limited overs history. He is cricket's version of those doe-eyed damsels of the silent movie era—surely doomed as the train advances on the slim figure tied to the railway tracks. At the last moment she wriggles free and heads for the arms of the lounge lizard with the smouldering eyes. Well, Allan Lamb has orchestrated similar cliff-hangers for England—from Sydney to Trent Bridge to Gujranwala. Somehow he finds his touch, timing and gaps in the field just as it seems he has failed to make the leap from passive occupation of the crease to pugnacious hitting. In just a single over, he has reduced Bruce Reid to squabbling with his fielders and Courtenay Walsh to inconsolable tears as England snatched improbable victories.*

*Yet Lamb is not just a batsman who has mastered the special demands of the one-day game. You cannot score three hundreds in a Test series against the West Indies without equal proportions of mental toughness, raw courage and technical ability. His England performances have fluctuated in quality—particularly in Tests abroad—but his century at Leeds against the 1989 Australians suggested he was close to maturity. The subsequent run of injuries that kept him out of the rest of the series was keenly felt: the side needed Lamb's cheerfulness and indomitable spirit as well as his runs. Those injuries also ended an interesting development in Lamb's career, as he had been tackling his first season as county captain with a surprising degree of professionalism, a commitment that was rewarded with the England vice-captaincy on the West Indies tour.*

*When Lamb was appointed captain of Northamptonshire, references to poachers and gamekeepers were trotted out in affectionate tribute to his approach to the rigours of the game. Lamb has never been one for the psychoanalyst's couch whenever the supply of*

*runs dries up, as befits a convivial character whose soul-mates number David Gower,*
*Ian Botham and Dennis Lillee—men who know their way around a wine list. Yet Lamb*
*surprised many by his effervescent approach to the job of county captaincy, and both*
*leader and club await with interest the next stage in an impressive career. Had he got*
*the disappointments of the 1989 summer out of his system?*

At the start of the season the gates were so big, and I was halfway through them. Then they slammed in my face. I was playing as well as I have ever done. At last I had got my first hundred in a Test against the Aussies and things were going well at Northants. I will never know just how memorable a season it might have been for me. I had barely had an injury in my career for England, and then they all piled up—torn ligaments in my left hand, torn tendons in my shoulder and finally a chipped finger. All of them done while fielding. You would have thought, after all those years facing the West Indies, I would have been injured while batting, but no. I felt like crying after the last injury, because that meant my season was over at the start of July. Ian Chappell had interviewed me for Channel 9 after my hundred in the one-day international at Trent Bridge and I told him that the best was yet to come. In the Leeds Test, I was full of confidence after my good start to the season. I played my shots on a flat wicket and I got a hundred. I was determined to get that hundred because I had got out in the seventies and eighties too often against Australia in the past. Now I am over the disappointment of all the injuries and I cannot wait to get stuck into the West Indies. I missed the England set-up very much, and it is a great thrill to be the vice-captain after seven years in the squad.

*I suppose you knew how the England lads were feeling as they kept getting hammered*
*by the Aussies.*

Of course. You end up with your confidence in shreds. I went through two seasons during which the media said I was just a good one-day player, and that got to me. I was looking just to occupy the crease, instead of having the confidence to play my shots, and I got in a rut. I was batting too carefully. I was lucky enough to be brought up on good, hard wickets in South Africa, and I am at my best when I am batting aggressively. Last summer the England boys were getting absolutely crucified on the TV. Although they tried to avoid the papers, they could not help themselves when they saw the various lurid headlines. Look at Nick Cook—he got back into the England side because he had bowled aggressively for us at Northants. But the spirits in the England dressing-room were so low that he did not do himself justice at all at Old Trafford. In the next Test at Trent Bridge, he stopped firing it in, gave it more air, and looked a much better bowler. And what about Graham Gooch? He has played the same way for almost all his career, and he has always been a candidate for lbw as he goes to play through the on-side. But he should not try to alter the way he plays just because he has got out lbw a few times against the Aussies. He just has to play his natural way. Dean Jones kept whipping the ball on off-stump through midwicket, but none of the Aussies told him to cut that shot out, in case he was lbw. I agree it is important for a little fine tuning here and there. I had a spell where I was out lbw a lot, and someone at Northampton whose judgement I respect told me that was because I was falling away to offside. He suggested I stood up straighter, that I was looking down the wrong line when I was leaning over. I got a hundred in the next innings. If you are moving around in the crease there is no way you can pick up the line if your head is not still. When Graham Gooch is playing well, his head is still. He should not worry about eliminating shots that have brought him so

119

many runs; we all have to keep confidence in the way we have learned to bat.

*You are a great mate of David Gower. How did the pressure of the 1989 series affect him?*

He had a depleted side for every Test because of injuries, and that is bound to affect anyone. Because of that, he lacked a bit of confidence and that changed the way he approached the job. His personality will never alter—and why should it? Mike Brearley was never one for waving his arms around and shouting on the field, so what is wrong with David giving a little nod here and there to a fielder and being himself? They were bound to make unfavourable comparisons between David and Allan Border, because the Aussies were winning; but they are different as people and as batsmen. Border looked a gritty leader from the front because that is the way he bats, whereas David is an elegant, wafty left-hander who is not as tight in his play. People say that David is loose, but what about his 7,000 Test runs? No, I reckon one of our major problems this summer was that the Aussies were allowed to get away with being aggressive. Their bowlers kept chirping our batters, but we are not allowed to say anything to the opposition because we will get slated in the media for being unsporting. If I was a bowler and I beat the batsman three times in a row, I would have something to say. When I played against Dennis Lillee, I loved the way he would have a go at me. It would really fire me up. Our bowlers should be allowed to show more gut feeling on the field. I do not mean swearing all the time at the batsmen, but saying something to the batsman as he passes when he has been lucky—just to ruffle him up a bit. It is the same in county cricket. We should be able to forget all about what went on out there over a drink after the game. The English are a bit soft. I like the way people like Ian Chappell and Tony Greig captained their sides.

*You seemed to have clearly-defined ideas about captaincy when you got the job at Northants?*

I will always thrive on a challenge and it brought me closer to the game. I was in danger of drifting away. I did not really feel part of the set-up at Northampton and I knew that I would not be able to carry on playing for much longer if I stayed on the outside. People say I changed, but I have always given a hundred per cent on the field—even if I have joked around more than others—and I expected the same from everyone. I felt the guys at Northampton needed a kick up the backside—more self-discipline. On paper we have the strongest side in Northants' history, and it has been even more frustrating this season when we have not performed consistently. We have just got to be more professional. Sides such as Worcestershire, Essex and Middlesex work harder at their game. If you have technical faults you must get into the nets and work at it: our blokes have not done enough of that this summer, especially as the nets have been up all the time because the weather has been so good. Apart from such frustrations, I really enjoyed the challenge of being county captain. It is something I need to motivate me. Now I'm really looking forward to being vice-captain on the West Indies tour, to work with the younger players, and, hopefully, be a better batsman myself with the added responsibility.

*Your one-day performances have been remarkable. How do you manage it, when other players of your talent fail consistently?*

One-day cricket is very easy. You just want wickets in hand near the end. The batter who is 60-odd not out after about forty overs has to be there at the end and be responsible for stepping up the tempo when he thinks the time is right. I have proved that you do not need to slog in the last few overs. You can get up to forty in the last four overs if you put away the bad ball and run hard to put pressure on the fielders. Eight an over is perfectly possible if you keep calm and let the fielding side panic. Of course, you need slices of luck, but far too often you see sides start off fantastically, then lose their way as they lose wickets. People think you have got to be hitting boundaries all the time but I have had slow innings where I have not given it a whack until near the end. At Trent Bridge, when I got that hundred against the Aussies, I did not think we had enough runs, so I waited until the last three overs, rather than the last five, before I broke out. We got about forty runs off the last three. You must not throw away your innings when you've got sixty-odd and then expect the tail-enders to score as fast as you could.

*How do you keep cool in these situations?*
Well, you do not stage-manage it, for a start. It just happens. I do not say to myself "Oh, it doesn't matter, I'll wait till we need 18 off the last over." I always like to look at between 100 and 120 off the last twenty overs and then, once the slog starts, I wait for the ball to go in all sorts of strange places and rely on the fielders getting downhearted. You try to forget about everything other than just building for the last few overs. Keep the target in your mind, and make the scoreboard tick over. I also think that the older you get, the better you are at judging things like this. When I look back at the times I threw my wicket away in a run chase . . .

*Which one-day innings was your best?*
It has to be that night game at Sydney in 1987, when Bruce Reid went for eighteen in the last over. I had been fiddling about for ages and I knew that if we lost that game it would be my fault. I just could not get going at all until near the end. Even then, we did not get enough off Simon O'Donnell in the penultimate over. I told myself if we could get a boundary off Reid's first ball, we had a chance. We did, and then I was looking to hit him for six. I knew I just had to go for a maximum, and I moved around in my crease to disrupt his line. He followed me with the ball and it was the wrong length—if he had pitched it up a foot more, I might have got a four to mid-wicket, but it was shorter, so I could throw the bat at it with a full swing. I put it over long-on, and that decided the game. I was really pumped up. The atmosphere was fantastic. But I watched the ball in that last over and I kept my head still: the same batting principles for any type of match.

*Has your brilliance in one-day games obscured your Test record?*
Yes it has, although nine Test hundreds is not exactly a failure. It is up to me to put it right over the next few years, starting with the West Indies this winter.

*Four Test hundreds against the West Indies must be some comfort to you.*
No one likes playing quick bowlers—we would all rather have a spinner or a military medium-pacer. But I have always approached the West Indies bowlers in a positive frame of mind. To a certain extent I feel they can be taken on; it is a matter of picking the right ball to hit and staying aggressively-minded. I just hope the wickets in the Caribbean will be better than those in 1986. They were shocking. Even their boys admitted they would have struggled on them against their bowlers. I could not have

worked harder on that tour in the nets against our bowling machine. At least it toned up reactions and got you used to short-pitched bowling. But there is not much you can do about a ball that lifts viciously off a length in a Test Match.

*So how can you bat with any hope of survival against the West Indies while playing aggressively at the same time?*

If you try just to stay there, Malcolm Marshall and the others will keep the four slips and the gully in place and wear you down. You have to try to spread their field and then hope to play normally. Once they take away the fourth slip, you can go for the big drive, and hope that if you get a nick it will go through areas that have been vacated. That is how *they* play the quicks. Why not us? We must also run sharp singles—just tip and run, like the Aussies have done against us this summer. The West Indies fast bowlers hate that. They get very frustrated at sharp singles. If the wickets are of the proper standard for a Test series, and if we approach the task positively, we can surprise a few.

*At least you won't be hassled over there for being born in South Africa. You have toured the Caribbean with no problems before. Have you given up hoping that the media will ever stop referring to you as a South African?*

They just do not seem to want to accept me as a England player; it is always "South African-born Allan Lamb". Now I just ignore it. I used to be bitter about that, but now I accept that it means nothing that both my parents are English—that I have done everything in my power to be recognised as an England cricketer. I have no plans to settle back in South Africa. We have just had a new home built in Northampton, our daughter is down for school here in 1992, and this is where I am staying—apart from trips to South Africa to see our folks. But they keep going on about it.

*Were you ever a candidate for the rebel tour to South Africa?*

The first I knew about it was when I heard who had signed. When I saw Mike Procter earlier in the summer, I said to him "Are you recruiting?" and he denied it. That was the last I heard until the day it broke. They would not have gone for me because it would be like taking coals to Newcastle. They wanted to see people they had never seen. But I would not have signed, even if I had been asked. I came over to play for England and I still want that; it means a tremendous amount to me. I would really love to play a hundred Tests for England, if that were possible. I am going to do everything I can to get somewhere near it.

# KEITH FLETCHER

**'Once, an Essex player had not tried in the field and I left him out of the side until he apologised. He would never have played again if he had not.'**

W HILE *England staggered from disasters at Leeds, Lord's, Old Trafford and Trent Bridge in 1989, the man who played a significant part in Australia's annus mirabilis was gracing such exotic locations as Newark, Leigh-on-Sea and Oxted. Keith Fletcher would have been astonished at the tributes paid by Allan Border to the inspiration gained from the Essex guru in two highly productive seasons with that county. Hardly a Test Press conference passed without an acknowledgement from the Australian camp that the English game still had at least one sage in its midst. Border made no secret that he came to Essex to learn more about English cricket and its major players. The campaign that triumphed so signally in 1989 started in 1986 when Fletcher was cosseting Essex to yet another championship. Border simply asked intelligent questions and Fletcher answered them.*

*So, as Fletcher took the Essex second eleven around the shires, England's premier batsmen were being exposed by subtle field-placing, sensible bowling and aggressive out-cricket that stoked up the pressure. In short, a typical Essex performance of a kind that has garnered nine trophies in the past decade. Despite the side's individual talent, they would never have dominated English county cricket without the leadership of Fletcher. In the last twenty years, only Mike Brearley has rivalled Fletcher's ability to get the utmost from his team, to conjure up improbable victories. All done with the minimum of fuss and maximum commonsense.*

*When Fletcher succeeded Brearley as England's captain in 1981, the job had passed to the safest pair of hands. But in India Fletcher allowed himself to be dragged down into a war of attrition with his opposite number Sunil Gavaskar, and the new chairman of selectors, Peter May, was unimpressed. Fletcher, England's best cricket brain and a far superior batsman to the deified Brearley, was gone. Fletcher kept his dignity and carried on inspiring Essex. Even in his last season of first-class cricket it was instructive to see*

*the slight figure scurrying around the field, fussing over his charges, ceaselessly plotting—still crazy about cricket after all these years and a healthy corrective to some jaded veterans who have picked up their benefit and gone through the motions. An hour with Keith Fletcher is worth many a coaching video or intensive net session. He assumes a professional cricketer can play the game, and is more interested in attitude. How did this patriotic Englishman feel about being the unwitting agent of Allan Border's marvellous summer?*

I am very pleased to have helped Allan, he is a super bloke. I appreciated that one of the world's best batsmen always gave Essex one hundred per cent. Allan captained Essex now and again and we always discussed field placings and opposition weaknesses. It takes time to learn the art of captaincy and Allan has finally come of age. For example, he knew all about Graham Gooch's desire for perfection and he capitalised on it. Graham worries too much about his batting; he wants the ball to go through extra cover all along the ground like a shell. It is no good for Graham if he nicks it to the boundary through gully. I never worried about where the ball went. I would say: "Look in the scorebook." Allan knew that Graham would fret when he placed two men close in on he legside. Sometimes it is a good idea, if only to make the batter think: "What the bloody hell has he done that for?" You might just lose your concentration for a second. I thought this series would be very tight and we would just nick it. I thought Neil Foster might win a Test for us, yet he has never bowled as badly in the last three years. The Aussies looked a team who knew what they were about, with a pattern of play, while we just drifted.

*How badly do you believe England batted?*

It was very disappointing. I look at their line-up and I cannot believe they kept being bowled out. They were unlucky with Allan Lamb's injuries, because he is a class player and he would have got a lot of runs. They needed someone like Barrington, Graveney or Cowdrey to come in and steady the middle order. Goochy is probably the nearest to those blokes because he sets out his stall to bat for a long time. But I reckon an opener will get done one out of three by the new ball. Then it's up to him to cash in when he has got through the early stuff. But it wasn't Gooch's year.

They played like one-day batters. They were all guilty of planting the front foot down the wicket and trying to play round it. Everyone has a first movement, whether it is back or forward, but it should only be a matter of an inch either way. Modern batters have too pronounced a front-foot movement. They get off-balance and cannot readjust. They are moving before the ball is delivered. The trouble is that you cannot get people to change at a late stage in their career. David Gower is one exception to this planting of the front pad: he is a fine player. He times the ball so well. He gets to twenty after just a few minutes and you do not know how he got them. He does play too much to square and behind the wicket rather than to mid-off, but you cannot really fault a player who has scored fifteen Test hundreds. It is good that he has not altered the way he has played. He is lucky that he is a left-hander, because he does not need to move his feet as much as a right-hander. A left-hander has to think about leaving the ball, rather than getting the foot to the pitch of it. If a right-hand bowler wants to bowl a left-hander off-stump, it has to be a great delivery to pitch outside and come back to hit the off peg. So a left-hander doesn't have to worry so much about defending that area.

*If these are our best batsmen, what hope is there for England?*

You must remember that a bowler like Terry Alderman is a rarity these days as he bowls wicket to wicket on a full length, at not much more than medium pace. We would be fending it off against the West Indies. I played against Terry Alderman in county cricket and he was a useful bowler but you would be more worried about the other overseas bowlers like Malcolm Marshall and Richard Hadlee. When I first started, there were quite a few like Alderman—Kenny Palmer and Andy Corran, for example—but their type seems to have disappeared. Kevin Cooper of Nottinghamshire is probably the nearest current English comparison. For the future we have just got to start at the grassroots, with the youngsters. The Under-19 side must be run in a proper, professional way. They must learn as soon as possible how to play cricket—how you go about building an innings, where the bowler should put pressure on a batsman.

*As you travel the country with Essex seconds and watch the first team at times, what is your view of the state of English cricket?*

There is the odd good young bowler, like Igglesden of Kent and Bicknell at Surrey. And I cannot understand why young Andrew is not regularly in Hampshire's first team. There are some talented batters around, too. I'm not biased when I say that our lad, Nasser Hussain, could become an ever better player than Graeme Hick. Nasser has so much flair—he can do anything. He seems to play any bowler as easily as shelling peas. He shows bundles of talent on bad wickets, and that is always important. I agree he looks loose at the start of an innings, but he does not often get out early. I would have picked him before Mike Atherton: I think he is a better player. There is now a perfect opportunity to blood young players on an England tour. A youngster going to the West Indies has not been through the times when they whistle it past your chin off a good length. He is fresh and everything seems a challenge. Youngsters might just surprise a few and get stuck in.

*Let's talk about the art of captaincy, Keith. Is one of its secrets to treat each player differently?*

You have got to do that. They're all individuals. There is no point in bollocking a player like John Lever, who would always give you everything; but occasionally you have to go for someone who has been stupid. Once an Essex player had not tried on the field, and I told him so in front of the others. I left him out of the side until he had apologised. He would never have played again if he had not done that. It is vital to be absolutely straight with your players and to pick the side to win each particular game, without any favourites. David Acfield is a very good friend of mine but I often had to leave him out to play an extra seamer. Yet he always knew where he stood with me.

*What is more important to a captain—good batsmen or good bowlers?*

The batters look after themselves but the bowlers have to be looked after. Batting is a selfish game but bowlers need everyone else in order to succeed. You must chivvy the bowlers along, because the team that sneaks a win out of a boring game wins championships. So you just have to keep your bowlers going, and make them run in for you.

*How does a captain make things happen on the field?*

I was lucky because I always fielded close to the bat, where it all happens. I would do things like changing the field just to exert pressure, if nothing was happening on a good wicket. I would go in at bat/pad, ask the spinner to bowl tight and just try to stop the batsmen scoring. Our two spinners, David Acfield and Ray East, were very reliable when we had men around the bat. We would tell them "don't worry if we get hit", and they were good enough to avoid bowling crap. We just wanted the batsmen to play differently, even if it meant going down the wicket and smashing the ball out of the ground. The essence is making the batsman play differently from the way he wants to play.

*It has been said that you used to chatter away at the batsmen from close in. Did you?*
Brian Hardie and I used to be close in at either side of the wicket and we would talk to each other. But we never talked directly to the batter—no sledging, honestly!

*How much did it help to be a batsman/captain?*
I used to think "now what do I dislike most when I'm batting?" and do that when I was in the field. Early on, I liked to assess what I thought should happen, when I was vice-captain under Brian Taylor. Brian's sergeant-major discipline was good for a young, developing team, and I would help him with the field-placing and work out what he was thinking. I learned a lot from the Yorkshire side under Brian Close in the Sixties. I liked his aggression, the way he would impose himself on the game. Nothing happens if you just stand around, waiting. You have to be single-minded and enjoy winning. Micky Stewart was another good captain when he was at Surrey. I did a winter tour once with him and I liked his bubbly ways and his tactical soundness. I think he was a good appointment as England manager, even if he does occasionally complicate a simple game. Basically, captaincy involves getting good players to perform to their best. I do not believe in scientific things like looking at charts to see where a batsman scores most of his runs. Neither do I care how good an off-driver someone is. He cannot keep thrashing it through the covers if you are bowling at his leg-stump. You work it out by watching a batsman at close quarters. Believe totally in your side, make them believe they are better than they really are, then they will perform above themselves.

*How bad are the current English pitches?*
When I first started there were a few bad ones. Many more of them turned early on, so I got a lot of valuable practice in playing spin. Every wicket in Yorkshire turned—in my second game, it turned square at Sheffield and they bowled us out twice to win by an innings. Nobody complained, because it was also a much more interesting game when the spinners were on. I find that there is a lot more talk about pitches today. People get away with leaving grass on the pitch, so that the ball goes through head-high off a length, or hits you on the shin from basically the same delivery. Some of the wickets in 1989 were lethal and stacked in favour of the faster bowlers; yet if a wicket turns before lunch on the first day, the umpires report it to Lord's. Yet we have had some fabulous games in Essex where the ball turns and techniques are tested—and no one gets physically threatened by John Childs.

*You have had experience of bad pitches on England tours, particularly the one to Australia in 1974/5 when Lillee and Thomson were lethal. That awful photograph of you being hit on the cap by Thommo at Sydney lingers in the memory. Were you frightened at any stage on those wickets?*
Slightly apprehensive, rather than frightened. That one off Thommo was short of a

length. It took off, hit my glove and was deflected onto the badge on my cap. Ross Edwards nearly caught me at cover! I think I would have worn the helmet if it had been available! Those wickets were green, bouncy with bare patches, and the one at Sydney was just like many of today's in county cricket. I don't care if we had had Peter May or Wally Hammond—you could not play that lot and succeed in those circumstances. The word went round that we could not play fast bowling, but the dice were loaded against us. Lillee exposed every area of your technique, while Thommo was just like Frank Tyson in his heyday. He was so unpredictable—you could leave four in a row, then he would glove you with one you just could not avoid. So we all got labelled. Dennis Amiss should have played another thirty times for England, but people said he could not play Lillee. Who could on those wickets?

*You captained England on just one tour, to India in 1981/2, where you got embroiled in dissatisfaction about the umpires and the slow over-rate. Do you regret the way you handled it?*

I do regret getting dragged down to Sunny Gavaskar's level and I just wish I could have played him when we had the regulation about a minimum number of overs per day. I just got so frustrated that we had no chance of getting into a winning position because they would slow it down so blatantly. And don't forget, they were only five-and-a-half hour days. At least with ninety overs a day you have a genuine chance of winning and you can forget about the umpiring standards and the slow-motion stuff. I wish we had not got so wound up about the umpires on that tour, but some of our batters were so fed up that they wanted to go home early. You cannot help moaning when you just know that Gavaskar was as plumb as old boots lbw early on and he goes on to get a big hundred. Then if one of your top batters gets hit on the front foot and the umpire's finger goes up instantly, that starts to grate on you.

*And when you came back from that tour, you were sacked from the captaincy. The manner of your dismissal wasn't exactly tactful was it?*

Peter May rang me at home one day and, as luck would have it, I was in the garden. It was ten minutes to three. He told me he wanted a change. I put the phone down and then it was announced on the BBC Radio news at three o'clock. I wonder what would have happened to that announcement if I had not been in my garden? I have never been told the reasons—I have hardly said six words to Peter May in my life—and I can only guess. I know they were looking to play Allan Lamb once he had qualified, and that they also wanted to get Derek Randall in; so I suppose it was a case of picking the best eleven and then selecting a captain.

*Perhaps the incident in the Bangalore Test had something to do with it, when you tapped off a bail in irritation at being given out?*

But that really was so innocent, just a gentle tap and the bails lobbed off. I was so furious at being given out, caught down legside, that I felt like knocking down the lot. I just think Peter May was determined to start afresh and there was no room for me.

*Just before you were sacked, you turned down the captaincy of the England team in South Africa. Would you have gone if you knew that Peter May was shortly to sack you?*

I think so. There was a lot of money involved—£47,000 tax-free. I would be a lot better off than I am today if I had gone, but at the time I felt it was not the right thing for an England captain to do. I knew nothing about the planned tour while I was out in India, and I was only contacted when they had already got to South Africa and it dawned on them that they did not have a captain. I asked for 24 hours to think about it, and we all know the rest.

*You had some great times with England, but I suspect your achievements with Essex mean more. What was the greatest day in your career?*
When we won our first trophy, at Lord's in the 1979 Benson and Hedges Cup Final. The year before, we had finished second in the championship, but now we had learned not to bottle it, and that summer we went on to lift the title. It was only a matter of self-belief. When Graham Gooch and Mike Denness walked out to bat at Lord's and the whole stadium rose to greet them, it was like a fairytale.

*And the future?*
There is nothing else I would rather do than this. I still love cricket and all its complexities. I have enjoyed this summer, looking after the second team, more than any other. The pressures of bringing on the youngsters are much different to the First Eleven pressures. What matters is that they learn the basics and adapt to the Essex way of playing.

# JACK
# RUSSELL

**'Merv Hughes gave me an almighty earful at Lord's and I gave it back. When I slapped the loose ball to the boundary I'd shout: "Now go and fetch that!" '**

I N recent years, England's cricket media has enjoyed as bad a collective trot as the hapless selectors. The flavour-of-the-month among the correspondents often becomes the busted flush after a couple of outings at the highest level. The selectors, those recipients of advice from all quarters, can be excused an occasional wry grin at the promiscuity of the media's preferences. But the writers and broadcasters were right about one player: Jack Russell. For two seasons before he was finally picked by England, Russell was clearly the most accomplished wicket-keeper in the country. The claims of others, spurious doubts about Russell's batting ability and the misfortune of playing for an unfashionable county all conspired to leave Russell thwarted.

It seemed he was destined to share the same frustrations as Bob Taylor, the keeper he closely resembles. At least Taylor's supporters had to acknowledge the genius and superior batting of Alan Knott. In the case of Russell there was no-one of that stature in contention. So he just carried on keeping immaculately for Gloucestershire while chiselling out valuable innings. Between 1986 and 1988, his batting average in first-class cricket rose from 26 to 31 as the media continued to bemoan his absence from the England team. Finally he was picked against Sri Lanka in the dog-days of the 1988 summer, and here the immutable Law of Sod played a part. By his exalted standards, Russell kept poorly, but he scored 94, the highest innings of his first-class career.

At the end of the 1989 summer he was still making runs for England and keeping wicket beautifully. He was so good behind the stumps that he was barely noticed (always the hallmark of the craftsman), while his batting developed into reliability in a crisis. He had a lot of practice in such situations against the Australians. Jack Russell will never be one of those cricketers who display their commitment to the cause by snarling aggression and jabbing of fist, yet his understated professionalism was the one major consolation for England throughout the Ashes series. An artist on and off the field, his *burgeoning talent with sketch pad has kept pace with his new status in world cricket. It seemed the last word in media hype to claim he was the world's best keeper before he had ever played Test cricket, but Jack Russell now ought to have the England gloves for the next decade. Had he ever despaired of getting his England chance?*

I did wonder if it was ever going to happen. A lot of players do think: "What more can I do?" But you just have to be patient and do well over a period of time. Last year I let the media forecasts get to me a little bit, so that it affected my form when I did not get into the England team. Now I am determined to keep performing to my best every single day, whether or not I am playing for England.

*Did the obsession with your batting annoy you? After all, a wicket-keeper is a specialist, just like a fast bowler. Bowlers are not expected to score fifties.*

I was frustrated about that, because if anyone had bothered to check my record they would have seen how my first-class total and average has increased over the years. I had one bad season with the bat—in 1985 when I averaged thirteen—and it was right that Steve Rhodes nipped in ahead of me and got on the England "B" tour to Zimbabwe. But since 1986 I have improved all the time. In 1988 I was not far short of 1,000 runs. That is not bad for someone at number eight.

*When at last you played for England, you were below your best behind the stumps and yet you just missed out on a hundred. Ironic, isn't it?*

I was really disappointed with myself on my first day in Test cricket. On average I drop one catch a season standing back but that day I missed two and got a finger to an outside edge. I just was not there mentally; I was not in the groove. You have to be relaxed, and have tunnel vision. You must grit your teeth and tell yourself you are going to catch the ball. It never crossed my mind that I was under pressure, because the Press had been talking me into the England team. I just was not mentally switched on. As for my 94, I was lucky to come in as night-watchman and get enough time to set out my stall. I was dropped on ten and after that I was not in a great deal of trouble. I cocked it up at the end, flat-batting a loose one to cover. My fault. A satisfying start to my England batting career, though.

*But it all came right with bat and keeper's gloves right at the start against the Australians, didn't it?*

I felt I kept really well at Leeds in the first Test. The ball was not coming through consistently at any one height. That slope there is a nightmare: when you are standing at the rugby ground end, the ball keeps coming past your shoulder when you expect it to be down by your knee. I did not let a bye go in a total of 600. The important thing is that I did not make a mistake.

*How many mistakes did you make in the Ashes series?*

As far as I am concerned, one. It was an inside edge by Mark Taylor off Neil Foster. It just carried to me as I was diving to my right. It was a nasty one, but on another day I would have expected to have taken it. Luckily it did not have a major effect on the game.

*Which stumping pleased you most?*

The one at Trent Bridge to get David Boon may have looked good, because I took it high to my right, but that was fairly routine—just a matter of waiting for it. The one to get Mark Taylor earlier in the day was more difficult. He ran down the pitch, the ball kept a little low, it turned out of the rough and the left-hander unsighted me for an instant. People think it is easy to stump someone when they are five yards down the pitch, but you have got to wait for it. If you rush things you are in trouble. You have to avoid snatching at the ball.

*How much of a strain has this Ashes series been for you as a newcomer?*
Mentally it has been the hardest summer I have known. Almost every day in the series I was on the field, either as a batter or keeper. That first stint at Leeds set me up for the series, because I kept well for two days and a bit. I was still going for every ball at the end.

*I suppose your batting has been as satisfying as your keeping, especially after being criticised for your two innings at Leeds.*
I did not bat to my ability at Leeds and I knew I had to do something about it to stay in the side. I will always accept criticism, but they were wrong to harp on about my inability to play the short stuff. I happened to nick one that did not really bounce as much as I expected. They unsettled me—I was into the unknown, batting for the first time in the ultimate Test series and I was not in the right mental groove for batting. In the second innings I could not attack, because we were trying to save the match at that stage, so they were bound to try me with a few short-pitched ones. Remember I am a keeper, so I cannot give it back to them. The first ball in first-class cricket I faced whistled past my nose, courtesy of Les Taylor, and it has been that way ever since. Yet I was not hit on the head at Leeds, or dismissed by a bouncer; I just flirted outside the off-stump. Left-handers do that a lot, no matter how good they are. I drove home from Leeds that night thinking about my batting and telling myself I was going to attack them and go for the boundary shot if it was on. The flak I got for Leeds helped me: it gave me a kick up the backside and I was going to be more positive. I was not batting well for Gloucestershire at the time and I thought I had nothing to lose by getting after the bowlers. The day before the Lord's Test I had a long chat with Alan Knott about my batting and he said that I had to bat as if my life was at stake. Real mental grit, geeing myself up all the time. After that I kept talking to myself while at the crease—the Aussies must have thought I was a real nutter!

At Lord's I also started to go back and across just as the bowler delivered the ball. I made myself play balls straight back down the pitch to the bowler, or at worst to mid-off. I did that to stop myself playing defensively to gully or square cover. There was no point playing a defensive stroke in that area with an angled bat, because you might easily get a nick. I wanted to show as much of the bat to the ball when playing a defensive stroke, so that made me play straighter. I also knew they would give me a lot of lip at Lord's because they sensed I would be vulnerable as a new boy and that they would try to beat me down mentally. Merv Hughes gave me an almighty earful at Lord's and I gave it back. That really helped me, it geed me up. When I slapped the loose ball to the boundary, I would shout "now go and fetch that!" and I really enjoyed the challenge.

*Was that half-century in the first innings at Lord's more significant than your hundred at Old Trafford later in the series?*
Yes, it broke the ice, helped build up my confidence and made me aware that I could

chip in with useful scores at Test level. I had often wondered if I would ever get a hundred in first-class cricket. I had got one for Gloucestershire in the Sunday League, but it is hardly the same with no one round the bat. At number eight, you are struggling to get too many hundreds unless you are in with a good batter on a good pitch and time on your hands. Night-watchman is probably the best opportunity. At Old Trafford, I tried to bat all day after being not-out overnight and John Emburey just coaxed me along if my concentration ever wavered. When I got to 94 I seemed to be stuck on it for an eternity, as thoughts of the Sri Lanka innings came back to me. I just blocked the singles. I could not have put more mental effort into the next six runs. I will never forget the shot: it was a pushed single off Terry Alderman that I played behind square leg. It was a half-volley, and I wonder if Terry bowled it deliberately. We played together at Gloucestershire for a season and we got on very well. Terry did not bowl too many half-volleys in this series, did he?

*So much for your batting, Jack—but you are primarily a wicket-keeper. Is there a formula to assess the art of keeping wicket?*

I suppose you have to possess that natural element. There are good keepers who are not naturals, but they do have that mental toughness. If you are not spot-on to take every ball, natural ability does not count. I try not to dive around too much—and people have been kind enough to compare me to Bob Taylor in that respect. Bob has been very helpful to me with technical tips—for example, he noticed in the Edgbaston Test that I dropped a couple of balls because I got up too early, so that my head and hands were too high. Alan Knott has been great on attitude. I do more work on my mind now, because I know that I can only keep wicket well if I am one hundred per cent right mentally. The mistakes I have made in my career have been half-chances where I have not been on the ball—where I would have made those extra three inches if my concentration had been perfect.

*I suppose the real challenge for you is standing up to the stumps?*

Yes, because I feel I am more in control of things. It can also be very difficult standing back to bowlers like Dilley, Foster, Walsh and Malcolm, because they make the ball dip so much after it bounces past the crease. It goes up and down, left and right as it dips towards you, and it is particularly bad on a ground where you cannot see too well because of the background. People may think that a keeper cannot even take the ball cleanly when he is standing back, yet they are unaware why the ball has hit him on the chest or thumb. But standing up is the real challenge. Alan Knott was again very helpful to me in getting used to taking balls at yorker length while standing up. Knotty told me that to be a Test keeper you have to be able to take balls that pitch on the popping crease and squeeze past the bat as the guy goes for the drive. He said if you can take them, you can take anything, because that really tests your reactions. If the ball pitches lower down the wicket you have time to assess the height. Now I get someone to mark out the yorker length when I practise and I take balls at that length for ten minutes every morning.

*What is the best stumping of your career so far?*

The one that was not given—Geoff Marsh off Ian Botham in the Edgbaston Test. It was the correct decision, but I was very pleased with the strategy—their batsmen tend to creep forward—and the way it was done. It went down legside and it was just a fraction too wide to get the ball back in time. Marsh went out, came back and changed feet so that his left foot was just back in the crease. If it had not been a foot too wide, I would have done him. Of the legitimate stumpings, I would pick out two and they were both off Phil Bainbridge, standing up to his inswingers. Jack Richards and Alan Warner were the batsmen, and they were both yorkers.

*A word on your artistic ambitions, Jack. You were a late starter with the sketch pad, weren't you?*

I often thought I could draw and paint but I did not think about it seriously until my wife bought me a small set of oil paints about five years ago. One day at Worcester we were rained off and I strolled down the banks of the River Severn beside the cathedral. I had bought a small sketch pad, some pencils, a couple of rubbers and I sat there and started to draw. I did a man reading a newspaper under a tree and it came out well. I kept covering up the sketch whenever anyone walked by, I was so self-conscious, but it came out the way I wanted. Then I started doing things in the dressing-room, and the boys would ask when was it their turn. I went to Pakistan with England, found there was a lot of time on my hands and started to draw. That was a fantastic challenge, because there was so much variety in Pakistan—the streets, the beggars, the grounds, the religious buildings. I could still be there now! My favourite commissions have been away from cricket. I have a big desire to paint landscapes, but time is the problem. It took me three whole weeks sitting outside Gloucester cathedral before I could get it right. At the moment I am not painting commercially, I am just building up my oils at home, but I hope to branch out in that direction later on. I have done a sketch of Don Bradman that came out in a limited edition, signed by the man himself, and my next sketch of a cricketer will be Ian Botham.

*What does sketching bring you, apart from a nice little sideline?*

Space and tranquillity. I get tense in the build-up to a Test, and it has been great to go and sit in a field. When I work on a sketch the whole world disappears: all I can see is that concept in front of me.

*So in the future, a few more exhibitions of your sketches—and what are your cricketing ambitions?*

To get a thousand runs in a season. To score a first-class hundred for Gloucestershire. To play at my very best every day—and to go through an entire season without dropping a catch. Not much to ask, is it?

# JAVED MIANDAD

**‘I am a fierce competitor and a proud Pakistani . . . I think some opponents get the wrong idea because I smile a lot. ’**

O F all current great batsmen, Javed Miandad is the one you would select to play for your life—provided he liked you. His touch is so sure, his judgement so impeccable, his options so varied that Javed Miandad's undoing often stems from those red mists that swirl around his head. The times when he resembles the artful dodger of the casbah will always bar him from a place in the Good Guys XI: indeed, he would be captain and manager of a rather different side, if selection ever got past the libel lawyers. When the storm clouds gather during games that involve Pakistan, this little man never stays on the periphery, tut-tutting about declining moral standards in world cricket. Umpires all over the world have experienced Javed's tendency to get his retaliation in first, while treating the laws of the game as simply the basis for negotiation. Yet he is a great batsman, unquestionably in the world's top three at the moment, despite a worrying back problem. The prodigy of sixteen delivered early and handsomely after promising much. The youngest to score a triple century, to score a Test double hundred, to reach 5,000 runs in Test cricket—the list is formidable and there seems much more to come. Experience of county cricket with Sussex and Glamorgan developed his technique even further as he gave wondrous exhibitions on unreliable pitches, all achieved with that street urchin's smile as he manipulates the ball into the most unorthodox, untenanted parts of the field. Javed Miandad enjoys irritating his foes, but he maintains he is basically an entertainer. . . .

I believe that you cannot play cricket properly unless you enjoy it. I do not believe in long faces. Cricket is for the future, not just for the day.

*And yet you are never slow to seek advantage for yourself on the field?*

People say so, but no player ever tells me that to my face. I am not aware of ill-feeling from the players and they are the best ones to judge. It all goes in the papers and things get stirred up. When they talk about Mike Gatting, they always seem to refer to Faisalabad and the incident with Shakoor Rana before they describe what he has done on the field that day. With me it is the same—I am a controversial character first, and secondly I might have played well that day.

*Let us talk about that Shakoor Rana incident and your part in it as captain of Pakistan. Did you goad Shakoor Rana to dig his heels in and demand an apology?*

You must realise that Gatting forfeited his chance of winning that Test by not climbing down earlier. It was not my fault that the game was so delayed. Gatting could have won the Test for his country and then complained officially, but he lost his advantage. The dispute was over a matter of culture. Our people are different from yours. They get involved in fights over the kind of verbal abuse Gatting used. When I played county cricket in England I did not mind the verbal obscenities; but the people in Pakistan took it personally when they understood the kind of words shouted at Shakoor. It's not as if Shakoor was umpiring in a Test for the money. He was getting peanuts. He was doing it as a hobby and he just wanted to be treated with some respect.

*What about the time when Dennis Lillee kicked you up the backside in Australia and you turned on him with your bat raised?*

That was in the heat of the moment. I was upset at the time because I was Pakistan's captain and he should not have kicked me, but it soon blew over. I did not think the authorities should have fined Dennis and banned him. It was not all that bad. We shook hands, it did not really bother us and we are now the best of friends.

*Are you saying that you are grievously misunderstood?*

Well, we all do things we shouldn't at some stage, and I am a fierce competitor and a proud Pakistani. That is bound to lead to misunderstandings and things that do not look too good. I think some opponents get the wrong idea because I smile a lot, and they think I am trying to get at them. But I love playing cricket. I like to enjoy myself and that means I smile a lot on the field. Why should people get upset at that?

*Let us talk about your batting. It seems to me that one of your strengths is that you know exactly where you want to place the ball.*

When I am batting I think a lot. I try to work out where the bowler wants to pitch it, and then it is up to me to adapt to his field placing and disturb his rhythm. It is a matter of occupying the crease for long periods and feeling confident. If you are tense, you do not play well.

*How do you approach batting on a turning wicket?*

By taking up the challenge first of all. You cannot expect to defend all day against class spinners on a pitch that helps them. They will get you out. I play as late as possible, and either play straight or follow the ball—it depends on how powerful a spinner I am facing. I do not want to play with the spin for one ball, then straight the next. It has to be one or the other, and stay in that groove. If I am playing straight, I tell myself not to worry if I miss the ball by a long way. That probably means it is going to be my day. I remember that all the pressure is on the bowler in these conditions because he is expected to clean up the batting, and he will start to get worried and send down some loose stuff if he does not get wickets quickly.

*How do you maintain concentration?*

I talk to myself and tell my partner to talk to me. I want him to tell me if I have played a bad shot. Sometimes when you are playing well you can play a bad shot and get away with it without realising it almost got you out. There should be no senior partners out there—both batsmen ought to keep each other going.

*How do you prepare for an innings?*

Well I am not a great man for net practice—about five minutes is all I want. I like to play ten shots on the offside and another ten on the legside and that is about it. Just to feel the bat on ball and play some well-timed shots is all I need. Then I sit down and think about the bowlers I am to face. Batting is basically easy: if you keep hitting the ball with the middle of your bat, you make runs.

*You were a boy wonder and made it. Many didn't, after showing similar promise. Why did you come through?*

I was very determined and I aimed high. I always tell a youngster to give all he has got in the first two years of his senior career. If he fails, he should get out and take up another profession. Do not hang around for several more years hoping to get better. It does not happen.

*When you scored 260 against England at the Oval in 1987, you looked desperately disappointed when you were caught and bowled by Graham Dilley. Hadn't you had enough after ten hours at the crease?*

I was after two records—the 364 by Sir Leonard Hutton at the Oval and the 365 not out by Sir Gary Sobers that remains the highest score in Tests. I want to beat that before I retire. That came into my mind when I got to 280 not out at Hyderabad against India, then Imran declared and robbed me of the chance. Whenever I pass a hundred in a Test, my mind sets itself for 366, not just two hundred. You only get the chance once or twice, and I know that I am capable of it. People ask me about Hanif Mohammad's 499, but I think that 366 in a Test is more impressive than 500 in a first-class match. I was really annoyed when Dilley got me out at the Oval because I had taken fresh guard while Imran played the shots and I knew that Dilley was going off with an injured ankle at the end of his over. With Neil Foster also injured, that meant England's two fast bowlers would be missing and it was set up for me. I had decided to bat in sessions and worked out that I would have my 300 by the close. With Imran having decided to bat on until lunchtime on the third day, I had the record there for the taking. But then Dilley bowled me a slower one and I pushed too hard at it. I was really annoyed at myself.

*What is your best innings in terms of personal satisfaction?*

It was a one-day innings against India in Sharja. Remember that a game between India and Pakistan is always special to us, in the way that England v Australia is for you. In the final, they got 245 in their fifty overs and we started badly. At one stage we needed nine an over and although Abdul Qadir helped me add a few, wickets kept falling at the other end. Chetan Sharma began the last over with us needing twelve to win and just two wickets left. I was on strike and got seven off the next three balls. Then my partner Zulqarnain was bowled. Off the fifth ball Tauseef Ahmed stopped the ball with his bat and we ran a suicidal single—he could easily have been run out. So I was on strike needing four to win. I hit a big six over mid-wicket. It was a pressure innings. I finished 116 not out, but only twenty of them came in boundaries. I had to run many sharp singles in great heat. I feel I won that game single-handedly, and I was very proud.

*In common with all Pakistani players, you are in favour of neutral umpires in Tests. Bearing in mind that you were dismissed lbw for the first time after 35 Tests in Pakistan, do you think there is a danger that neutral umpires might be more inclined to give you out that way?*

Everyone worries about the standard of umpiring when they tour, and neutral umpires would solve that. As for the lbws—I am not often out that way wherever I play. In three series in England I have been out lbw only once, in the last series in West Indies not at all, and the same applied to the last series in New Zealand. That is another myth about me.

*Getting those two hundreds in the West Indies in 1988 must have been a major boost.*

If you want to be reckoned in the game as a batsman, you have got to do it against the best attack in the world. They really test your technique, your courage and your temperament. It was about time that I got hundreds against them.

*You have not exactly been a raging success as Pakistan's captain, as it passes back and forth between you and Imran. Have you given it away for good now?*

Yes. I just want to play as a batsman now and serve under Imran. The young players in the side look up to us and I want to do what is best for the team. I was not really happy as captain, and after achieving the ambition in 1981 I was not all that bothered about leading my country again. I think Pakistan will be a great side soon. All our batsmen are young and we have a balanced bowling line-up as good as any in world cricket. We have two fast left-arm bowlers in Wasim Akram and Saleem Jaffer, then there is Imran Khan. We have the leg-spin of Abdul Qadir and the off-breaks of Tauseef Ahmed. So if it turns we have two terrific spinners, if the ball swings we have Imran and Wasim, and if the pitch is fast and bouncy our three pace men are sharp enough. Our wicket-keeper Saleem Youssuf is good enough to bat in the first three, and we have several all-rounders. I think Pakistan will soon be on par with the West Indies. We now have the bowlers.

*What can England learn from Pakistan in developing young players?*

Test cricket sorts you out, but we never kick out our young players even though they are out of form. We stick with class. Some English experts blame overseas players for causing the standards to drop, but surely playing alongside Viv Richards or Richard Hadlee must have helped English county players? The biggest names in English cricket now are English players, and yet the standard of their national side is very low. Overseas players are irrelevant.

*You had to leave the New Zealand tour early in 1989 with a serious back injury. How did it happen, and is it going to clear up?*

I was having fielding practice on the morning of a one-day international when I bent down to pick up a ball and the back just locked. I had been troubled by back problems for a few years, but this was much worse. I had treatment from a Harley Street specialist and he ordered a complete rest from cricket for six months. I have done a lot of swimming and weight training and I will be ready for the next round of Test matches.

*Ready to fulfil a few more ambitions. What are they?*
There are two of them. To beat Sobers' 365 in a Test and the record Test aggregate of runs set by Sunil Gavaskar. I am about 3,000 runs short, but I will do it. It is important to me, so I will just keep going.

# JACK SIMMONS

**'As I limped back to the pavilion, 40-odd not out, I heard a member say: "Old Jack still enjoys it—they're going to have to shoot him, aren't they?"'**

IF Sir Neville Cardus were alive today, his fanciful pen would do flowery justice to one cricketer who until he retired in 1989, rendered a great service to his beloved Lancashire. For Jack Simmons is as much a part of Lancashire's woof and warf as the twitching net curtains down Coronation Street. Jack was an anachronism, a spinner still thriving in an age when seam bowling dominates, a genuine sportsman at a time when it is fashionable to get your pragmatic retaliation in first, a balanced human being who only uses the word pressure when the conversation moves on to more important matters like unemployment or death. The only pretentious act of Jack's life was try the Cambridge Diet a couple of years ago. But the reduction of that comfortable girth soon brought howls of protest from cricket's conservationists. Now he saves the fruit salads and white wine and soda for the winter—a summer without a dip into the Jack Simmons Fish Supper Guide would be unthinkable. He regularly sees off the youthful challenge of Mike Gatting in the Trencherman of the Year contest, but no one deserves more his seat at top table. Jack thrived on hard work out in the middle and his statistical status as the second-best all-rounder in Lancashire's history underlines his value. Yet beneath the genial banter there is a strong, competitive streak. Over the years Jack has sold his wicket dearly from all parts of the batting order, and with his unrelenting, miserly slow-medium bowling, he has one of the outstanding records in limited overs cricket. His flair for captaincy found its outlet a decade ago, on the other side of the world, when he led Tasmania to an improbable victory in the Gillette Cup final, ensuring an important psychological breakthrough for that Cinderella state's players as they tried to come to terms with superior opposition and inherent feelings of inferiority. With his deep love of cricket, his battle-hardened temperament and his unforced ability to inspire younger players, Jack Simmons would seem to have been ideal captaincy material for Lancashire. Why does he think he was passed over for the job so many times?

I've been close to it a few times, I've been vice-captain for years. A few people said it was because I didn't go to the right school—there was a time when that was important at Old Trafford—but I don't think that was the case in my time. I was most disappointed when John Abrahams got the job; I was forty-three, but my age was irrelevant because since I turned forty I've played the best cricket of my career. There is no substitute for experience. In the last few years my bowling has developed a lot more flight and guile and I'm still taking my share of catches. After my success as Tasmania's captain, I was asked about the Lancashire job when I came back to Old Trafford. I said it was different over here, because we're all professionals and didn't need an old head so much. Perhaps I talked myself out of the captaincy by saying that, I don't know. I suppose it's my biggest disappointment in cricket, much more so than not playing for England, because the Lancashire captaincy was more realistic.

*Perhaps your unpunctuality might have told against you?*
Yes, it's true I tend to be a few minutes late, but people forget that I'll stay on for more than an hour in the evening when all the others have gone. That makes up for being a shade unpunctual earlier in the day, in my book. Anyway, I may be easy-going, but not on the field.

*Are you surprised that your career has lasted so long?*
To a certain extent, but I'm a great believer in enjoyment helping the time pass quickly. I've loved the life of a county cricketer, meeting up with old friends on the circuit, catching up on all the gossip. There *is* a generation gap for me now, though. I've noticed it in the past couple of years as the likes of Norman Gifford and Keith Fletcher have packed up playing and I find myself looking for the umpires for a chat when I walk into the bar. They're the same age group as me and we have the same attitudes to the game. A lot of the younger players don't even watch the cricket now. They walk around with those Sony Walkmans on their heads, listening to music.

*Has the leg-pulling from the youngsters got more painful in recent years?*
Not really, although they do call me "Uncle Jack" or even Grandad at times! I think there is still respect. I feel good when I've had to face up to responsibility on the field and come through it well. I'll always take the flak when the batters are handing out the stick and the younger bowlers are not keen on getting whacked. It's important to me that I can still do the job and not worry about being hit for six. It is natural for me to aim for line and length and then build on my confidence to be able to land the ball on the spot. The younger bowlers know I can still do that.

*Has the biggest change in your time been in behaviour on the field?*
Yes—and sadly there's a lack of natural sportsmanship now. I can't name ten who "walk" today, whereas when I started in 1968, you'd be hard-pressed to find the same amount who would stand there and brazen it out. I blame the extra money involved, the current social attitudes and the experience of English players who go abroad in the winter and see how little the umpires are helped by the modern cricketer. The Aussies will blatantly tell you they don't walk, and they don't expect you to give it away either. It's the same in Pakistan and India. When I started with Lancashire, I was told: "Son, you walk here and don't forget it." Only once have I stayed when I knew I'd touched the ball. It was in a Sheffield Shield game in Australia when I was captain of Tasmania. I

got so incensed at the opposition batsmen turning round at the end of the over and admitting they'd nicked it while justifying their refusal to walk off, that I decided to stand my ground. I tried a pull shot, followed the ball round and gloved it to the wicketkeeper. He and I were the only two who knew categorically that I'd gloved the ball, but I stayed put. Then I thought "What have I done?" and got out soon afterwards. I deliberately hit the ball in the air.

*Have you been tempted to follow the modern trend in English cricket and leave it to the umpire to decide?*

No, because we ought to help the umpire if possible. I'm also proud of my good name in cricket and I want to live up to the standards drummed into me all those years ago. Once Paul Downton caught me and I walked without waiting for the umpire to make what would have been a very difficult decision. The Middlesex lads said to me afterwards "Jack, you didn't hit that," but I'd heard a noise. I went off in preference to being called a cheat.

*Is that why you were so annoyed at Stuart Fletcher in the Roses match against Yorkshire in 1987 when you were suspended for a week after publicly calling him a cheat?*

There were contributory factors that made me cranky that day. I was annoyed that Yorkshire didn't seem to want to risk defeat in going for victory. I'd been on the Cambridge Diet for a few months as well as packing up smoking, so I was frayed at the edges. Above all, my mother had died two days before the incident and it hit me hard. She was to be buried next day and at the time of the Fletcher incident I had taken a few wickets and wanted as many as I could get in that innings as my own personal farewell to my mother. Their last pair were together, they were hopelessly adrift of the run chase and we had plenty of overs left. Fletcher got a big thick inside edge, it looped off his pad and the catch was taken close in. The umpire said not out and none of us could believe that Fletcher hadn't joined us in walking off, because it was such a routine dismissal. So I walked down the pitch and called him a cheat—the first time I've ever done that. I said nothing to the umpire, incidentally. Well, Yorkshire hung on for an undeserved draw and I stayed livid for the longest period of my life. After the game a reporter caught me on the dressing-room phone, making the funeral arrangements, and he asked me if Fletcher had cheated and I said he had. Guess where I went that night? To speak at a dinner in Huddersfield—where Stuart Fletcher learnt his cricket! I was still seething and everyone there knew it. So the balloon went up and my comment to the reporter was printed. I suppose it was fair enough that I got a week's suspension but I would have taken my case to the Players' Union if I had been fined. Many members of the Lancashire committee said to me "You were bloody right, Jack." Stuart Fletcher and I have settled our differences over a drink, but the fundamental point about that row is that it would never have happened at the start of my career. The batsman would have been off like a shot.

*So you are not exactly genial Jack out there?*

I'll give someone the long stare if I think they are out of order, especially the cocky youngsters who might be thinking "who's this old bugger then?" I don't go in for all this sledging stuff—the only thing I've ever said to a lucky batsman is "have you backed any horses today?" I pride myself on my competitive streak. If I was told that the batsmen needed just one run to win with twenty overs left, I'd battle like hell to get them out. If I'm the last man and we need 200 to win, no one will get me out easily—and I'll make sure my batting partner feels the same way. You see, I was given responsibility early on when I played in the Lancashire leagues. At the age of nineteen I was a professional, the only paid player in the side, the bloke who has to win the games. I ended up opening the innings despite being the youngest player in the team, and the responsibility did me a lot of good. By the time I broke through into county cricket at the age of 28, I'd been through a hard, competitive school and I was mentally ready for the first-class game.

*In Lancashire you're an institution, but over in Tasmania you're still a folk hero after your deeds as captain in the late Seventies. Did it feel strange to be so idolised so far from home?*

The biggest thrill of my career came when we won the Gillette Cup. I ran off the pitch, punching the air like a footballer, for heaven's sake. I ran straight to my wife to give her a big hug and a kiss, oblivious to the sight of my rival captain, John Inverarity, standing alongside with his hand out, waiting to congratulate me. We'd broken through—all 600,000 folk in Tasmania knew that at last their cricketers were somebodies. That warmth between the people and myself has lasted ever since. I never need to hire a car when I'm out there, one is always placed at my disposal and I'm treated like a king wherever I go. Last Christmas I took some young Blackpool cricketers to Tasmania and we were treated superbly. I'm very proud that they remember what I helped them achieve all those years ago and I have to admit there's still an emotional pull coming. I keep wondering whether I could achieve as much again if I were full-time coach or manager, or was it all a fluke? I'd love to find out one day.

*I suppose the biggest challenge was to get the Tasmanian players to believe in themselves after being the whipping boys for the other State sides.*

That took two years. They were so defeatist when I first joined them. I talked to them about positive attitudes and they would turn around and say "There's a party on tonight, Jack—are you coming?" Now I've never been one to miss out on a party, but I'd chide them, saying they were about to play in a first-class match, that it could be the highlight of their careers. They would say "Yes, Jack, but we're going to get beaten anyway, so let's enjoy the piss-up." I still went with them to the parties, but I think they didn't drink so much when I was around!

*Winning a Sheffield Shield match for the first time was another major breakthrough.*

And even sweeter, because Western Australia were the top side around. I have never been so tired walking off a cricket field that day after Roger Woolley and I had added so many runs to win by four wickets. We faced a big target in the final knock and I knew they were so unused to a big game that there was no point in aiming too high. So I told the lads just to bat through a session at a time, because they lacked the confidence to bat for an entire day. We had four sessions to get the runs, the wicket was easy-paced and the atmosphere from the crowd was fantastic. They kept pouring into the Devonport ground as news of our performance spread around the island. Roger and I played and missed a lot—I've got a grainy video of it somewhere—and we needed luck to pull through. But we did it and the joy was unbelievable. David Boon was twelfth man for us that day—he was only a boy, and I've watched his career with great pride. He came to me for coaching and he was almost like a son. David couldn't get enough of cricket and

146

he deserves his success. It still takes a lot for a Tasmanian player to get picked for Australia. The other Aussie players give them a bit of stick still—they think it's just bush country—but there's a lot of talent on that island. They are in the same position as Western Australia a few decades back—and look at them now, they are the top state.

*I know that we all love to pigeon-hole players, but the "Flat Jack" description is a little out of date now, isn't it?*

I'm glad to say that I'm a far better bowler than in the days when I'd tie up one end by firing the ball in at just under medium pace. That's not what I'd call spin bowling, and I've been very happy at the way I've adapted in recent years. I was proud to be Lancashire's Player of the Year at the age of 47 because I'd kept pace with the modern game. Gone are the days when I could bowl tightly at the likes of Tom Graveney, Colin Cowdrey and Geoffrey Boycott. They would play me "through the V", stroking the ball straight to mid-on or mid-off, and I'd settle for not being taken apart. Today someone like Mike Gatting would reverse sweep a good-length off-break, or Ian Botham would simply hit me straight out of the ground. The way that batsmen improvise nowadays means the bowler has to come up with something fresh or he is smashed out of the firing line. I've simply got more confident as I've got older; I watched how the likes of Ray Illingworth, Derek Underwood and Norman Gifford could compete by offering more subtlety and extra flight and I've tried to do the same. I've become more philosophical—if I get hit for six, so what? When it's a batsman like Ian Botham, I feel it's a privilege to be on the same field. I've seen Botham play some astonishing innings and I've loved my duels with him. He is a remarkable cricketer, a great natural talent.

*Isn't your career a classic example of the value a county can get from a good spinner?*

We keep turning up for pre-season training, don't we? We're no different from fast bowlers in the need for a strong pair of legs and a big backside to help us keep going. A good, experienced spinner is harder to hit than a medium pacer. By and large we are more accurate and the spinner should have a few men out in the deep for the mishit. The medium pacer doesn't usually bother with that, so that if his field is pierced, it's often another boundary. There are still some good spinners around, even though modern captains seem to be obsessed with seamers. John Emburey, of course—although he seems to be lacking in confidence. I rate Vic Marks very highly, a slow bowler rather than a spinner in the Emburey mould. Vic gets Somerset out of the cart time and again and I don't think he gets the credit he deserves. He flights the ball so well and he has a well-disguised quicker ball. As for me, I'd like to be remembered as a spinner who got over a thousand wickets in first-class cricket at a time when we weren't fashionable rather than as Flat Jack of the limited overs game. I'm pleased I've survived when so many class batsmen have shown their improvisation by messing up a spinner's line and playing him through unorthodox areas. It eventually dawned on me that bowling the same six balls in a row isn't enough.

*Despite the way the game has changed, do you still love it as much?*

Oh yes, I still get a thrill coming off the field having done well. At Old Trafford we're grooming Dexter Fitton to take my place in the first team but I shall continue to make it difficult to pick him instead of me for as long as possible. That's not to say I won't help him, because I will always advise a team-mate, but my professional pride keeps me going. I remember a couple of years ago I had to bat with a runner because of an injury.

They sent out Graeme Fowler, which wasn't a bad deal, considering he's just about the fastest thing on two legs in the championship. Anyway, I managed to scrape a few with Graeme running for me and I limped back to the pavilion with forty-odd to my name—not out as well. I overheard a member say to his mate: "You know, old Jack still enjoys it—they're going to have to shoot him, aren't they?" Do you know, I think they might have to!

*Did you think you might still be playing county cricket at the age of fifty?*
I finally had to give way at 48. Lancashire need to give Dexter Fitton first-team experience, even though I set out my stall to stay in the side. I know Ray Illingworth came back for Yorkshire and played in the one-dayers when he was past fifty, but I'll miss not playing in the three-day matches. In the field I always contrive to have young lads on either side of me if there's any chasing to be done, but I can still catch them in the gully and my arm's still good—I ran out Bill Athey from mid-on last season and I loved telling him he shouldn't take risks against me! It will be like losing an arm. I will miss the fun in the dressing-room, the occasional day when it all works on the field, and the friendly faces on either side of the boundary rope around the county circuit. I suppose at this stage I'm like the woman who is heavily pregnant: I've at last got used to the inevitable.

# CHRIS TAVARE

**' I am less patient than I used to be; I want to see a few more runs on the board in my first hour at the crease. '**

CHRIS Tavare's recall to the England team in 1989 after a five-year absence gave the wags a chance to dust down one of cricket's hoarier jokes: *The scene: the obligatory desert island.*

*The year: 1989.*

*The marooned survivor is at last rescued, just before he eats his devoted Man Friday. He bombards his rescuers with questions. Is Margaret Thatcher still monarch of all she surveys? Are the Prince of Wales and his beautiful bride still living happily ever after? Has Ronald Reagan answered a question yet at a Press conference? Is Chris Tavare still batting for England? When the last question gets an affirmative, he says: "Sod it, I'm staying here."*

This is the kind of jibe that Tavare himself would enjoy. Despite an apparent ascetism, his dry humour does include a healthy amount of self-mockery. He knows his barn-door defence has driven many cricket fans to distraction, yet he is too tolerant a fellow to defend himself with any great zeal. So the statisticians punch the computer button marked Tavare and out tumbles the damning evidence: The only batsman to fail to score a single run in an hour twice in the same innings; the slowest fifty in English first-class cricket; the second slowest half-century in all first-class cricket. Truly a stone-waller in the Whitehall class.

When Tavare was brought back to stiffen England's middle order, many Australian players and their travelling media were astonished. They could only recall a limited batsman of inexhaustible patience and minimal footwork, a man who had bored for England. When he twice fell cheaply at Edgbaston, the Aussies shelved their analogies with paint-drying and expressed relief that once again sleep would not come easily during an England innings. All that was unfair to Tavare. By that fourth Test England badly needed some resolution sandwiched between the butterfly charm of David Gower

and the macho efforts of Ian Botham. Tavare's ability to play for the team and to draw the teeth of penetrative bowling was widely admired. His unselfishness has been a byword in the England ranks; Ian Botham, his very antithesis, never tired of praising Tavare. Eighteen of his thirty-one Tests saw him open the innings, a position for which he did not care, yet he never uttered a word of complaint. When the game's situation demanded, he could smoothly go up a gear and play dynamically, as Bruce Yardley found to his cost at Melbourne in 1982.

Chris Tavare has never been one to trumpet his virtues via the mass media, so few outside the masonic inner circle of county cricket would be aware of the quality of his cricket brain. He has been one of the sharpest tacticians in the English game in recent years, yet he only had two seasons to prove it. After guiding Kent to a couple of one-day finals at Lord's, he was cruelly sacked in favour of the latest member of the Cowdrey dynasty. Tavare kept his own counsel on that piece of blood-letting, stayed another four years at Kent, then linked up at Somerset with his great friend from Oxford days, Vic Marks. With retirement approaching, was Tavare getting rather skittish in his approach to batting?

I do like to get on with it earlier now. I am not as keen on batting long periods as I used to be, and I use a lot more bottom hand to punch the shots away. When I moved to Somerset I decided to enjoy my cricket a little more and not get so wound up in technicalities. I am less patient than I used to be; I want to see a few more runs on the board in my first hour at the crease. I used to restrict myself on certain shots, telling myself that I would play a few more as my innings developed, setting myself to bat for a long time. Now I play them a lot earlier. I have never been a great square cutter, but now I am setting myself for the shot. When I have played well for Somerset, it has given me more satisfaction than at any other time in my career. But I have had to come to terms with being more inconsistent.

*Were you surprised to be recalled by England in 1989?*

I was, because most of my best knocks had come in the one-day games and I had been inconsistent in the championship matches. It was nice to be back in the England fold again, but I did not take my chance, and that was that. The 1989 Aussies were just like any other Australian side with their tails up. They were very confident and aggressive, as you would expect when their batsmen keep piling up such big totals.

*What differences in the Test Match atmosphere did you notice after an interval of five years?*

It remains a very big occasion and a very public one. On the county circuit there is a bit of a crowd and a small group of journalists, but in Tests you are so much more open to public scrutiny. The television is on all the time, all the major cricket writers from both countries are there—and that is an extra pressure you tend to forget about when you have been out of it for a time. You just have to accept criticism when it is justified, and hope your team-mates appreciate you. After all, you get the accolades when you do well. Success is so important in today's society, and cricket is part of that society.

*How did you steel yourself to ignore the barracking when you were in one of your obdurate moods?*

I have always been a good concentrator—all that pacing around the wicket helps. It only bothered me when I played badly. The worst time for England was the Lord's Test of 1984 against Sri Lanka, when Chris Broad and I added 49 in 27 overs between lunch and tea. It was a good, flat wicket and I got bogged down. Chris got sucked into the criticism, but as the senior player, I must bear the responsibility. Chris just missed out on the tour to India, and that innings against the spinners told against him. I felt a little guilty about that. The press wanted someone to blame after Sri Lanka played so well against us. We were expected to hammer them after being badly beaten by the West Indies, but the wicket was easy-paced and we just could not get their bowlers away against defensive field-placings. I was out of form as well: I got away with it at the Oval, when the fast wicket and the speed of the West Indian bowlers allowed me to play the ball away through the gaps, but that did not work against bowlers of a slower pace at Lord's.

*What happens to you psychologically in such circumstances? Do you fight the temptation to throw your wicket away?*

That is a difficult one. It is still a Test Match, and you want to bat in the way that gained you England recognition. In that innings against Sri Lanka, I finally lost patience, took on the leg-spinner and was caught at long-on. On other occasions I have had the likes of Ian Botham, Allan Lamb, Derek Randall or David Gower blazing away at the other end, so there was no need to do the same. For most of my time with England we needed an anchorman at one end because we had so many strokemakers. But I was not always slow. My two Test hundreds (at Delhi and the Oval) both came in reasonable time.

*That 89 you made at Melbourne in 1982 had much to do with England winning the Test. Was it a pre-arranged plan to get after Bruce Yardley?*

We felt the Australians were getting away with using Yardley both as a wicket-taker with his off-spin and also as a stock bowler. He was tying up one end so that the fast bowlers could have a prolonged rest. We decided to try to hit him out of the firing line to ensure the seamers were brought back early and that would tire them out quicker. It worked that day. I could not always bat like that in a Test—it all depends on the relevant responsibilities. But it was nice to show the other side of my batting.

*In more than half of your England appearances, you had to bat out of position as an opener. How big a problem was that?*

I have always wanted about twenty minutes to get myself mentally prepared to bat, so number three was always my preference. It was difficult being in the field, standing at slip, concentrating on the possibility of a catch, then dashing off to get ready to open the batting. I like to sit down, get my mind right about the bowlers and assess how the wicket is playing. If we won the toss and batted first, that would be the same, as there would be no real difference between opening and going in at number three: either way, I had enough time for mental preparation. Having said all that, it was a great honour to play for England and I would have batted anywhere. I was always aware that, had it not been for the ban on players who had gone to South Africa, I would not have played so many Tests.

*You may have struggled to up the tempo in some Tests, but that never seemed a problem in one-day matches. What was your mental approach to the one-day innings?*

Simply a matter of *having* to get on with it. In the longer game it is a case of picking the time to go up a gear, but you have no choice in the one-day matches. You just pump yourself up and try to make it happen. You cannot get the adrenalin flowing quite so easily in the three-day games, because they happen so regularly.

*How do you stop getting too keyed up, so that you lose judgement on your stroke selection?*

I find that happens to me more and more these days. I have bursts of adrenalin and it is hard to rein myself in after playing a lot of shots. It is easy to lose control, so you try to get into a pattern of play that makes you feel confident and in command.

*Is it true that you were quite a shot-maker in your early days in Kent?*

I used to play a few shots and then get aggressive later in the innings. But when I went to Oxford, I soon realised that I could not get away with so much against better, quicker bowlers. If I wanted to make a living out of cricket, I had to adapt. I used to have a huge backlift, and in my first season with Oxford I struggled with it against the quicker bowlers. Then I started to work hard at my defence, because I knew I just had to get used to spending long periods at the crease. I aimed to be there for an hour, then think about increasing my range of shots.

*Your grip on the bat has attracted a lot of attention over the years. Basically, the top hand doesn't face the bowler like it is supposed to. The palm grips the bat on your side. How much has that restricted your strokeplay?*

Not a great deal. If you look around, there are all sorts of grips and they do not stop batsmen playing freely. As a youngster, my grip was similar; otherwise I would not have been able to adjust to the fine tuning I adopted at Oxford. I lost a bit of power—not due to my grip, but because I used less bottom hand. I found that too much bottom hand was hampering me against the quicker bowlers, so that whenever I played an attacking shot, it was noticeable that the top hand alone provided the power. I would have played that way irrespective of the grip.

*Is there one outstanding memory from your career?*

That is easy. The day I batted with Ian Botham at Old Trafford against the Australians in 1981. That was the most amazing, moving experience of my career. It was not just because of Ian's batting, but the way he transformed the atmosphere. We had been pretty boring on the Saturday morning, but as soon as Ian walked out on to the pitch, the crowd roared him on. Once he got going, the atmosphere was absolutely electric. He played a couple of sketchy shots over cover, then Mike Whitney missed that horrible steepler at mid-off. But apart from that it was an outstanding knock in technical terms. I just played my usual way at the other end and tried not to be too distracted by the fantastic atmosphere. I always loved batting with Ian: you can have a laugh with him, he relaxes you, he appreciates his partner and gives a lot of encouragement. He has a great natural talent and has turned matches that you have almost lost. It was a privilege to bat with him that day at Old Trafford.

*You left Kent after batting very well in the 1988 season and seeing them miss out narrowly on the championship. How big a wrench was it to leave?*

153

Huge, after putting my heart and soul into Kent cricket for so many years. I also appreciate I left myself open to criticism for leaving in the year of my benefit. I have never made public my reasons for going, and I shall not do so.

*Some feel it was because you were sacked as Kent captain after failing two years in a row to win the NatWest Cup.*
That was not the case. I know that for sure.

*You were criticised for taking off Derek Underwood in the 1984 final when he had established a stranglehold over the Middlesex batsmen. When he came back, it was too late and you lost off the last ball of the game. Was that a tactical error on your part?*
If it was, I had been making the same mistake for the past two seasons. Richard Ellison had six overs left and I wanted to break that up, because I did not want anyone having to bowl six overs on the trot when the pressure was on later in the innings. They still needed six an over throughout the last ten, in poor light. They needed seven off the final over, and it came down to the last ball of the match. I felt perfectly happy about the tactics and have not thought about it since. Why change the formula that had got us to the final two years in a row?

*How much did you enjoy captaining a county side?*
I got a great deal of satisfaction out of getting the best out of players, going to Lord's twice in a row, and getting into the habit of winning big games. It takes time to learn the captaincy trade, but I was fortunate to have the advice of experienced men like Alan Knott, Graham Johnson and Bob Woolmer. A captain does not have all the answers; the lines of communication must remain open.

*How long will you stay in the game?*
I only signed for Somerset for one year. I will not be playing much longer, because things outside cricket are becoming just as important. I am far more relaxed about what I want out of cricket now and I know that career doors tend to shut as you get older. My cricket career might be dictated by events outside the game. When you have played professional cricket for any length of time, you are not really exposed to the business world. But my slight experience of it tells me that money is tight and that people expect results. Rather like modern professional cricket.

*Has the standard improved in your time in the English game?*
I believe it has. When I joined Kent, a handful of sides were very successful. But now all seventeen can give the others a good game if necessary. It is so much more competitive. Every county side has learned how to play the one-day game in particular. I find the one-day game is so pressurised now. The older players say that they played more and still produced great performances, but we often end up exhausted after a one-day match or the final afternoon of a championship game. Cricket needs a mental input as well as a physical one, and if you are drained you have problems. In other words, bring in four-day cricket, so we can all play properly and treat each game as a special occasion. We should not be able to think "tomorrow will do" if we fail today.

# RAVI
# SHASTRI

**'I always try to remain a sportsman, but if my side has not given a hundred per cent on the field, I am very difficult company. '**

MANY *talented cricketers consistently under-achieve due to the pressing need for a frontal lobotomy, but Ravi Shastri will never come into that category. He has always appeared a hard-headed cricketer, fully aware of the game's practicalities. When he toured England for the first time with the senior Indian side, he was just twenty, yet he met Test Match demands to the manner born. Even then he was earmarked for the captaincy of his country. Shastri has simply bided his time for that honour as it passed between Kapil Dev, Sunil Gavaskar and Dilip Vengsarkar. It was no surprise that, in his first Test as captain, Shastri led India to a sensational win over the West Indies in 1987, and few would bet against a long tenure in the job. Shastri's all-round skills, a dignified calmness that masks loathing of defeat, and an air of detachment from his team-mates all equip him for the special demands of Test captaincy. The son of a doctor and a university professor, this graduate in commerce from Bombay University has never allowed himself to be sucked into the modern maelstrom of surliness and synthetic aggression. His deportment in the colours of Glamorgan has been equally impressive. A county hardly noted for the calibre of its recent overseas captures finally managed to find a jewel in Shastri. Colleagues positively jostle with each other to rhapsodise about his keenness to help the most inexperienced player, to embrace willingly the responsibilities of the well-paid star turn. Many felt Shastri was ill-served when Glamorgan signed Viv Richards in 1989 but the Indian accepted the situation philosophically. He knows that at 27 he has more top-class cricket left in him than King Viv, especially now that illness has delayed the West Indian's Glamorgan debut for a year. A left-arm spinner good enough to score Test hundreds in the Caribbean can view Viv's occasional pryotechnics on the county circuit with a fair degree of phlegm. It seems odd that a batsman of Shastri's technical competence and coolness should share a record with Sir Gary Sobers that cannot be surpassed for cyclonic hitting—sixes off every one of a six-ball over. There are many*

*other contemporaries ahead of Shastri that one would pick to stand alongside the great Sobers but the Indian did it while plundering the fastest double hundred in cricket history. It was January, 1985, Bombay v Baroda in the Ranji Trophy, and the unlucky bowler purveying flattish left-arm spin was one Tilak Raj. Predictably, Shastri's memories of that over remain undimmed.*

It was a flat wicket and he was bowling quickish left-arm stuff, not the traditional Bishen Bedi style. Tilak Raj was more of a batsman but he was one of the hardest guys to score off in the leagues in New Delhi, so it was no piece of cake. He had already bowled Sunny Gavaskar for 49 that day and when Sunny told me he was soon going to declare I thought I would go for broke. I was also in very good nick—a few days earlier I had batted a long time to get a hundred against England in the Calcutta Test which followed a century in a one-day international against them. To the first two balls of that over, I went down the track and hit him over long-on, and the third went flat over mid-wicket as he fired it in at the leg stump. The fourth six was the best of all. The keeper went down the pitch to talk to the bowler and I guessed he had told him to fire it down the leg side. I went even wider, I was ready for it and the ball ended up ten seats back over the square leg boundary. For the first time I started to think about the Sobers record and the fifth went a long way, between mid-on and mid-wicket. By then the bowler was in quite a state and I knew the ball was in his court so I had to guess what he would try. All kinds of permutations were possible—a bouncer, a full toss—so I tried to get into a position where I could get a bat on it whatever he bowled. He sent down a yorker on the off-stump. I was outside leg at the time. I reached across and flat-batted it over the sightscreen at long-on. I had to lean into the shot and it never rose more than thirty feet. I did a little war dance of delight, not just because Sobers was one of my heroes but because I had been criticised for my slow batting in the previous Test and it was nice to show another facet of my game.

*You were hardly known for the flashing blade at the stage in your career. You were an orthodox, correct batsman.*

Well, I had always known I could whack the ball if the occasion demanded it, but at that time the only way I could get a big score was by playing correctly. I have developed my shots as I have got older. The experience of county cricket has helped.

*You are an all-rounder of acknowledged Test class, but isn't there a danger of falling between two stools and not doing yourself justice?*

It is not easy. I do not see any all-rounder in world cricket managing to be brilliant with both bat and ball for more than about two years at a time—it is just too much of a physical strain. In my case it is particularly hard because I am now batting at number three for India and I cannot then go out and bowl thirty overs to the standard I set myself. In a sense my batting orthodoxy tells against me because I have to bat against the new ball, but at least I could hold my own in the first four for India if it ever came to it and I did not bowl a ball. No one can carry on performing miracles as an all-rounder year in year out. The great Sobers needed a rest and that's why he batted at number six in the days when it was less pressurised. Ian Botham, who has been a magnificent all-rounder, has had mediocre series with the bat or ball, even though his overall record is tremendous. The physical demands of Test cricket have contributed to the aggressive way that Botham, Richard Hadlee and Kapil Dev have batted over the years, because they know they cannot bat for the best part of a day, then be expected to fire out the top

157

order with the ball. Only Imran Khan among the recent great all-rounders batted like a front-rank specialist. But even then he would come in around number seven after a long rest.

*Your bowling seems to be getting flatter and more mechanical: are you worried about that?*

Yes. I want to get more wickets as I approach my peak. I need to be active in the game so I must develop in my bowling. I am very strong on the mental side of cricket. I like to watch videos of batsmen I am due to bowl at, and look back on games where I bowled well and work out why. Then I get in the nets and try things out, even on my own if necessary. But the efficiency of the Test player is declining because we do not get enough time off to practise and refine our technique. If I could manage six months off, I would be a better bowler after ironing out in the nets what had gone wrong in the previous year. Now I find I'm trying things out in matches that I would rather attempt in the nets. That is asking a lot.

*Therefore your spell in county cricket doesn't help your desire to sort out your bowling in the long term.*

It is a different part of the learning process, though, and I will be a better cricketer for it. The cold weather is a problem. If I field a stinging straight drive it hurts me more than if I were English. I have to learn from such a tough environment. It is a great education coming up against so many great batsmen.

*How long do you intend to stay in county cricket?*

As long as I am motivated. I will not go through the motions, I will tell the side before they spot that. The physical aspect is not as hard as the mental one—a sportsman should be fit, after all—but playing all the year round is hard. There are no problems about competing in the Glamorgan side with Viv Richards, when he is fit next year. We have been friends for years. I have admired him so much, it will be a privilege to be in the same dressing-room. I think Richards and Botham have been the two great entertainers of my time.

*How do you manage to keep your emotions in check on the field when the atmosphere is so highly charged?*

My parents were very hot on discipline right from the start, but do not be fooled that I am always cool. My friends will tell you that I hate losing and that I snap back at them if they try to console me. I will always try to remain a sportsman and play within the rules but I would throw my shirt in to win a game. If my side has not given a hundred per cent on the field, I am very difficult company.

*I suppose the West Indians are the current side that really concentrate your mind?*

Yes. I always want to do really well against them and I am proud that I have scored hundreds over there in Tests on my last two tours. The adrenalin pumps automatically against them, yet as soon as the tour is over I wonder how I got through against that fast bowling barrage. You have to accept the constant pounding and work out the best way to combat it. I believe you should play within your limitations against them, and that means in my case staying there to wear them down. I believe that they will get you soon enough if you throw the bat, because they are just too good. I am proud of scoring almost a thousand runs and taking fifty wickets against the West Indies in Tests. They remain the true yardstick of ability.

*Will they remain so?*

I am not so sure. They have been lucky enough to have some great batsmen in their first six so that they could afford the luxury of four fast bowlers without needing an all-rounder. Soon their batting will not be strong enough for that, because everyone has an evening in their career. It is only a matter of time before they have to reshape the balance of their side. I also believe that spinners will come back into the mainstream because fast bowlers are being burned out by too much Test cricket. A genuine paceman cannot last very long now unless he is superbly fit and rations himself. Cricket is just like life. Things come round in cycles—and the spinner will return.

*What is it like being the object of so much attention in a country like India where cricket seems so important?*

The burden of expectation is huge, and you get mobbed if you venture into the street. I am not married so I am obviously the subject of all sorts of written fiction, but you just have to live with it. They turn against you very quickly if you fail. You get used to being booed as you walk out on to the field. I simply say to myself: "You've got the salt, you've got the onions, now show them you can do it." I like the challenge of turning boos into cheers. Throughout my career I have tried to make things happen. I am a great believer in destiny. When I missed out on the World Cup final in 1983 because they preferred the off-spin of Kirti Azad, I told myself I would make up for that. It was worse because we won the World Cup after I had played well in the earlier rounds. Every day after that, when I stepped on to the field for India, I vowed that one day I would play in a final. I finally did—in Australia, when India won the World Championship, featuring all the Test countries, and I was voted player of the tournament. I was hungry for success and that was sweet.

*The captaincy of India seems on the horizon for you after being talked about in that capacity for years. Do you really want it?*

Yes. It was a great thrill to beat the best side in the world on my debut as captain when Dilip Vengsarkar was injured. I am modest in many matters but I honestly think I'm good at the job. I have led every Indian team at various stages in my career, and as a believer in destiny I think you get what you deserve. Luckily, I have age in my favour. I would rather do it in my own time than lose it while still young. I can tell you that in the next three years, India will have one of the best sides in the world. We have had a pretty good decade—winning the World Cup and then reaching the semis in the next one—but that is just the start. Hirwani, the leg-spinner, will be a force, Manjrekar and Azharuddin will make stacks of runs, and we have a young batsman in Bombay called Sachin Tendulkar who is sent from upstairs to play the game. He is only fifteen, a right-hand bat, five feet four inches tall, but I tell you, he's going to be a great player. With players like him around, it would be a pleasure to lead India.

# PAUL
# DOWNTON

**'There are people around who want to damage you on the field because of the pressure to get results. Four-day cricket must be the answer.'**

IT is one of English cricket's ironies that a player of Paul Downton's ability and equable temperament should have aroused so much adverse comment in recent years. He is a man of unblemished sportsmanship, a sound batsman, a wicket-keeper good enough to stand in 22 consecutive Tests. Why do so many from the game's periphery judge such a civilised man so harshly? A combination of circumstances, certainly. Playing for Middlesex has never been a hardship when the port is passed around at England selection meetings and, under Peter May's chairmanship, there lingered the suspicion that nice chaps with impeccable table manners had more cause to look out for the envelope stamped London NW8. That is no fault of Paul Downton's, however, and anyone who saw his staunch batting in the West Indies at the outset of his Test career and against the same opposition in the 1984 series needs no reminders of his technical orthodoxy and steely temperament. Perhaps the timpani that greeted his introduction to county cricket crashed too loudly, too prematurely. When Downton pulled off a superb legside stumping off the medium pace of Asif Iqbal before the unimpressionable eyes of Alec Bedser, the then chairman of selectors marked him down for future greatness. Two months later, in September 1977, Downton was picked for the England tour of Pakistan and New Zealand while still a law undergraduate at Exeter University. Bedser, lapsing into uncharacteristic hyperbole, said the stumping off Asif had smacked of genius. At that time, Alan Knott and Bob Taylor deserved such a tribute rather than a twenty-year-old student, and Downton knew it. Those two set such a standard that any young pretender had to be out of the top drawer and Downton became the umpteenth to suffer premature eulogies. When he finally forced his way into the England side ahead of Knott and Taylor, Downton dropped a crucial catch at Trent Bridge in his first home Test. Allan Border ended up highest scorer in the game, Australia won by four wickets in a low-scoring contest and Downton was sent back to the county treadmill. Shades of Fred Tate and the Old

*Trafford Test of 1902. Downton was 27 before he settled into a long run as England's first-choice wicket-keeper, with Bob Taylor announcing his retirement because he had been so impressed by his successor's performance in the first Test of the 1984 summer. Yet within two years Downton had relinquished the gloves, as England embarked on a policy towards wicket-keeping that smacked of pins and blindfolds. When Downton has been subsequently recalled to the national colours, outrage became the predictable response. Luckily he is a balanced individual, with a proper grasp of life's perspectives, but surely even his serenity has been ruffled in recent years.*

Inevitably you get depressed when things are going badly, and you are aware of what people think of you because of the intense interest of the media nowadays. I remember Mike Hendrick giving me some down-to-earth advice when I made my home debut in the Trent Bridge Test, the one that nobody ever lets me forget because I dropped Allan Border. He told me simply to look at my selection on a daily basis and not worry about the future, just get on with the job. I was never afraid that I was playing in my last Test and just went out to enjoy it.

*Most England keepers in recent years have suffered from a lack of coherent policy towards the job. Could the current incumbent ever feel safe for the entire series?*

Not really. But don't forget the selectors were incredibly spoilt for so many years by having two such brilliant performers as Bob Taylor and Alan Knott. It was a fantastic achievement for Bob still to be keeping for England at the age of 42, and he and Knotty were so consistent. After them, anyone would suffer by comparison. We have all been in and out, haven't we? Jack Richards came in to bolster the batting, then he suffered a finger injury. Bruce French had the same problem. It did not make sense to me that Jack Russell went to Pakistan in 1987, but then had to give way to Jack Richards for the New Zealand tour a few weeks later. Just before that, I had come out of the pack for the World Cup, after batting well for Middlesex on some very good wickets at Lord's. Then I could not get a run in that competition. I was run out in the first match against the West Indies when feeling fine, but after that I had little chance to do anything other than come in with a few overs left and try to crash it around. It must have appeared a strange selection, but I am sure I would have scored some useful runs if I had had more time at the crease.

*The vituperation reached its height when you were brought back for the one-day internationals against West Indies in 1988. After doing well in those games, were you thinking "up yours" to your critics?*

Human nature to say yes, I suppose. I am not unduly sensitive about it, but it would have been nice if my value in those games had not been glossed over, after my defects had been minutely examined when I was selected. I felt that my plus points would be ignored in the way they were over-praised as I was making my way into the England side a few years earlier. We tend to need heroes and villains, don't we? Every writer needs an angle; you cannot just submit a bland report on a day's play any more. You then have the bandwagon effect—a young player gets talked into the England side after a few good innings, then after an early failure he is consigned to the rubbish bin by the same writers who pushed for him. It is very easy to spot players and get them in the England side, but much more difficult to keep faith with them after a few initial disappointments. That is why I felt terribly sorry for Jack Russell when he eventually made it. Most of the pundits were saying he was the best in the world before he had ever stood in a Test.

That put a lot of unfair pressure on him. I know that most of my Test career is behind me, but I still keep hoping. I was out of it for eighteen months between David Gower's last Test as captain in 1986 and my recall for the World Cup, and the difference in atmosphere was marked. In 1986 everyone was running for cover after we had been hammered in the West Indies by a superior side and the ludicrous allegations about women and drugs started to flow. We were all branded and Gower carried the can. When I returned to the fold, I was hugely impressed by the corporate solidity of the squad under Mike Gatting and Micky Stewart—two similar characters who made you feel you belonged, that they had kept in touch. I still think that is the same even though Gatt's no longer captain, so I tell myself that if I play consistently well there is always a chance.

*I have often thought that few of us are qualified to assess the merits of Jack Russell compared to yourself or Bruce French or anyone else, because it is such a specialised part of the game. Do you feel that way when the flak is flying?*

Absolutely right. No one other than another keeper knows what the fellow is thinking as the bowler runs in. Keeping wicket consistently well is the hardest aspect of first-class cricket because your errors are noticed and highlighted. A bowler can have a bad spell, a batsman plays a bad shot, but somehow such defects are not magnified. You are like the goalkeeper in soccer: you are distinctive because you wear pads and gloves. Few understand what it is like to expect to field 600 deliveries a day, only to be told you have had a bad day if you misfield a couple of them or spill a difficult, diving catch. Mental fatigue is the greater problem because your body gets into a particular shape for six hours of cricket each day. You have to learn how to relax in between deliveries, then go through the distinct mental process of focusing your mind as the bowler starts to run up. At the start of your career it is very difficult to learn how to concentrate behind the stumps for a day and a half.

*You shout a lot behind the stumps, don't you?*

I am a quiet sort off the field, but I feel that is expected of me when we are out there. A side needs someone to bubble, to jolly them along—Graham Barlow was brilliant at that when I first joined Middlesex. I now see it as my responsibility to ensure things do not go stale in the field. Even though a lot of what I say is just cheer-leading, I try to make sure we do not just go through the motions.

*Do you consider yourself a specialist keeper or a batsman/keeper?*

I am very wary of such categorisations. I have always been useful with the bat and the gloves but once you start to get runs you are categorised. The day I stumped Alan Butcher off Asif Iqbal (my first victim in first-class cricket, incidentally), I had already scored 31 not out, going in at number ten, but all the talk was about my stumping. The image suggested that I was the latest find from the Kent wicket-keeping stable and much was made of me standing up to Asif, compared to Knotty who preferred to stand back to the medium pace. My attitude is the same as it was then—I got into a county side as a specialist keeper and I've stayed there for the same reason. It is a point in my favour that I can bat but I would rather be thought of as a keeper. Although I have opened for Middlesex, there is an extra physical dimension involved if you also keep wicket. I suppose the ideal place for a keeper who can bat is number six: you don't want to be padded up half an hour after your innings has started, or have to bat out the last ten overs of the day after keeping wicket.

*All your contemporaries in county cricket can bat to a reasonable standard compared to previous eras, even if no one can do it as well as Les Ames. Does this lack of a specialist per se indicate a levelling off in standards of wicket-keeping?*

I don't think so. There is a greater emphasis on everyone getting a few runs these days. There are hardly any tail-enders who will give it a whack if the ball is tossed up. They are now encouraged to go to the nets and battle it out. The same applies to the keepers.

*How much does it bother you that you are considered more of a one-day performer at international level, rather than a contender for the five-day Tests?*

I try not to think about such divisions of ability, but I will say this: It is harder to keep wicket in the one-day game than in any other. People play to patterns in the longer games, whereas in the one-day version anything can happen and the ball careers around all over the place. You can get the batsman taking chances like backing to the leg and trying to force it away through the offside—in that case the bowler will try to spear one in around his legs or in the bowlers' footholds. That causes visual problems for the keeper, with dust flying, the bowler tearing in, the batsman swinging the bat and the ball not always in your line of vision because it is coming into the batsman's body. You get tested far more in those type of games than in a longer match that is less pressurised.

*Any other examples where we might not appreciate the art of the wicket-keeper?*

Well, here is one, courtesy of Alan Knott. He pointed out one day that although it looks horrible when a keeper misses a stumping with the batsman stranded yards down the pitch, it might have been rather more difficult than it seemed. Knotty said: "Always look where the ball has pitched before you say it's an easy stumping," and he is right. Consider one where the batsman leans forward, is beaten on the outside edge, lifts his back foot and you flick off the bails. That is easy because hardly anything has hampered your line of vision. But it is far more difficult to take the ball that is pitched a yard short of the popping crease or if the batsman has moved down the wicket and you have lost sight of the ball. Your brain is telling you what ought to be happening, but you have no time to adjust if the ball shoots through off a full length. In comparison, a legside stumping that you saw all the way may look impressive but is easier because the ball has only disappeared for a split second.

*How do you cope with the more brutal aspects of the modern first-class game?*

As a travelling circus, the English game is still enjoyable because there are so many friendships to cherish. But there are people around now who want to damage you on the field. It has become exaggerated by the pressure to get results, resulting in poor pitches. The balance has gone too far. We need better wickets and a longer game. Four-day cricket must be the answer.

*Do we play too much cricket?*

I am a great believer in improving the quality by rarifying it, by making each game important. At the moment all the games fall into each other, so you don't have time to practise, to stop and think about your technique. Unless you are going for the championship, it can be just a continuous roadshow and you are hardly galvanised by the sparse crowds for county cricket. When the season's gone flat for the side, you are playing for yourself and the man who reads the scores on his way to work. I like the

Australian system. They play fewer games, practise much harder and do their absolute damnedest to make it all count when they play a match. It must be nice to have an inner calm about practising well, to be properly prepared. In England we are not really near that level of preparation because we play too much. Batters get into the habit of thinking: "There's always tomorrow." They play around fifty innings a season. We must ensure that the class players look forward more to playing, to be more responsible about their talents.

*Has your winter work as a stockbroker helped you be more analytical about the game?*
Certainly I have become more aware of the need to produce results by utilising all available resources and data. In cricket, unlike commerce, there is no-one around to say: "You better produce today or you are on your bike." Now I would not want to go that far, but at the moment the actual essence of daily production for a county cricketer comes down to that player's own pride. We should be more aware of what we are trying to do. A modern product has to be worked out that is in tune with today's world. Test cricket must be preserved, but sponsors are not going to continue forking out for other forms of professional cricket just for the sake of it. Four-day cricket makes huge sense to me because the product will be fresher, the players less stale. The way the counties are run is out of tune with the modern world. Thirty people on a general committee is simply homage to democracy. An inner caucus should run the show, imbue the proceedings with greater professionalism and be seen to do so.

*The only time I have ever seen you really angry in public during your career was in June, 1988, when you had been summoned to Lord's in the wake of Mike Gatting's sacking from the England captaincy after the allegations of misbehaviour at the team's hotel. I recall you reading out a statement that left us in no doubt that you resented having to go to Lord's.*
I was very annoyed. In trying to do the right thing as they saw it, and being thorough in their investigation, the Test and County Cricket Board created a new story and gave the papers a spurious follow-up. I was one of four players called in, even though every newspaper account correctly stated that I left the gathering after one drink with Gatt on his birthday. I can still see our four mug-shots on the Six O'Clock News and the obvious suggestion was that we were implicated. It would only have needed a phone call the previous day to ascertain our accounts, yet I was dragged into a mucky story. My family were involved, the girl in the shop on the corner had a good titter—all because the inquiry was badly presented. That was not the happiest day of my cricket career.

# JOHN
# LEVER

**'I have found in recent years that a minority of fans would rather shout insults than support their side. I shall not miss any of that. '**

WHEN *cricket historians of the Twenty-first Century seek to analyse the ideal English professional of our age, they should stop at the name LEVER, J. K. John Lever epitomised the best qualities of the county game. Just as the Lancashire and Yorkshire pros rendered great service on and off the field between the wars, so did Lever for Essex in the age of the portable phone and the Ceefax scores. He was a captain's dream: loyal, shrewd, uncomplaining, talented, phenomenally fit and a stickler for the highest standards of integrity. John Lever just needed to be wound up at the start of each season and he would then provide his own motivation. His ability was unquestioned—a left-arm opening bowler who could swing the ball devastatingly late into the batsman. His fitness was legendary, proof indeed that a dedicated quaffer of real ale and the occasional puffer of a cigarette can still bowl a thousand overs a season. The man who started for Essex in the year of the Beatles' infatuation with the Maharishi was still running in as pimply adolescents were fainting at Bros concerts. Not even a burst stomach ulcer stopped him taking a hundred first-class wickets in the 1983 season. Only the presence of Mike Hendrick and Chris Old prevented him gaining more than 21 England caps as the ideal seamer behind Bob Willis and Ian Botham during Mike Brearley's period of influence. It was a measure of the universal respect held for John Lever that Bishen Bedi's allegation that he had cheated during his first Test was derisively dismissed. Despite Lever's sterling efforts for England, he remained predominantly an Essex man. He and Graham Gooch were the cornerstone of Keith Fletcher's assaults on trophies, as Essex shed their image of strolling troubadours and got used to the taste of champagne. While becoming a dominant side, Essex also managed to retain a human face during all that success, and John Lever did more than anyone to juggle the ball of professionalism with those of sportsmanship and communicable enjoyment. When Eddie Hemmings hit the last ball of the 1989 Benson*

166

*and Hedges Cup Final to the boundary to win the trophy, even the Nottinghamshire faithful were sorry that Lever was the unlucky bowler. It felt disturbingly significant that John retired to the world of teaching at the end of the season—at a time when players of his sunny disposition were becoming rather thin on the ground. Did he feel he was leaving the professional game at the right time?*

It would be so wrong for me to say that the fun has gone out of the game, but it *has* changed a helluva lot. If you cannot keep a sense of humour and still try your hardest, you are losing out. That has always been the Essex way and I feel we never lost sight of our responsibilities as entertainers. Very few batsmen walk nowadays: the umpires really have their work cut out. There is more pressure than ever on bowlers to get every ball right in the one-day games. The hardest day of the week for a bowler is on Sunday, when you have to bowl 48 deliveries in the right spot. Every bit of concentration goes into those 48 balls, and if you stray a couple of inches down the legside, that is a wide—and you are avoiding the captain's eyes. And you cannot switch off when you are not bowling—you must be alert in the field. If you have done your job right on the Sunday afternoon, you are shattered on the Monday morning. The days of letting the number eleven have a slog have gone. Even if helmets had not been adopted, modern bowlers would prefer to stick it around your ears, rather than run the risk of being slogged for six. Also the spectators have become, like the counties, hungry for success. It is easier to sell a winning side to the sponsors. I have found in recent years that a minority of fans would rather shout insults than support their side. Sometimes it resembles the Australian crowds, who are occasionally funny but invariably rude. I shall not miss any of that.

*Let us get the sadness out of the way first—that final ball to Eddie Hemmings in the 1989 Benson and Hedges Cup Final. Was that the lowest point of your career?*

It was the most devastating moment I have known. I felt responsible for not picking up the cup, for losing it with one delivery. That night I bowled it 30,000 times and it was in the right slot every time. It made no difference that we had beaten Nottinghamshire off the last ball in the Nat-West Cup in 1985. I had failed in my job. I had already dropped two catches, the second one an easy chance in the gully that went straight in and out. That was to reprieve Derek Randall, but when he got out to Derek Pringle next over, I felt I was in luck. They needed nine off the last over—a bit tight, but they had two new batsmen in. I had managed to bowl Chris Tavare leg-stump off the last ball in the semi-final when Somerset started the last over needing ten, so I was reasonably confident. When I bowled a "dot" ball to Eddie Hemmings, perhaps I thought we had won it. So they needed four off the last ball and we changed the field three times. I knew that Eddie would try to play inside out, so I had to fire it in at his pads. I thought that if I got the line slightly wrong he would nick it, so I brought fine leg up and put third man back. If I had put fine leg back, I would have been happier aiming at his leg-stump, or even outside it; but with the man up to save one, I could not really afford to give him anything loose in that area. That was my big mistake. I did not follow Eddie as he backed away, and it pitched around middle and leg, so that he had enough room to throw his bat at the ball. He got an outside edge to it, and although it all then happened very quickly, it felt like slow motion to me as Brian Hardie ran after it, then gave up the chase. It was an awful moment. I should have had a sweeper out there on the point boundary. I also bowled it in the wrong area. It is long day for the result to come down to the final ball, and I felt desperately sorry for the rest of the team.

*That delivery underlines the importance of concentration in cricket, doesn't it?*

Absolutely. If the ball goes for four, the whole of that over has been wasted. You have built up the pressure with five accurate deliveries, then the concentration goes and the batsman is off the hook. If the first one disappears, you are trying to drag it back for the rest of that over. If you are tense, you cannot exert pressure on the batters. I have never been more nervous than at Leeds in 1986 when I was recalled by England after four and a half years. I was brought back to exploit the conditions at Leeds, but I bowled down the hill, I over-pitched and tried to bowl too fast. Finally a guy in the crowd shouted "Come on, John, pretend it's Essex!" and only then did I relax.

*You were lucky enough to play under the captaincy of Mike Brearley and Keith Fletcher. How similar were they as captains?*

Fletch studied the batsmen a little more. He was absolutely brilliant tactically. He made me very lazy as a bowler because his field-placing for me was so shrewd. When I got to a Test, Mike Brearley expected me to have ideas of my own, and that came as a bit of a shock! You have to play with Fletch to realise how much he knows about cricket. He is not a complicated bloke; he just talks commonsense and you end up saying "Now, why didn't I think of that?" He did not always handle people right when he started as captain, but he soon treated us as individuals and with respect, so long as you gave him everything. He liked a laugh and he always knew when to stop the skylarking and get on with the job. Allan Border's success this year against England has a lot to do with Fletch. When Border played with Essex, he studied what Fletch was doing and talked deeply with him. It is easy to have team meetings in which you talk about the opposition, but then you can go out on the field and forget all about it. Border has not done that—every batsman has been pressurised by him in specific ways. Fletch was brilliant at pressurising batters.

Brears shared with Fletch that priceless ability to get people to play for him. You bowled those extra overs for him, even though you were in trouble. Some bowlers need to be patted and cajoled, others need a kick up the backside. Brears did it very well with Bob Willis and Ian Botham; he showed confidence in them and they responded. Many people think that Both just came on to bowl and did it; but he needed encouragement and guidance as well.

*But wasn't Botham equally good for Brearley?*

He was a godsend to the captain, because he never knew the meaning of defeat and he never wanted to stop bowling. Any side that Both played in had his total support; that is why he is so popular. In Brearley's day, he bowled aggressively and he could swing the ball at speed. Like all the best bowlers, the fast outswingers got him stacks of wickets. He would have got anyone out at that stage—forget all that stuff about Test cricket being short of the Packer players. As a batter, he was high class, and the extra confidence gained from taking five wickets was reflected in his batting. When he makes the first ball disappear, many a good bowler has had to think: "What am I going to bowl now?"

*When you at last played for England at the age of 27, much of the gloss was taken off your great start by claims that you had swung the ball illegally by applying grease to it. Twelve years after all that fuss, was there anything in the allegations?*

Absolutely not. It was Bernard Thomas's fault that the row started. Both Bob Willis and I were profuse sweaters in humid conditions, and Bernard had the bright idea of giving us each a strip of Vaseline gauze to keep the salt out of our eyes. I put two thin strips over my eyes, but Bob put a great wodge of it over his forehead and, of course, it did not stay on. It plopped over his eyes first over and he threw it away. Mine only lasted a couple of overs and that was thrown aside as well. Then one of the umpires pounced on the offending strips, showed them to Bishen Bedi, the Indian captain, and he marched over to the Pressbox and denounced us as cheats. Of course, this had nothing to do with us about to go three-nil up in the series! What is more, Bishen alleged that I had probably used the Vaseline at Delhi when I took ten wickets in my first Test. Now it had taken me years of practice to learn how to swing the ball and I resented Bishen's sour grapes. Even my family were besieged at home because of all the kerfuffle. It was ridiculous. We even used the balls offered us by the Indian Cricket Board instead of our own—and I was delighted that it swung all over the shop at Delhi. I even got three lbws out of the first four batsmen in that first Test—and visiting bowlers do not get too many of them in India. You will always get such snide comments when a swing bowler has a great day. Bob Massie had to contend with that when he took sixteen wickets in the Lord's Test in 1972. He later told me that he had no idea why he swung it yards that day; it was freakish. If he was using something to help the shine, why didn't he clean up on other days? Everything was right for him just once. Why assume he was cheating?

*How did you learn to bowl the one that swings in to the right-hand batsman?*

It took me two summers and two winters, in my early days. I had to stick at it because I knew that this was the way to get good players out; otherwise you are just slanting the ball away from them and there is no surprise factor. Because I was not a natural swing bowler like Gary Sobers, I had to plug away—tell myself not to fall away when I got tired. You have to keep the wrist cocked and push the ball with index finger and second finger across the body. Keep your head still and follow the ball down the wicket. At the instant you release the ball, the hand must be behind the ball, not to the side, otherwise it will go straight on to the slips. If you lose your action, you lose the art. Some days it goes faster than others; you have to adapt accordingly. You just hope the ball will hold its line until the last moment, then duck in. It is a matter of finding the right pace to bowl it on any given day. The great merit of swing bowling is that you can get wickets anywhere in the world; you are not hampered by the amount of grass on the pitch. Imran Khan and Malcolm Marshall are devastating in any country.

*England would seem to be the spiritual home of swing bowlers. Why are there so few today?*

The current crop of wickets do not help. The larger seam on the Reader balls will help the guy who zips it around off the seam, rather than the one who relies on subtlety of movement through the air. One-day cricket demands that the bowler keeps it tight, so that you have to drop it in on the legs rather than pitch it up and try to make it swing. It is obvious that a good swing bowler expects to be driven, because he is pushing the ball up to the batsman, trying for late swing. That can be expensive if the bowler's timing is out.

*How did you manage to stay fit for so long?*

Some might say my long run-up helped! I ran a long way simply to get rhythm, to start a sequence of events that would allow me to bowl six consecutive balls in the right

170

area. In the process I obviously had to be strong in the legs to maintain that, so I joined Bob Willis in running to keep fit. It was easier when I was a lad, but by the time I got in the England team I had to keep up the standard of fitness. As you get closer to your thirties, that does not happen automatically. My bowling action helped—there was never a great strain on my back or knees; it always felt right. I also looked after my boots and padded them to avoid shin soreness. Basically, it was a case of being professional.

*It seems that the 1989 Australians have been more professional than England. Do you see it that way?*

I honestly do not believe there is all that much wrong with us at the moment. I cannot tell you why our best batsmen (and they *are* the best ones) keep getting out. It is easy to say "sack the lot of them", but the new ones do not have the same pedigree. You should bring young players into a successful side—as we have done at Essex—and get them to follow the example of good pros. Don't put them into a struggling Test team where confidence is so low. The Australians have filled their boots when they have batted, and then attacked us in the field. Dear old Kenny Barrington would have been proud of the way Steve Waugh has just batted us out of the game with big hundreds. Kenny managed several England tours, and he was a great one for telling us that we had to cash in when the conditions favoured us. He was a great man, Kenny. He would think nothing of standing in a net for an hour, throwing you a ball to make sure your timing was right. During a Test, he would sit there living every ball, with the Union Jack in his thoughts. When you went out there and batted or bowled badly, you would think: "God, what would Kenny be thinking now?" You wanted to please him. We had so much respect for him that we would battle extra hard to make him proud of us. Kenny was absolutely priceless and we all loved him. I am just grateful that I was lucky enough to play for men like Kenny Barrington, Keith Fletcher and Mike Brearley.

# VIC
# MARKS

**'The media make too much out of captaincy—"Gower's Goons", "Gatt the Prat" and all that. It seems ludicrous that so much criticism is concentrated on a comparatively trivial matter. '**

A GENUINE slow bowler has needed to be philosophical to survive this last decade of English first-class cricket—a time of heavy bats, shorter boundaries, green wickets, extra stitching on the ball's seam and serious damage to batsmen's fingers. Vic Marks survived and smiled. The smile was never a wolfish one, like Ian Botham's, or one of Mike Gatting's Holbeinesque efforts. It was a wry smile, a humorous acceptance of the fates that decreed Vic Marks should play his slow off-spin on a home pitch where the mishit six is as common as surly car-park attendants at that cramped Taunton ground. If Vic had been employed at the Oval, or Leicester or Bristol, his bowling average would have been appreciably lower than one in the early thirties. Many more rash batsmen would have perished on the boundary edge to his deceptive skills, instead of plopping eight and a half ounces of leather into the River Tone. Marks would greet such brutality with nothing more histrionic than a furtive glance to see how many of his team-mates were guffawing at this latest outrage. His farming lineage had equipped him with the necessary stoicism to cope with the roughest treatment and to plan fresh strategies after the obligatory stare at his boots while the umpires rummaged around for another ball. Often that new strategy involved even more flight and guile and, to those reared on ersatz spinners firing the ball in at around medium pace, a spell from Marks was a reminder that the art of spin bowling revolved around subtle changes of pace, angles of delivery and—above all—temptation.

Victor's batting was less interesting but more modern in its rugged unorthodoxy. He was a genuine all-rounder at county level—a man who played countless innings of great character and altruism. Significantly, his last three innings for England (of 83, 74 and 55) were played in trying circumstances in Pakistan in 1984, when the team had been ravaged by illness, injury and Press innuendos. Above all, Vic Marks was a good man to see on the county circuit. Despite deserved England recognition, one feels that the less

173

*frenetic pace of county cricket suited him. He was sentimentally attached to the more chivalrous precepts of the game, enviably lucky to enjoy the gift of friendship and subtle enough only to discuss his involvement in the Christians in Sport Movement with like-minded individuals. Marks never rammed his own point of view down anyone's throat; he just lived a code of conduct that was greatly admired. Like Mike Brearley, this Oxford graduate in classics never patronised team-mates who could barely manage to complete the Sun crossword before their nocturnal beefburger and vat of lager. When Victor retired in 1989 to write with characteristic whimsy on the game for a Sunday newspaper, English cricket lost one of its most endearing figures. Did he have any valedictory words of comfort for the endangered spin bowler?*

The pitches are crucial. The standard of spin bowling has declined in my time because bowlers are being flattered by inferior wickets. We do not seem to have that grounding whereby we play county games on uniformly good, hard, dry surfaces. When bowlers perform on a typical flat Test wicket, they are astounded that the ball does not zig-zag around off the seam as in county games. Groundsmen are not always encouraged to prepare the best surfaces for county games. Some home captains get angry because they cannot possibly zoom up the table if 350 is the usual innings total. So result wickets are prepared—and that does nothing for the game's long-term welfare. In terms of legislating the spinner back into the mainstream, I can only suggest four-day cricket. Hard, dry pitches that would last four days would mean spinners taking a more significant part in the proceedings. I would like to think that county clubs would naturally insist on good surfaces for the four-day games because their sponsors would need to be attracted for the last two days as well as at the start. If the pitches were satisfactory, there would be no debate about the quality of balls and the extra stitching on the seam.

Tactically, spinners are not being used in the proper manner in the English game. They ought to be used in an attacking vein, not as stock bowlers. Look at John Childs with Essex. When he gets the ball, he knows that he is expected to get wickets, so he bowls aggressively. He does not think: "Oh, we're short of bowlers, so I'm going to have to bowl twenty overs and keep it tight." He is on because Essex think he represents their best chance of taking wickets.

At Somerset, I have been used too defensively in recent years because there was no one else, rather than because I was the best bet for wickets. I've become an aggregate rather than an average bowler, trying to forget how much they cost.

*Do you always want to bowl?*
Pretty much. I do not like fielding all that much! When I was about eleven I used to bowl fast around the wicket, but soon it was clear to me that I was suited to spin bowling.

*Do you see yourself as a flight bowler rather than a spinner?*
That suggests I don't spin it! My weak physique has something to do with it, because I cannot bowl it any other way. Just watch John Emburey throw in like a bullet from the boundary. I wish my right arm was as powerful as his because it would give me more bowling options. I would like to fizz it through a little quicker at times, but it comes out of my arm at its natural pace. So I cannot bounce it like Eddie Hemmings, and have to rely on extra flight. I'm also smaller than Eddie and Embers, so I have to throw it up more.

*How should a slow bowler react when he is on the end of a hammering?*

First, he must look at where he is being hit. If he is being hit in unusual areas, then he is losing control. You have to live with being hit straight back over your head, but avoid being cut or pulled. No spinner likes being hit through the covers after the batsman has stepped away to leg, or if he continues bisecting your legside field. Zaheer Abbas was a master at playing me "inside out"; so were Paul Johnson and Trevor Jesty. They both sweep and lap well, too.

*What is your attitude to being smashed for six?*

Well, I don't say "well bowled!" like Bishen Bedi used to do! When you get hit for six, invariably it is a perfectly respectable delivery, so you tell yourself it was a good shot to a good ball. That is a slightly soft option, because there is a big hitter at the other end and it is up to you to combat him. You must take some preventative action to stop the ball going out of the ground. That is preferable to saying: "Well, it was all right leaving me, captain," or "Pity I'm a slow bowler and I can't bounce him." You have to do something to keep him guessing. Try to watch how he sets himself up for the big blow in the previous couple of deliveries. Observe his movements just before you deliver the ball: is he winding himself up too much? Is he committed too early to the front foot? Is there a chance of a legside stumping as he advances on you? One of the frightening aspects of all this is that there are some batsmen who are perfectly capable of doing it to you every ball. People like Ian Botham do not exactly have an in-built reserve.

*You are not what I would term a "clench-fisted" cricketer. Have you ever displayed outward signs of excitement or elation?*

On the rare occasions when I get a wicket, it is true that I react rather sedately compared to others. But that doesn't bother me. I am a fairly low-key person, and you have to be yourself. When I first played for Western Australia it was pretty clear that I was the odd one out. Graeme Wood, my captain, asked me where I fielded, and when I replied that I could not throw very well and did not fancy the slips, he settled on square leg—a good compromise, I felt. Off the third ball of my first game, Andy Hilditch was unlucky enough to chip one to my right and, as luck would have it, I dived, threw the ball into the bowler's end and, after a cock-up between the batsmen, Hilditch was run out. Not many batsmen have perished to the demon Marks throw, I can tell you! Anyway, I was savouring the moment, when suddenly ten Aussies came pounding down on me, surging all around me in joyous celebration. This rarely happened at Somerset! That same year I prepared to bowl my first over in grade cricket in Perth: the field seemed to my satisfaction, and I decided to start. Suddenly, from deep backward square leg, I heard this thunderous shout. I stopped, wondering if he was unsure of his place in the field, ascertained all was well, and prepared to bowl again. As I wheeled in, he started up again: "Come on! Knock him over! Get stuck in!" Yet I was not exactly Dennis Lillee—I was only bowling gentle little off-spinners! That sort of thing tends to happen more in grade cricket out there, rather than the Shield. The Shield players seem aware that mindless yelling from seventy yards away does not have a great deal of impact on proceedings.

*You played two seasons of grade and Shield cricket in Western Australia. Did you see anything out there that would aid the English game?*

I was most impressed by the competitive nature of four-day cricket. By that, I do not mean sledging or shouting on the field, I mean the way they prepared themselves for the Shield matches.

There was a pattern for all ten games—two evening net sessions, than a talk on the eve of the match—so that when you actually started the game, you felt fresh and tuned up mentally. You knew you would then have a week off, so, to use their terminology, "everybody put in". Even I dived around in the field! The fast bowler could really slip himself, whereas in the English version, you often have to rest your fast bowlers on the last day of a county match because an important one-day match is coming up the next day. In Australia it is competitive all the time, even when the opposition is 300 for one. The fielding side still battles on, while in similar circumstances in a county match, you would be waiting for the declaration and going through the motions. You would have decided not to burn out your strike bowlers and conceded the ascendancy. In the four-day game you just have to learn how to bowl people out on good wickets.

*So we play too much first-class cricket in England.*

I think so. This season we had a stretch of 25 days out of 28, and that cannot help you relish the special occasion as they do in Australia. There they play around eighteen innings in a first-class season. The captain in county cricket also runs out of fresh things to say, as I know only too well. At times, what you are seeking is not always what is best for the game: you look for stamina and perseverance rather than flair. County cricket can become attritional, so that the dogged side can beat the more talented team near the end of a hard season. Now there is virtue in that, but it is over-balanced against those players who have something special to offer, yet find themselves weighed down by the sheer volume of cricket.

*How did the Somerset captaincy affect you?*

I was lucky to have a tremendous support group, with magnificent senior players and a very supportive manager in Jack Birkenshaw. But I still occasionally got lost for ideas and became dejected after a couple of bad days in a row. The supporters' perceptions have changed so much in recent years. Every county expects to win something now; a few years back, Somerset followers would settle for beating Yorkshire once every three years or so, but now the hunt is on for a trophy. I think the media makes too much out of captaincy—"Gower's Goons", "Gatt the Prat" and all that. It seems ludicrous to me that so much criticism is concentrated on a comparatively trivial matter, like bowling Neil Foster from the Pavilion End at Lord's against Australia. As for the personal aspect of captaincy, I did not go in for all that back-slapping stuff because it simply was not me. You spend so much time in a dressing-room that you are quickly found out if you put on an act. Geoff Miller discovered that, when he followed Eddie Barlow as Derbyshire's captain. Geoff was not the type to follow Eddie's disciplinarian line, and when he failed at that, he rightly reverted to his own genial ways.

*I can understand that you do not want to make too much of your involvement with Christians In Sport in case some might think you are being "holier than thou". But has your support of the movement influenced your attitude to playing in South Africa?*

I have never considered going there. From a moral standpoint I would not go if by some chance I was offered a trip there to play cricket. It is naive to say that sport and politics should not mix; the fact is that they do. Some will say that my view is just a gesture; but, like sanctions, I believe it is a worthwhile statement to make. Having said that, I would condemn nobody for going to South Africa.

*You have been lucky enough to have played with some great cricketers down there in Taunton.*

Some staggering cricketers. The overseas players signed by Somerset have been brilliant—Viv Richards, Joel Garner, Sunil Gavaskar, Martin Crowe, Steve Waugh and Jimmy Cook. Each one a great player. Around 1978/79 Viv was phenomenal, the best I've seen for batsmanship. Then there was Ian Botham. We have all run out of things to say about Both, and yet, to my great annoyance, he is younger than me! When this history of twentieth-century cricket is written, there will have to be a chapter on Both.

*So how do you leave active service in the English game?*

The overall size of each county staff has risen dramatically in my time, so it must be healthier. The overseas players have not had a detrimental effect on numbers of playing staff, and they have undoubtedly improved standards. In general, county cricket still contains many honourable men who get on well with each other and compete in an acceptable way. I shall miss many, many aspects of the circuit. I hope that groundsmen are one day placed on the same financial level as other club officials, because pitches are so important.

# GRAEME FOWLER

**'I would like to see Sunday cricket turned over to the best of three slogs lasting ten overs each. The public want to see the ball disappear out of the ground. '**

NO matter how long he stays in first-class cricket, Graeme Fowler will always appear the youthful, artful dodger. As he approaches that touchstone of long service, the benefit year, Fowler still has the air of the chirpy fledgeling embarking on an exciting adventure. He would be perfect for one of those twee advertisements extolling the virtues of health foods or ideal in the lead role for a remake of The Picture of Dorian Gray. No day seems too long for him, no ball is ever simply accompanied to the boundary by him. Fowler has been one of this decade's great chasers of lost causes in the outfield, the kind of fielder every bowler wants in his side. As a batsman for Lancashire and England he has opened the innings with unorthodox flair, bravery and phlegmatic good sense. There have been tighter techniques on display at the top of the England order, but a batting average of 35 in 21 Tests for a weak side against the likes of Imran Khan, Richard Hadlee, Kapil Dev and the Caribbean juggernaut gives cause for satisfaction. The technicians may have winced at some of Fowler's methods, but you don't take a hundred off the West Indies, then a double hundred from the Indian spinners on their own midden, without a nodding acquaintance with the rudiments of batsmanship. Fowler played all his Tests during the period when Graham Gooch was banned for his South African connections and it is ironic that in his last series he averaged almost 55. Yet soon he had more pressing matters to consider than regaining his England place. Six months after making 201 in the Calcutta Test, Graeme Fowler's life was falling apart. He had a broken neck, with the prospect of a life in a wheelchair, and his marriage had collapsed. Yet a year later he had scored more first-class runs in the 1986 season than any other player qualified for England. It was typical of Fowler that he would come through the harrowing months of 1985 a stronger, more rounded character with his sense of fun even more acute.

I'm just a kid at heart, I suppose, so that helped me put things in perspective. It all depends on your mental attitude and there are still days when I wake up feeling black and moody, just waiting to have a go at somebody. But I tell myself that something good can always come out of any situation. If you want to enjoy yourself, have a look around and you will find something to enthuse about. Since 1985, I've made a conscious effort to enjoy myself because I know what it's like to be bloody miserable—and there is nothing worse.

*How desperate were you during those bad times?*

Awful. I can't tell you how black it was. I did some things that were evil that have affected people ever since and will do so for the rest of their lives. No matter how often I apologise to them it will never be enough. It took me a long time to come to terms with being such an utter sod and I shall never forget how I hurt people who didn't deserve it. All I can remember is that just a few months after scoring a double hundred for England my life was crumbling around my ears and I was living in someone else's house with no prospect of playing again.

*How did you break your neck?*

It stemmed from a car accident in 1978. The hospital didn't bother with an X-ray so I didn't know that two bones had been broken. Seven years later I was taken ill during the Kanpur Test, the last I played in. I was treated for a virus when in fact I had a broken neck! When I came back to England I told Lancashire I just had to sort out the injury and a specialist told me that two bones were crushed and disfigured. My neck started to feel worse automatically after I had been officially told what was wrong—like seeing blood when you've hurt your leg. So I tried all sorts of physio and traction with different weights but none of it worked. I just tried to keep going during the 1985 season, getting more and more depressed. If I had had any brains I would have taken off the entire season to get it right. I should not have kept quiet about it, because when I was playing so badly I could not then offer my broken neck as an excuse. I had dug my own grave and had to get myself out of it. I had restricted movement, there was little strength in my hands and I could not feel comfortable in any position. I was awful mentally, in no state to play professional cricket. If you dive for a ball in the field, not knowing if you will get up again, you are in trouble. We came to Liverpool for a county match in July and the roof caved in. I jumped up for a ball in fielding practice and the nerves trapped in my neck. The muscles went into spasm, and the left side of my body was semi-paralysed. I lay on the ground for half-an-hour and would not let anyone touch me. I remember lying in the ambulance listening to the drivers talking football as my head banged against the side, feeling absolutely miserable. That was the end of my season, apart from a few failed attempts at a comeback.

*How did you pull yourself around?*

I spent that winter sorting out my neck and my personal life, telling myself I had a great deal to prove as a cricketer and human being. Come the start of the 1986 season, I found I was captain twenty minutes before the first county game at Hove. I went out there, scored 180 and loved every minute of leading the side for the first time. I never looked back after that all summer. Since then everything has been a bonus for me.

*One of the problems for you during that black period must have been your immaturity, the fact that you lacked much experience at coming to terms with the down side of professional sport?*

180

That's right. Everything had come so quickly to me. Within a year of getting a regular place in the Lancashire side I was picked for England and off on the tours. I had studied physical education at Durham University, done all the silly things like staying up all night, spending my grant within the first week and getting drunk for days. I would not have been able to cope with the disciplines of county cricket if I had joined the staff at 18. As it was, it took me long enough when I eventually became a professional. I did not play cricket until I was twelve. All I used to do was ride my bike, play with my dog and kick a football. I only played my first game of cricket because I was bored on the beach on holiday.

*So when you first played for England in 1982, you were not really ready for it?*

Not at all. It never crossed my mind. I had hardly opened the innings for Lancashire at that time, and when the England captain Bob Willis rang me at Old Trafford, I thought: "What's he want me for?" When he told me I was in the England team at Leeds against Pakistan I thought no more about it and bowled along in my seventeen-year-old Triumph 2000. The gateman did not believe me and would not let me in. When I finally got through, Ian Botham thought I was some young lad carrying an England player's gear into the dressing-room! When he saw me getting changed, it dawned on him we were in the same side. Hardly anybody knew of me. I was new to county cricket and I reckon I was only picked because I kept getting hundreds off Warwickshire, Willis's county.

*But you made 86 in the second innings—a typical Fowler innings, full of good shots and a lot of playing and missing.*

I was determined not to be overawed. I went out and played my normal game. I was so raw: I knew nothing about what constituted a good score for a Test Match, that the Headingley wicket was unsatisfactory, that the Pakistanis were a good side. What I do remember about that first month as an England player is that the tax I paid was equivalent to my grant for a full year at Durham. Things were certainly different!

*I remember that you were often beaten all ends up during that Test debut but you just kept on playing your own game. Do you really not worry about the previous ball when it has just turned you inside out?*

You cannot afford to. It has gone. Being left-handed has a lot to do with this. With the ball being angled across me by a right-hand bowler, I am always a candidate for the waft outside off-stump. So is a right-hander when a left-hand bowler is operating over the wicket, but there are fewer of them. If I was a right-hand bat, the ball I played and missed at would probably hit me on the leg and that does not look so bad as missing the ball which lands in the keeper's hands. But why should I worry when I hit fresh air if a right-hander is not worried if the ball bounces off his pad after he has missed it?

*Yet you faced immediate criticism about your technique when you came into the England side. That really got to you when England went to Australia in 1982/3, didn't it?*

Yes, I felt overawed on two different levels. The Press complained to the tour management that I was being unsociable and unco-operative, even though the captain Bob Willis had told me at the start: "Don't talk to the press, they'll stuff you." Having been on the circuit for just two seasons, I hardly knew any of them anyway. I was

181

---

unaware of a professional cricketer's responsibilities. I had only ever done one interview before I played for England. I was out of my depth, but it was more serious in terms of my batting. I did not realise that people thought I had a dodgy technique until I played for England. When I saw my Leeds innings on video I was not too impressed either. I did not like the way I played or even the way I ran between the wickets, and it came as a huge shock. When we got to Australia I tried to play like an orthodox England batsman and it was a nightmare. I had never analysed how I played before, yet now the management were telling me I should not hook, that I was offering an angled bat to the slips when I tried an off-drive, that a drive to a rising ball off the back foot would only end in a nick to the slips or keeper. I was confused, short of runs and encouragement. Finally I thought: "Sod it, I'll play my own instinctive way and if it doesn't work out, at least I've been true to myself". In the Brisbane Test I battled away for nearly six hours for 83, but then gloved one to Rod Marsh down the leg side. I got told off for trying to play it down the leg side because I would have only got a single to fine leg anyway. By that time I was standing up for myself and pointed out that tucking the ball off the hip for a single is a bread-and-butter shot, and that if I can do that a hundred times, I have scored a century. In that class of cricket you do not get a hundred via 25 balls that go for four, you do it with bread-and-butter shots. I was not the only one being untrue to his instincts. Ian Botham was furious at himself for checking his hook shot and getting out, caught off his glove. Against bowlers of the quality of Rackeman, Thomson and Lawson, you could not afford to theorise and play in a way foreign to your instincts. There just was not enough time.

*Is that the only time you have faced concerted attempts to change the way you bat?*

Well, Peter Lever used to try when he was Lancashire coach, but we never saw eye-to-eye on a professional level. He once told me I had no sort of technique, because to a ball pitched on my off-stump, I could play through mid-off, extra cover, mid-on or mid-wicket. I told him to try setting a field to that! Once in the nets he said: "That last ball, you pushed at it, you didn't defend and you didn't attack it. It was a good ball and you played a nothing shot." I pointed out that I just pushed a good length ball for a single to keep the scoreboard ticking and that was my main job as an opener. What Lever wanted was six identical forward defensive shots to six successive balls pitching on a good length on the off-stump. As a former fast bowler, his idea of perfect cricket would have been nought for nought at the end of that over. But modern cricket is not like that. The days of playing through the V have long gone.

*You played all your Tests during the period of the South Africa ban, yet there were some pretty good fast bowlers around to discomfit a weakened England side. Your last Test innings was 69 in India, then Graham Gooch came back and you were out. Do you feel bitter that you never played when everyone was available?*

All I ever tried to do was play well for Lancashire, and if anything else came of that, so be it. But I was the senior opening partner for England in 1984—I even got on the front row of the photograph—so I cannot have done too badly. In my last two games for England I scored 201 and 69 and my Test average is still better than Allan Lamb's. I think I can hold my head up. During my time Peter May, the chairman of selectors, used to say the same thing at every team dinner: "Welcome, gentlemen, nice to see you all—you are currently the best England players available." I did not like that because I used to feel that the chairman agreed with many that Gooch would have been in the side instead of me if he had not gone to South Africa. I must admit it would have been nice to play for England in a Test Match when the whole nation was considered, but there you go.

*One of my abiding memories of your England career is the terrible stick you took from the West Indies bowlers in 1984. Did you get any satisfaction from your performance?*

I enjoyed the challenge and I am proud that I got a hundred against them in the Lord's Test. But they did wear me down and I got annoyed about spending so much time with both feet off the ground fending off the short-pitched stuff. I was never frightened, but it was not the cricket I had been brought up to play, where the bowler tries to get good players caught behind or in the slips or lbw. The stumps would have to be seven feet high before the West Indies bowlers could hit them. I have a photograph of me that summer in which I am shaped like a question mark, with the ball a foot away from my head and I am a foot off the floor. When I retired hurt at the Oval after Malcolm Marshall hit me on the forearm, Ted Dexter said on TV that a legitimate way of playing that type of bowling was to wear a chest protector and let the ball hit you. Jim Laker also said that Brian Close used to let the ball hit him *without* a chest pad. I am afraid that is not an option. Nobody in their right mind could let a cricket ball hit them at the speed Marshall and the others propelled it. Many just did not appreciate how difficult it was against them. When they were on a roll they were phenomenal—we felt like we were pissing in the wind. On the eve of the one-day series against them, we had our usual team meeting and Andy Lloyd and I were advised how we should play against their quicks. Early on we were to keep the scoreboard ticking against Joel Garner and Malcolm Marshall, then we had to watch out for the way Eldine Baptiste angles the ball in and hits the seam regularly. The conclusion was the man we had to get after was Michael Holding, one of the greatest of fast bowlers! You cannot smash a guy like Holding over the top or glide him prettily through the covers. These blokes shoot bullets not blanks! That same summer, we were licking our wounds in the Edgbaston dressing-room after our first annihilation and Bob Willis said: "The only way we'll beat this lot is to play them on bad wickets." I told him we would therefore need about forty batsmen for each Test because we would be carried off at regular intervals. Bob, a great fast bowler, did not understand batting or batsmen. Slow turners were the only answer against the West Indies.

*In contrast, the trip to India must have been very pleasant for you?*

Apart from the early political disturbances, yes. David Gower was very imperturbable during that period and I really enjoyed his style of captaincy. He may fly off the handle now and then when the piano wires go twang, but he has never done it at important times. As a left-hand batsman himself, he was good for me because he experienced exactly the same problems I did. You know, the casual waft and all that. The cricket on that Indian tour was nice—tactical, a stern mental test, but you could set out your stall and play properly. Allan Lamb is an instinctive player and that is why he is so impressive against the West Indies—he likes the ball coming at him quickly. I enjoyed having to think what the Indian spinners were trying, how they set their field, what shots I had to eliminate, how hard I had to concentrate. A pleasant change from the wearing-down process at the hands of the West Indians. I batted for nine and a half hours in Calcutta for my double hundred and it was fascinating to bat for so long with Mike Gatting. He is an absolutely brilliant player of spin. I could pick their leg-spinner Sivaramakrishnan about eighty per cent of the time. I reckoned he had a top-spinner, a googly and a leg-spinner. Gatt said there were two different googlies, two flippers and a couple of leggies and proceeded to prove it. He could see how each individual ball varied within the categories. He must have eyes like a rat! During that long stand at Calcutta, we enjoyed a shared sense of communication that was like a close friendship. Only batsmen who have been through something like that will know what I mean. We kept encouraging each other, fighting fatigue, the heat, the humidity, a raging thirst. Gatt's confidence and enthusiasm just rubbed off on me. At the end of the second day, he alone kept me going and in the last over of the day he did something I will never forget. I was 140-odd not out, having batted all day and he was comparatively fresh, having been there since tea. Off the first ball of the final over, he tickled one down to fine leg and I set off for a single. He sent me back and I asked him why. "I'll play this over," he said, "You've done your bit for the day." I can't think of anyone else who would have done that. Magnificent.

*So a double hundred against the Indian spinners, to go with a century against the West Indies. How would you compare batting against Richard Hadlee and Imran Khan during that period?*

Imran always had these theories about how to move the ball using different grips and positions at the crease and he used to swing the ball at speed, invariably away from my bat. But I would choose Hadlee as the superior bowler. He never gave you anything loose and he had a fantastic memory. Once I got out to him at Liverpool when I flicked a half-volley outside leg-stump, to be caught at fine leg. Next year I asked him what was the worst ball he had ever bowled at me, to be told: "Last year at Liverpool—and I got you out with it." He must remember every bad delivery he bowls, not that he sends down all that many of them. He just never gives you any peace.

*After all your ups and downs with the England team, what are your views about the way our top players are treated by the selectors?*

We have some fine players in this country, but with all the nerves and pressure involved in playing for England, you should not also have to feel "if I don't get fifty next innings or take a few wickets, I'm out." How hard do they want to make it? Derek Randall and Geoff Miller always used to play the current Test as if it was their last; they felt they never got enough encouragement to feel part of the team. There was never enough stability to help them relax and give of their best. There are a few current cricketers who have played just once for England, and that cannot be right. If you're good enough to be picked for one Test, surely you are good enough to get a second chance. I have no personal axe to grind, but when only Graeme Hick outscored me in 1986, it seemed odd that I never got a phone call or a letter from the selectors when I had been playing well all season and England were in the process of losing two home series. I know I speak for the rest when I say that the England players of my time have had no faith in the selection process.

*Away from the Test scene, how would you improve the English domestic game?*

It is our duty to provide entertainment, whether it is a dogged five-day grind or a one-day thrash. At the moment I feel the players are not being allowed to do that in the way they would like. So many petty things are hampering us. The spectators do not care if we bowl sixteen overs an hour or twenty-three, so long as the quality is there. Instead of a diversity of competitions we are getting too much that is similar. What is the real difference between a one-day game lasting 55 overs a side, or sixty overs or forty overs with run-ups allowed to be lengthened? Not much. I would like to see the Sunday League turned over to the best of three slogs lasting ten overs each innings. Do not worry about the length of bowlers' run-ups; it is a batsman's game and the public want to see the ball disappear out of the ground. On Sundays, we should have coloured clothing and an orange ball, with kids coming to the games in replica kit so that they can identify with their team. Make it a family day with barbecues and live music and an air of enjoyment. It should not be a day for the specialist, it should be given over to the public. For the rest of the week, we can play proper cricket. At the moment, we play too much similar cricket day after day.

*And what's right about the game in England?*

It is a great way to earn a living for a start. I love playing cricket, to do a job that people appreciate when I get it right. It is not like an office job when you know you have had a good week but there is nothing tangible to prove it. If I get 30-odd in a one-day game, people stand up and applaud me into the pavilion. If that is not a boost to the ego, then what is? The day they stop applauding will be a sad day for me. I love the performing aspect of it all, I suppose, because I have always been a fan of the rock world. I played the drums in a schoolboy band and I have loved to feel I was a performer on the cricket stage. I even like after-dinner speaking! What I really like about English county cricket is the feeling of camaraderie among the players. They have a gusto and an infectious sense of fun, despite all the grumbles and the travelling. Somehow the humour is all in tune, whatever the dressing-room.

*I cannot see you as a county coach when your playing days are over. Any thoughts about your future when you finally start to look your age?*

I will never be a coach. A lot of former players want the game to stop evolving because it clouds their own past performances. I hope I would never fall into the trap of thinking that the batsman who got a hundred against the West Indies faced inferior bowlers than I did in '84. I feel my life will move away from cricket when I retire. Over the last few years I have spent a lot of time in Perth, Western Australia, and I have had great satisfaction from teaching autistic children how to swim. I get on very well with kids, and the autistic ones have a great deal of love to offer. I had so much reward from teaching them. Working with children like that and my own personal experience brought home to me that there are many good things about life if you are prepared to look for them.

# DICKIE BIRD

**'I will defend the umpire against anyone. They are all fair and honest men doing their best. I would even defend Shakoor Rana. '**

AND they say there are no characters left in top-class cricket! Harold "Dickie" Bird is the genuine article. Nothing that Dickie ever does could be other than naturally idiosyncratic. By common consent he is the world's best umpire. Cricketers from all the Test-playing countries aver that when Dickie gives his decision it is automatically accepted, such is their respect for him. How he manages to merge the appropriate faculties to reach his decision in a split second remains a mystery, for Dickie is a chatterbox, an insomniac, a man who never seems to be in the proper relaxed frame of mind to get it right. He proves that great umpires are born, not made. No one would ever suggest that an adjudicator in such a high-profile sport should spend so much time on the high wire of taut nerves, arm-flapping angst and agonies of indecision. The first threatening cloud of a session induces enough melancholia in the Bird breast to satisfy even Henrik Ibsen. Dickie's magisterial predecessors like Sid Buller and Frank Chester would never display such fallibility. Over and above his brilliance as an umpire, Dickie has one outstanding characteristic—humanity. He is loved by all and he will readily laugh at himself—not a trait ingrained in everyone born and reared in Yorkshire. The players look forward to seeing him because he makes them laugh, the media recognise his approachability and the public warm to his agonising as he stands on the boundary edge, lamenting "Why does it always happen to me?" Only Dickie could succumb to the call of nature halfway through a Test Match session, only Dickie's shin could intercept the Exocet progress of a ball, leading to the melodramatic collapse of the stricken umpire. We laugh with him, as well as at him. Does he deliberately defuse the tension out in the middle by playing a role?

Well I do fuss around, trying to be human, sharing the tensions with the players. I know how uptight they can feel out there and it's important to me that they hold me in respect. Do you know, I've never had any problems with those who were supposed to be

187

a real handful. Look at Dennis Lillee—great lad, never a moment's trouble with him. He and Rod Marsh were the first ones to ring me last winter when I went out to Australia. They asked me to come and stay with them—and they were supposed to be the terrors of umpires. Ian Chappell has been a great supporter as well. To me he was a gentleman on the field. He wrote in his book that if it ever looked as though the game was going to boil over, I'd twitch my arms out, say something daft and everyone would laugh and relax. You see, I'm married to the game. I nearly got wed on two occasions, but it didn't happen and although I would have loved a family, I have no regrets. I've given my life to cricket. The players know that and I think that is why they respect me. Treat them like professionals and they will respond the right way.

*You say you've never had any problems out on the field—but what about Clive Lloyd in the Edgbaston Test of 1984? After you warned Malcolm Marshall for intimidation, the West Indies captain threw the ball away and made it quite clear he thought you were wrong.*

At least I was being consistent. I've always been very hot on intimidation and I warned Malcolm because he had gone round the wicket to Paul Downton in his two previous overs and he was obviously trying to soften up Paul. Ian Botham was on strike when I spoke to Malcolm and although Ian never minds bouncers, it was getting out of hand. The West Indians weren't too happy about it, but I was applying the letter of the law and I said to Malcolm, "Look, you're a far better bowler when you keep the ball up." He proved that afterwards. He ended up thanking me for that advice. Clive Lloyd may have been annoyed at the time but he has always said it's up to the umpires. I would like to see all umpires being strong about intimidation and I wish the players would help us more in that area.

*Do you still feel close to the players after all these years?*

Oh yes. I talk to all of them out on the field. I wish there wasn't the massive appealing that we get nowadays. Everyone seems to be shouting "catch it!" when the ball lobs up. But I suppose that's part and parcel of the modern game. It still means everything to me when players come to me at the end of the game and say "well done, Dickie".

*Who walks these days after getting a nick to the ball?*

Not many, although there are a few great sportsmen. Ian Botham is as good as gold about that. He is a great man, whatever he gets up to away from cricket. John Abrahams was a tremendous sportsman. He was batting once for Lancashire when he got the faintest touch on his glove. I couldn't have given him out, but when someone stifled an appeal, John walked. There were a lot more like John Abrahams when I started in the first-class game, but I still think that by and large we can hold our heads up in England. Non-walkers must realise they can't have it both ways, though. If players stand there, fair enough, but if they get a rough decision they must walk straight off and save their moaning for the dressing-room. Eddie Barlow once told me that he was a non-walker, but if he ever got an unlucky one, he would never complain, even in the dressing-room. He was as good as his word about that. The ones that worry me are the selective walkers—they go after scoring a hundred, but not when they're on nought. Having said all that, there's nothing in the laws to make someone walk.